Low Man on
the Totem Pole

LOW
MAN
ON THE
TOTEM
POLE

H.V. MacArthur

MCP
BOOKS

MCP Books
2301 Lucien Way #415
Maitland, FL 32751
407.339.4217
www.MillCityPress.net

Printed in the United States of America

ISBN-13: 978-1-49849-927-9

CONTENTS

INTRODUCTION

"Make the world more beautiful. You should leave the world more beautiful than you have found it when you were born — then you have done some service to existence."

—Osho

You Are Great

First of all, thank you for taking the time to read this book. Time is a precious commodity. And you investing your time in this book is something I take seriously. I'm not sure what your situation is. You may be a parent with young children. You could be juggling more than one job or staring at a fork in the road of your career. Maybe you're looking for your calling in life, or you're out of work struggling to find a way to make a living. I don't know. But I know what you choose to do now and in the future matters greatly. You matter greatly.

How do I know? I know because you exist. I believe how we choose to make a living affects not just ourselves and our families but also the global economy. I might as well tell you now, come clean: I'm an optimist. A neurotic optimist but still an optimist.

I first started thinking about this idea of everyone's greatness in my twenties. Early in my consulting career, I was working for a travel company. One of my first assignments was to travel around and train employees to provide good customer service. I always found that to be an odd focus for companies. The reality is nobody needs to *learn* customer service. We all go out of our way for others when we feel safe and motivated to do so. So instead I focused on helping employees get out of their own way so they could show up as their best selves regardless of whether the customer was being a jackass or not. And let's face it, there are a lot of jackass customers out there. You, in all likelihood, have been a jackass customer. I know I have.

But I digress. This particular trip had landed me on a little island down in the Caribbean. When I arrived at the resort where I'd be doing the training, I was greeted by an American woman who was hospitable yet formal. She and her husband ran the place, and she had set me up with my room.

As I took in my surroundings, I noticed a few details. My hostess smiled widely, but somehow that smile never seemed to reach her eyes. She didn't speak with her driver, an island native, for the entire twenty-minute trip to the room. Nor did she acknowledge him even after he dropped us off and brought in my bags.

She gave me some time to settle in, and returned later with dinner and some questions about the class I'd be delivering the following day. When I told her that as part of the course I'd be asking all participants to think about their life's purpose, she stopped me with a bit of a laugh, then gave a serious warning. This type of lofty thinking would be too "out there" for the staff, she said. She went on to explain they were a simple people, and requested I focus on things such as smiling, saying hello, and going above and beyond what the guests expected.

It was a tough call for me. On one hand, I disagreed with her assessment. I believed in my core that all people could identify with wanting meaning in their life and connection to that through their work. I also believed every brain was capable of understanding that work is one of the main ways we can add meaning to our lives. But I was also in my mid-twenties, with scant experience to test my theories and no research to back up my instincts. I also desperately needed this gig to go well, because I needed this, and more, just to pay the rent.

I'd recently been laid off and "volun-forced" into consulting for a living. To top it off, I knew I was laid off because they didn't want me there. You see, I was good at my job but just as good at calling out the things I thought the leadership sucked at. I did so eloquently enough but nonetheless managed to piss off all the wrong people. So I was struggling with whether to follow my instincts and teach the class the way I knew would connect with and inspire the audience or whether I should comply with the request of my faux-friendly hostess, who would surely report back to the powers that be whether they should continue hiring me.

This was the dilemma I wrestled with the following morning. The class was set up in a shady picnic area right on the beach. More than thirty people showed up, all native to the area, all with English as their second language, and all with jobs the world considered manual labor. Their expressions told me everything: I was just another foreigner coming to tell them how to do their job. My hostess stood off to the side, smiling, but I felt anything but supported. "Watched" was more like it. My gut felt like it did the day after I realized I'd been laid off — that powerless feeling that my security lay in the hands of somebody else, and that somebody didn't get me and wouldn't have my back if things went sideways.

The hostess introduced me and instructed the group to listen because I came from the corporate offices and was a customer service expert. That made me cringe even more. I'd been on the receiving end of these types of lectures, whether because of my age, gender, or position. And all I thought about the people being introduced as the experts I was supposed to listen to was I was about to listen to some jackwagons who'd probably never worked a real day in their lives discuss something they learned in a classroom somewhere. But damn it, I needed a job, so I launched into an overview of what we'd cover: how to greet guests, the company's customer service principles, and how to handle complaints.

But something happens to me when I teach a class. It's no longer me doing the talking. Instead of me in charge, it's like the class comes through me. Something takes over, and the rest of the world disappears. The only people who matter are those in front of me. I connect at a deep level. Something about what I sense about the people in the audience tells me what to pull out of my brain and share.

I've heard this called "being in the flow." It's not a conscious decision. During this time, I stop thinking about me. I stop thinking altogether, really. It's like I'm completely open and connected, and the audience is selecting what they need most in that moment. So on this occasion, I focused on talking about knowing how to identify your "pyramid of purpose," or your POP. I'll discuss this later, but the majority of the session talked about how to connect our day-to-day activities with our larger purpose — that what we call work is just a brick in the pyramid of our purpose, and how every guest interaction is an opportunity to support building that purpose or detract from it.

I didn't know how my hostess was handling my detour from what we'd agreed I'd discuss. I also didn't care. I wasn't thinking about my job security. I was watching a group of men and women wake up right before my eyes. I was seeing their energy pick up. There was laughter, note taking, and lots of questions. I don't remember exactly what they asked, but I remember feeling connected and useful.

Of course, some disengaged, and I could see they were having a hard time keeping their eyes open in the tropical heat. I have no delusions that I'm some magical creature who can summon the greatness everyone harbors inside themselves. But the majority connected to what I was saying, and that was enough to keep the channels open. I made sure I covered all the points I agreed to with my hostess. After all, they were good points; I just took a different path to them.

Afterward, there was applause. The way I see it, this is never about me, and it wasn't this time either. The group was simply acknowledging the relief they felt at being understood. And that's one of the greatest sensations we can experience—no longer feeling alone or lost but connected to others, often who we may have thought were so different from ourselves. So it's that feeling they were applauding, and I silently applauded them for allowing themselves to be open to it.

The driver from the day before approached me after the class. His accent was strong and his English broken, but I got the meaning from his smile and thank-yous. In the meantime, I saw my hostess approaching. I snapped back to reality, and that nasty knot in my gut filled me again. Was she going to complain? Would I be losing a future gig because of this?

Then the driver showed me something that made all my anxiety melt away. He held out his handout from the class. He had been taking detailed notes. On the back, he had drawn a pyramid. At the top of the pyramid were the words "Be a good father." There was more, but I couldn't read it, nor could I quite understand what he was saying to me now. But when he looked at me intently, tears in his eyes, and pointed to the top of his pyramid, I knew I had helped him connect to what mattered most to him.

The hostess interrupted us, and I politely let her know I'd be with her in a moment. The driver began speaking excitedly. From what I could make out, he had saved enough to buy a home. Two of his kids were in school. He knew how to fix cars and his wife liked to paint. I still struggled to understand his words, but what was clear was he was proud of himself. He was proud to share with me who he was. I knew he was feeling his greatness. And that is an amazing thing to see awakened in someone. For me, there is nothing better.

The Struggle Is Real, but So Is the Opportunity

Afterward, I met with the hostess. I could tell she was ill at ease. She acknowledged the morale boost the class had provided the team and then detailed what she wanted to make sure I emphasized in the next session. I listened and took notes. I could see she was struggling with how to balance her need to guarantee results and look good as a leader. So I listened with compassion. Because in that moment she was my audience. She was the one selecting what was needed right then. And I was in flow with her and helping her to find her greatness.

Here's what I believe are the two biggest issues facing workplaces today. First, a majority of us have been told not to believe in our greatness (or we've been told our greatness is tied to the money and titles we earn and not to our unique gifts or talents). Second, we have a business structure that relies heavily on people-managers who have no clue how to develop people, yet they are held accountable for how employees perform. This sets up the perfect storm of stress, fear, and resentment.

But I believe with every fiber of my being that each and every one of us has a special gift, a talent. A unique talent nobody else possesses. Sure, you may be one accountant among a bazillion accountants on this planet. But not one of those other accountants views the world the same way you do. It may be that you grew up in a dysfunctional home, and that gave you a lightning-quick ability to spot patterns and gaps like nobody else. I don't know. But I know there's something special that only you bring to the table.

I also believe we are obligated to bring these gifts into the world. You may think your piece of the puzzle is small, but no matter; a puzzle isn't complete without every piece. So it's important we all bring our unique puzzle pieces to the table and out into the world, and in that way I believe we will be better able to take care of each other and the planet.

Think about it. We are in unprecedented times. Technology, and especially the Internet, has radically changed the way individuals can make a living. Today, if you live in South Africa and happen to be gifted at making sweaters, you can make those sweaters and connect to a population, say in Alaska, who can use them. Through advancements in travel and shipping, you can now sell your products practically anywhere in the world. I understand there are still politics and laws to consider, as well as equity of the distribution of resources, but for a moment let's just sit here and bask in the potential of what technology has wrought for us.

This means we are no longer hampered by the idea that there are only a certain number of careers open to us. It means entrepreneurship is not just for the rich, lucky, or few. All this information and access means no less than the freedom to create our own destinies. Who knows, we may just go back to trading for goods and services vs. relying on money. Then money, the so-called root of all evil, would become obsolete. Who needs the middleman? Instead, resources, products, and services would be the only things that hold value, and everyone would have something to trade with. I told you I was an optimist.

Still with me? Now for the tough news: as wonderful as my vision for the world and the human race is, there are several things that are currently getting in the way of all that—mainly our own ability to change.

Change Is a Skill Not an Event

The truth is change is not just an event or process; it's a skill. A mandatory skill. I remember being brought in by companies to do training classes on change management back in the day, meaning before 2008's economic downturn. Back then, if a department was reorganizing or a company was changing direction or leadership, it was a *big* deal. My job was to come in, teach people how to deal with the stress of change, train leaders how to cope with resistance to change, and try to minimize the time people spent running around like scared ants who just had their well-organized assembly line stepped on.

It was like people were on the beach building sand castles or whatever. And then a big wave of change came and sucked them out to sea, spun them around, and then spat them back on the sand. They wanted me to come in and calm everyone down enough so they could get back to working in the sand. One and done. At least for a while.

Things are different today. Technology, the economy, and globalization have created constant and rapid change. People have been sucked out to sea and are being spun around. The problem is they are upset with all this wave action and waiting to get tossed back to the sand. What we need to realize—and embrace—is *there is no more beach.* We are in the ocean. The waves are going to keep on coming. We need to stop worrying about our precious beach sand and get good at surfing the waves.

But even waves have patterns. There is predictability in change. The first step in learning to thrive in this environment is to understand how radically different today's world is. Companies long ago banked on the fact that if our parents and grandparents had been customers, we would be too. Tradition, loyalty, and reliability were the competitive edge. Now what matters is whether you are seen as innovative, unique, and "trending." People care less about reliability and more about self-expression and creativity. Who needs a TV that lasts for twenty years when the technology that powers it will be obsolete in eighteen months?

Things changed pretty quickly after the economy did its financial do-si-do. All of a sudden, companies adopted layoffs, reorgs, leader changes, and strategy shifts as a way of doing business instead of as occasional events. So where does that leave employees and managers? Well, a lot of them are left feeling stressed, overworked, and underappreciated. Mainly because we are still viewing our careers and work in the reflection of the gold retirement watch.

INTRODUCTION

When Did This Trend of Change Get So Crazy?

Truth is, things started changing after the unfortunate events of 9/11. A wave of negative financial impacts hit several big industries, and all of a sudden we saw people getting laid off left and right. No longer were layoffs a sign that a company was fighting for its life. Instead, they became a way of remaining flexible in a volatile, seemingly unpredictable economy, and sharing risk between employer and employee.

I was one of those first few to receive my layoff papers a few months after 9/11. I remember feeling like a social pariah as people averted their eyes during my slow and lonely walk to my car, cardboard box and potted plant in hand. Fortunately, I was one of the lucky ones who saw it coming, and I was able to have a job lined up pretty quickly afterward. Or so I thought. Two months after taking the new position, I was laid off again. I know all about being pelted by successive waves of change.

Today, just about everyone has a layoff story or two to share. But there's a silver lining to this new employee-employer relationship. It opens up opportunities for us to play the field a bit, diversify our skills, gain new experiences, and qualify for jobs based more on talent vs. time in service. Employees have begun to understand the only thing that guarantees employment is a clear business need for the skills we're offering.

What About Loyalty?

Loyalty used to mean employees stayed with a company for years, their whole lives if they could swing it. That was considered a sign of a good work ethic. And if you were caught interviewing for jobs or having a résumé circulating, you might get called into the HR office for a talking-to, or worse. It seems some leaders haven't let go of this ideal. And that strikes me as not quite fair. If companies no longer offer the "security" of the proverbial gold watch retirement package, then how can they expect the stability of an employee base that is signed on for life? In the new reality, loyalty is based on performance not tenure. That means managers and employees partner for as long as it makes business sense. Take a look at Daniel Pink's book *Free Agent Nation* for an in-depth view of this trend and how it can enrich the workplace and careers of employees.

Change is not going away, so we'd better get good at it, plain and simple. And being good at it doesn't just mean reacting well when change happens to us. It also means tracking trends and seeing change before someone delivers the news to us. How good are you at seeing what's going to happen? It's not about predicting the future, but it is about paying attention to what's going on and playing out the various scenarios.

Tough Love Is Still Love

So why this book? Because I love employees, and I love work. To me, what you do for a living is a direct expression of your internal state. It can be the most beautiful expression of your authentic soul or it can be a revelation of how trapped and helpless you feel. This book is for the CEO of a company as much as it is for the person who cleans restrooms. I believe all people's expression through their work is a chance to love the human race and help it thrive, or to chip away at it and help bring it down.

To me, there is nothing more beautiful than watching a hairdresser obsess over each strand so their client's hair perfectly frames that person's face, or seeing a sanitation worker artfully unloading trash bins, or witnessing a CEO light up at the opportunity to take a business into the future in a way that elevates everyone working for her or him.

But as much as I love each employee, I think people need to wake the hell up. Too often we enjoy playing the victim of our circumstances—be they the unfairness of why we got passed over for a promotion, why our ideas aren't being taken seriously, or why the so called "they" are keeping us down. We abdicate our power and choose to sit in the passenger seat, bitching about how the car is being driven or where the driver is taking us, all the while refusing to get in the driver's seat ourselves.

I'm no different. I struggle every day with fear and a story that casts me as the victim and someone else as the villain. I have to actively shift my thinking toward what I can choose vs. what is being chosen for me. I grew up hearing I was a "have-not" and that opportunities were just not available to me. So every morning I wrestle to let hope, not fear, write my story for the day.

I am also fully aware certain things may hold me back or slow me down. I'm also aware certain things play in my favor. My focus is not on obsessing about what I have and don't have working for me. My focus is on being who I am and my purpose.

I might as well come clean and tell you that none of what I'm about to share in this book is based on scientific research or intensive case studies. It's all based on how I see the world through the coaching work I've done for the past twenty years and the observations I've made as an employee and people-manager for a few more years than that.

I recommend you take from the book what works for you, what makes sense, and what speaks to your instincts. Dump the rest. If it doesn't resonate with you, then it's not for you. And that's perfectly fine. My hope is you find at least one or two nuggets that make the time you invest in reading the rest of this book worthwhile.

PART 1:
Shift to a
Business Mind-Set

CHAPTER 1:
Mind Your Mind-Set

"Your work is going to fill a large part of your life, and the only way to be truly satisfied is to do what you believe is great work. And the only way to do great work is to love what you do."

—Steve Jobs

When working with a person or a team, the first thing I want to know is how each person approaches the mind-sets I see people move through during the course of any given day at work: fighting for their safety, looking good to the powers that be, and being strategically helpful for self and others. Once I know which one of these three mind-sets they live in the most and what triggers each one for them, then I can help them transition more smoothly through each of them.

We're All Wrestling with Fear

Why aren't we more strategic? Why don't we just follow our passions? Why do some and not others succeed at living the life they want and doing the work that most fulfills them? Over the years, these are the questions I've constantly wrestled with.

I began to notice a pattern in just about every employee I encounter in the workplace, regardless of title. It's not rocket science, and it may seem similar to other theories of human behavior. But it's helped me navigate many sticky situations, and several others dig themselves out of a career mudslide.

I find people tend to operate on a sliding scale from fearful to loving mind-sets. The more insecurity present, the further down the fear scale a person's mind goes. The more hope and confidence the person possesses, the further up the scale toward big-picture strategy and helping others the person focuses.

All We Need Is Love?

I call this book a tough-love letter to the employee in all of us because I think love is the one thing people want to experience through their work, but no one is willing to say that out loud. After all, *love* is the four-letter word that causes many of us to get uncomfortable. Drop the *f* bomb in the workplace and we might get a stern look, but more often than not, we'll be deemed honest and straightforward. A cut-through-the-shit kinda person. But love? That will get a groan and eye roll, and we won't win any points. Why?

Because we're told to leave our personal lives out of the workplace, to be professional. We're told not to take things personally. It's just business, after all. Yet in the same breath, we're told to be engaged, motivated, and to give 100 percent. Everyone seems to be afraid that if we start uttering the word *love* we'll start hugging each other for hours on end, singing "Kumbaya," and getting lost in a self-help circle of trust.

How are people not seeing the contradiction in this approach? Maybe when we worked in more of a factory system, when we needed people to be satisfied with repetitive work that required little to no creativity, this was necessary. It certainly would have been helpful in shutting down the individual's curiosity and passion. But in today's work environment, we need highly engaged individuals regardless

4

of which position they happen to sit in. And engagement requires love.

When we love what we do, we are more likely to operate in "the flow." When we love what we do, we are using our unique gifts. This also means the work itself is a reward, and we are less consumed with (often) meaningless titles. We get energy back from the energy we invest, which reduces burnout. Instead, our work feeds our spirit and we have more zest and purpose in our lives, with more of our authentic selves available to our loved ones.

Does that mean we do everything on a volunteer basis for no pay? No. When we love ourselves, we also treasure what value we bring to the table. We don't shy away from negotiating for our skills and services. Instead, we understand we bring a value that we can be proud of. We are aware of how much our services can command based on supply and demand, not on worthiness. We know we're all worthy.

I love what I do. I love who I am when I'm doing it. I love the people I do it for — even the ones who challenge and sometimes irritate me. It is love I take into the negotiating room. To me it is about investment. I'm investing my heart and soul. That, to me, is priceless. So when I'm discussing money, I'm looking at what my services tend to command in the marketplace and how much my client stands to gain in return on investment, as well as how much they have available to invest.

I disagree with the adage that the nice girl doesn't get the corner office. I'm big on being a nice girl. It has never stopped me from going after what I believed aligned with my purpose. But somewhere being nice got confused with being a doormat. Confidence, true confidence, is the side effect of genuine self-love not puffed-up bravado or ego.

I'm not talking about cockiness or thinking you're better than someone else. That's just a cover for insecurity, demonstration that people haven't discovered their true purpose and therefore need "proof" of their worthiness through titles and money. I'm talking about knowing your purpose so clearly that you understand your innate worthiness, that you love yourself enough to allow your gifts to shine. That you love your gifts and your purpose so much that you are not willing to sell them to the highest bidder or squander them by taking the easiest path. You are precious with your gifts. You get that you are the warden of these gifts and therefore the only person who has responsibility to make sure they are properly expressed in your lifetime.

The more people love themselves, and the more they cherish their uniqueness, the more they will find themselves in the slipstream of life. Not that life will be easy or fair. Not that they will be guaranteed riches. But they will feel connected, content, and at ease. They will have a sense of calm and the ability to focus on what needs to get done vs. focusing on fighting with themselves, others, or reality.

I say the word *love* in a business setting, and I can sit back and watch everyone squirm. Instead we toss around words such as *trust, loyalty,* and *teamwork.* But not *love.* Leave that four-letter word out of it. Why? What is it about the word that brings about such a strong reaction? And I'm not talking about just a roll of the eyes. I'm talking about leaders warning me *never to say the word again,* telling me I'll lose credibility. "I'm looking for practical tips," they say, "not some touchy-feely emotional binging."

But the reality is if the practical tips worked by themselves, you could just buy a Management 101 book for all managers and employees, mandate they read it and comply, and then watch as all your problems are solved. There's certainly no lack of Management 101 books out there. I know; I've read most of them. So have most of your crappiest managers. So what's missing?

I don't buy this is strictly an intellectual issue. I believe it's a crisis of self-worth, self-care and, dare I say (yes, I dare), love. Love and hope are desperately missing from our workplaces. Our work is intimately connected to who we are, how we live, and whether we prosper and thrive. How does that not have something to do with love?

When I'm coaching people, my goal is to determine what fears are holding them back and to think of ways to get them back to a state of love. This is where their brains will be clear, where they will come up with ideas and strategies that help themselves as well as others, and where they will see opportunities beyond and within the obstacles.

Following, I describe the three core mind-sets. Once you are looking for them, you will be surprised how easy they are to identify based on a person's reactions to others or the environment (see diagram). We all slide along this continuum at different times in our lives depending on how much we are coming from fear vs. love.

MIND-SETS: SAFETY → LOOKING GOOD → STRATEGIC/HELPFUL

SAFTEY

- **Concerned With:** Protecting their turf, reputation, job security, saving face or untrustworthy, avoid sharing ideas or anything that might put the spotlight on them unnecessarily, follow
- **Behaviors:** May withhold information for the sake of retaining control, accuse others of being underhanded procedures to the letter without considering impact
- **Result:** Builds reputation of being uncooperative, others may perceive them as not caring about what is happening outside of their immediate territory, tends only to see problems vs. opportunities

LOOKING GOOD

- **Concerned With:** Building or reinforcing their status and own reputation
- **Behaviors:** Will be "conditionally helpful," only assisting when they can receive credit or the other person either boosts or at the very least doesn't threaten their status. They tend to do work that produces tangible results but doesn't always move the business forward, competitive for individual accolades and time in the spotlight, known for bragging about themselves
- **Result:** They can get rewarded for doing good work when they are gaining "fame" or kudos but will be breaking trust of those they may deem not as important, or may not realize how their bragging and trying to look better than others is damaging trust and credibility, especially if others of perceived importance give accolades or points; however, the bigger picture is rarely seen

STRATEGIC/ HELPFUL

- **Concerned With:** How to produce the best long-term results for all involved
- **Behaviors:** Makes decisions based on a strategic vision and how things will support the organization, clients, and themselves, reaches out across boundaries to uncover needs and make connections, creates future plans based on trends and seeing opportunities where others see challenges
- **Result:** Builds a reputation as a collaborative and strategic leader, people tend to reach out and share information with them on a regular basis, work is done on behalf of others in a strategic manner, challenges are turned into innovation opportunities, while still building own credibility and achieving personal goals

Safety Mind-Set: Drowning Mode

When our sense of safety feels threatened, we go into survival mode and fear escalates. It doesn't matter whether the threat is real or not. The thing that matters is we perceive ourselves as being under threat. I like to compare this to how someone acts when drowning. What do people look like when they are in the middle of drowning? Are they calm, cool, and collected? No. They're flailing around, panicked and deathly afraid. So what happens when a lifeguard swims out to save them? Does a drowner politely greet them and thank them for taking the time out of their busy day to swim out to help them? No. In fact, lifeguards are trained to view drowners as dangerous to them and to themselves.

I've never seen a lifeguard swim out to a drowning person and then get offended that the drowner wasn't more appreciative. Have you ever heard of a lifeguard telling a drowning person, "Until you can figure out how to be a bit more respectful, I will not be dealing with you. I'll be on the beach when you're ready to be a decent human being"? Of course not.

Well, believe it or not, a lot of us are in drowning mode in the workplace — and in life. But on dry land, nobody tends to recognize drowners as drowners. On solid ground, surrounded by walls and no physical threats, we're expected to show up as pleasant, open, and helpful human beings.

So what does a person who's drowning on the job look like? They're usually pretty obvious. They tend to be territorial, aggressive, or controlling. People will usually describe them as jerks, assholes, or bitches. We don't recognize drowners as panicking and afraid. We see them as jackwagons. And the worst part is their fearful behaviors trigger our own defensiveness, which brings out the jerk versions of ourselves. It's a crazy, fear-filled roller-coaster ride.

So what is it that triggers this fear? Work is directly tied to our sense of survival. In what would commonly be described as "civilized" communities, most of us are lucky enough not to be faced with surviving actual physical violence in our day-to-day lives. So the primary survival threat to our existence is connected to job security.

Over the last ten to fifteen years, jobs have just become less secure. More and more companies are moving away from long tenure — and the job security that affords employees — in favor of employment flexibility. Adding to the instability is the general state of the economy and even advances in technology. It feels like the Wild West for many out there, and their behavior gets more and more defensive.

So how are we handling this new reality? I see people either refuse to admit there's a problem and hope it all goes away or fight tooth and nail to hold on to whatever "territory" they think they have in their jobs. If they shut their eyes to the problem, what I call the turtle approach, they'll do things that increase their risk of losing their job, such as avoiding difficult discussions and even avoiding work altogether. If they fight for territory, what I call the tiger approach, they show up as difficult to work with, unlikable, and not worth the effort it takes to work with them.

All of us get triggered to go to our safety mind-set at some point in our lives. We all worry about our financial security to a greater or lesser degree. And the more that fear drives our decisions and view of the world, the more time we are going to spend in this mind-set.

The plus side of the safety mind-set is it can cause an adrenaline rush and knock us out of our comfort zone, spurring us to claw our way back or even reach greater heights of accomplishment in our careers or even our lives. But spending long periods of time in this mind-set will create high levels of stress that will eventually detract from our performance and negatively affect our overall health. There's nothing wrong with landing in this mind-set from time to time, but we don't want to live here.

The key to pulling ourselves out of the safety mind-set is self-love, hope, and confidence. Though external factors can do a lot to lift us out of our safety mind-set, the most reliable way out is to direct ourselves back to a place of calm through the thoughts we choose, no matter what our current circumstances. Here is a step-by-step guide to extracting ourselves from this potentially detrimental mind-set.

Step One: Be Aware of When You Are in Safety Mode

The first critical step is to be able to identify why and when we are operating in a safety mind-set. Pay attention to how you feel when thinking through this lens. What behaviors are your go-tos? What situations tend to be your Achilles' heel? The more in tune you are with this, the easier it will be to kick into a more rationalizing approach to the situation.

As Shakespeare wrote, "Nothing is good or bad. Thinking makes it so." My mother—the most fearful, safety-focused person I've ever known—used to quote this regularly. I think she rationally knew this to be true, but years of being taught to be afraid of the world made it hard for her to believe she could have that much control of her life. I like to think me watching her engage in this internal struggle is what set me on the path to figure out how to move from knowing something to believing it and then acting upon it. It's quite a powerful thing to willfully change one's mind.

This step requires you to work your muscle of self-awareness. Not such an easy thing to do when we've been emotionally triggered. That is, when we perceive a threat, we tend to react with our most rehearsed response instead of stepping back and thinking through the best approach. But if you can start to track when and how you get triggered, you can start to rehearse new responses. Yes, you can retrain your brain. The more you practice observing, acknowledging, and shifting, the more automatic these behaviors will become. Treat it like advanced driving lessons. It's one thing to drive in light traffic on good road conditions. It's a whole other level to be able to handle crazy drivers in a blizzard.

Step Two: Change Your Story

The next step is starting to recognize when other people are operating from this mind-set. The goal here isn't to stop them or change them. At this step, simply get good at spotting the behavior and crafting a different story about it and the person. This is about making sure you don't let them drown you with them. Instead of them being jerks, resistant to change, or territorial, tell the story of a drowning person. They're scared and panicked. Yes, that guy who yells at everyone, and the woman who puts down her employees and tells them their ideas are ridiculous, are drowning. And their behavior is rarely intentional. In fact, it is highly reactionary.

There are two critical things to remember about step two. First, just because you are telling a different story doesn't mean you are agreeing with or excusing the behavior. You are simply telling the story that keeps you in lifeguard mode as opposed to getting drowned and taken down with them. Second, you may or may not be able to keep them from drowning. But you absolutely can keep yourself from drowning and ensure you keep showing up as your best self. Your goal will be to set respectful boundaries for yourself, as well as to throw a safety line to the person you see struggling. Your communication will focus on educating the other instead of prosecuting them.

This step requires the skill of empathy. Empathy is not about agreeing with people's behavior choices. It's about rationalizing them in a way that allows you to connect to what they're feeling. Feelings and emotions have gotten a bad wrap, but they're the universal language of humans. We've all been scared, angry, shocked, or sad. When we tell the story of the drowner, we automatically relate to the feeling of being scared and not knowing what to do. That doesn't mean people should have license to yell at others, but for that moment, we stop seeing the yeller as the enemy and start seeing her or him as another human in trouble. That empathy is what causes our brains to calm down and go back to being objective, strategic, and creative.

Step Three: Focus on Helping vs. Judging

The third step is identifying whether or not your particular lifeguard skills can help save the other person from drowning. Sometimes we have to accept our limitations. It may be that your goal has to remain simply not to add to the problem and to preserve your own capabilities. But when your default is to show up with love instead of fear, you may realize there is some help you can provide and that the other person is open to your approach. People can sense when our motivations stem from genuine love or fear. If you are determined to "put people in their place" or keep them from hurting your reputation or feelings, other people will see you as a shark and not a lifeguard. At the end of the day, you can't force someone to accept your help, but you can control whether you are there to help them or hurt them. Remember that.

Looking Good Mind-Set: What Do Others Think of Me?

As we move out of the safety mind-set, we're still operating from a sense of fear. But it tends to stem less from a perceived threat to our safety and more from feeling a threat to our social acceptance. You may think that's not a big deal, but it is. Being ostracized from our social circles is still tied to our need to be protected by our "tribe."

So what does someone look like who is primarily focused on looking good? I'll tell you, and I'll tell you what I call them, but before we go there, I want you to remember if you're a human being, you definitely have had your own moments of worrying about looking good. In fact, most organizations encourage us to be hyper-focused on how good we look to our bosses and the powers that be.

What makes it difficult to spot someone operating from a looking good mind-set is they present themselves as what

I call "conditionally helpful." The truth is the majority of us are operating from this place most of the time. The workplace even inadvertently encourages us to act this way. Think about it. Most performance reviews are centered on people proving they are good performers to their bosses. They have to *look good* to the powers that be.

Now don't get me wrong, I'm a *huge* fan of performance management. You'll see a whole big chapter dedicated to it in this book. However, I see it as a way for bosses and employees to learn a common language to better discuss how to partner to get work done, and not as this weird paternal dynamic of trying to win favor with the boss. We'll discuss how to make performance management work for you later in the book.

So when I'm being conditionally helpful, I'm basically doing all the right things and working well with others as long as doing so doesn't threaten my reputation in any way. Say I'm working on a project with Susan. We meet and discuss our ideas. It seems clear that we both have something to contribute, and there seems to be enough credit, opportunity, and glory to go around. So Susan thinks I'm pretty awesome. I was nice, friendly, and even complimented a few of her ideas. How cool am I? The coolest. And I genuinely think she's pretty cool too. The cat's pajamas. The bee's knees. My homey.

Then one day Tyrone, our boss, stops by my desk. He says he's noticed the creeping scope of the project and is concerned about whether we'll meet the deadline. Now, if I'm operating from the looking good mind-set, my focus is on not disappointing Tyrone. If that's my focus, what do you think I'll do?

Well, this is tricky. I know I don't want to look like I'm throwing Susan under the bus, but I also don't want to take any blame for things not going as Tyrone expected. It's important to note Tyrone doesn't even have to express disappointment. The fact that he's a manager is enough to trigger my looking good fear because of the perceived power he holds.

So I say things such as, "Yes, I've been talking to Susan about the project. I was concerned too. But we talked through it, and I think she gets why we need to be on top of this. I'll keep you posted and make sure we make that deadline." Tyrone nods and moves on.

You probably know exactly what I did there. I threw Susan under the proverbial bus but not in a noticeable way — just enough to cover my own ass without getting any blood on my hands. Later, when I see Susan, I tell her, "Hey, Tyrone stopped by to talk about the project and his concerns about the scope and deadline. I let him know you and I already talked about it and have come up with a plan. He seemed to be okay with that. I let him know we'd keep him updated."

Susan walks away thinking I'm pretty swell, and she's probably glad she gets to work with such a cool teammate. That is, until she goes to lunch with Antonio. Turns out Antonio overheard my conversation with Tyrone. So when Susan has lunch with him the following day, he gives her all the dirt. He does this because people who are worried about looking good make sure they protect their "tribe" from looking bad, as well. This often gets mistaken for loyalty. It's not; it's self-preservation.

In my experience, the number one way people bond in the workplace is over mutual dislike of someone else. And when we tell our story, we want to be convincing. It's tough to convey the weird undertones of what I did when speaking with Tyrone. So to capture that feeling and tone, Antonio will feel the need to dramatize events. This triggers Susan's fear of not looking good to Tyrone. So what does she do? Well, she finds a way to get in front of Tyrone and subtly shares her side of things. "Hi, Heather mentioned she spoke with you about the project scope issue. I'm glad you're aware of things. In fact, I think you may want to be aware of a few things about Heather. I'm not sure how trustworthy she is…" and the story goes on.

So with all this looking good behavior going on, you might wonder who's focused on the work. I'm focused on looking good, and the work is second, at best, on my list of priorities. Susan is focused on defending how good she looks, so her time is spent bitching with Antonio and defending herself to Tyrone. And who knows what work is getting dropped while Antonio comes to Susan's "rescue." And Tyrone? Well, he's probably focused on how to hire better help.

One of the biggest pains in the ass all managers have to deal with is helping the grown adults they employ play well with one another. And what's tough about that is how fearful most managers are. Think about it. The majority of managers get promoted into leadership positions because they were good at performing as individuals. You have a great deal of control over how good you look when it's just you. It becomes a lot harder to manage your image when your reputation depends on whether other people do a good job. So what do a lot of managers do? They start controlling and micromanaging.

Step One: Self-Awareness

How do we move out of the looking good mind-set? The first step is…you guessed it…recognizing we're there. This is tougher than recognizing when we're operating in the safety mind-set. The safety mind-set doesn't tend to feel all that good. The dangerous thing about the looking good mind-set is when it's working, it feels pretty awesome. Just look at the advent of social media.

We take a selfie and post it on Facebook, Instagram, or whatever our platform of choice may be. Then we keep coming back to see if anyone likes what we posted. *Will enough people like it? Does anyone like it? Should I take it down so no one else sees how few people like it? Wait, a bunch of people like it? Woo-hoo. I look good.* What a high.

This roller coaster sets up a punishment/reward cycle that stokes our addiction to looking good. This is why I see people bend over backward and beat themselves down to win favor from managers, who are likely just as dysfunctional, which is why they are overly critical and defensive. But that one "Atta boy" is enough incentive for employees to sell their souls just to win the favor of a random person the company assigned as their superior. And the more critical the boss, the more people compete, backstab, and manipulate to get those "Lookin' good" carrots.

All this activity leads bosses to think they "look good" because their team fears them and is super busy. But here's the thing: Rarely are they truly productive. Even if the team does produce something, several dead bodies are typically scattered in the wake. It's hard to put a price on the impact this has on morale and engagement, not to mention missed opportunities for collaboration and creative genius.

So we have to be vigilant about noticing when we are prioritizing doing things to please others above servicing the greater good. If you name-drop or use "The boss is asking for xyz" to drive work, you are motivated by looking good. If you are more concerned with the wrath or approval of your boss over delivering the best result for the business, you are concerned with looking good.

Step Two: Change Your Story

Next, we need to stop overvaluing looking good. It's one thing to recognize what we are doing, but it's another to stop wanting to do it. As I mentioned, being in safety mode tends to feel stressful, and most others don't support us operating there. Drowning sucks. But looking good and winning points with the boss feels awesome. Getting promoted rocks.

But you're playing a short-range game. Vying for that little annual merit increase because the boss approves of you is a beggar's strategy. We'll discuss later how to play the long-range game. But let's be clear: Looking good takes *a lot* of energy. It's exhausting and stressful. At any minute, we can fall from grace. Often, for us to look good, someone else has to look bad. And maybe the worst part: all this posturing rarely has anything to do with our actual purpose.

A woman once approached me after a class to ask for help getting promoted. She explained she had been passed up for a promotion and the person who got promoted wasn't half as good or knowledgeable as she was. I asked her what she wanted. She said she wanted to be a director, the next title up from her senior manager position. I asked her why. She looked at me like I was asking the dumbest question ever. I repeated my question. She stuttered and then said, "Well, to be successful, of course."

That is the saddest answer I could hear, and I hear it all the time. I pushed back, much to her frustration. I pushed her for a better answer than that she was on a hamster wheel of success that somebody else created a long time ago. What did she care about? After a few more questions, it all came tumbling out. She loved music and believed if she were able to create ways for everyone to access and create great music, the world would be a better place.

Now that was a purpose. I could see by the light in her face that those words were connected to her true purpose. She was excited again. I asked what having a director title had to do with that. She paused and said she honestly didn't know.

I explained there was nothing wrong with going after vertical positions higher up in an organization. But to do so just because someone else told us that's what success looks like is just playing the looking good game. But if she were motivated by her genuine purpose, then she'd see a vertical title change may or may not be the next, best move. And if it were the next, best move, then she would focus more on how to get there rather than being resentful about being passed over this time.

Her ego was concerned about the person who was promoted over her. But if she were focused on loving herself and demonstrating love through her purpose, she'd see not getting the position as a detour as opposed to an attack against her worth.

She explained she'd been demotivated the past few months because she didn't get the director position, even though she'd recently been put in charge of a project that could directly affect her ability to work on a software platform designed to help people publish their own music. She also admitted the software skills were probably a more direct route to increasing her capability to command more pay than a director position would be.

The beauty of the new workplace is there is more than one way to make a living. If money is critical to your path, then there are several ways to go about getting some. And there is nothing wrong with an executive leadership position being part of that. But it doesn't have to be. That's the point. People are making money selling chainsaw art online. That wasn't happening fifteen years ago.

Step Three: Focus on Helping vs. Judging

The next step is to recognize when a colleague is consumed with looking good. It's not that hard, actually, because they often come across as self-serving ass kissers and ladder climbers. They tend to be good at managing up because they are obsessed with those in power thinking highly of them. The other side of that obsession is anyone without power or perceived influence is often ignored, discarded, or — worse — used.

All this behavior can easily trigger us to come from a place of judgment. And that's not good for anyone, because if we are busy judging them, we are less likely to act strategically or be effective lifeguards. We must tell a different story than those people being self-absorbed or selfish. Instead, see these people's fear, and have compassion for those who haven't figured out who they are and what their authentic purpose is. As high as they may get from looking good to the "right people," it is an exhausting and stressful game they are playing.

Know they are not coming from a place of confidence and self-love no matter how cocky or self-assured they appear. Like ducks, they may appear calm above water, but their legs are moving frantically below the surface.

Your goal is to help them feel safe and confident in themselves. Look for their genuine talents. Pay attention to what gives them energy. Watch their body language. When people are doing what they are meant to do, their faces are soft and joyous. Their bodies are relaxed and open. It's almost impossible for them to stay guarded when they are in their flow. And if they see you are not threatened by their greatness, if they get you will not threaten how they look to others, they'll begin to trust you.

They will show you more and more of their true selves. Now this doesn't mean you forget they are still somewhat in drowning mode. They may start to swim and then suddenly get scared they aren't looking good, and this may cause them to revert to survival tactics again. You should expect this. Don't be offended or disheartened. And most of all, don't let your own fear of looking bad because of their behavior trigger your defensiveness. Your ultimate goal is to keep showing up strategically helpful, to keep showing up as your best self regardless of how others around you are showing up.

Strategically Helpful Mind-Set: How Can We All Level Up?

We all have moments when we are being strategically helpful. But what does that mean? It's when we are calm and focused on solutions instead of getting credit, when we're balancing our own goals with the needs of the greater whole. It's not about being a martyr. You don't sacrifice what you need or want. Instead, you use your creativity and strategic thinking to align your needs with the needs of those around you. This is where collaboration is most useful. This is where your ideas and choices serve to elevate *everyone*, including yourself.

When I first start coaching people, they usually show up eager and "coachable." They seem humble and willing to learn. But it can sometimes feel like a bit of a show. They seem to want to "look good" as coaching recipients. Often they are feeling attacked from the get-go because they were told they needed coaching. To save face, they try to appear compliant and agreeable. It's not until I start poking at their hot buttons that I start to see their real feelings.

I'd much rather see their anger than their "good behavior." At least we are dealing with authenticity when we get to their anger. After all, I'm coaching their reality, not the fantasy they have of how they are perceived. It is fantasy that has set them up to look delusional and disconnected from those who deal with them every day. And I'm not talking about people who are unsuccessful or totally disliked. The majority of people I work with tend to have one core issue that's infecting everything else, either subtly or completely. I rarely come across someone who's impossible to help, or a total mess.

In fact, I'm no different than the people I coach. I'm just as human, even though I'm the one coaching. This is another reason I loathe being introduced as any kind of expert. I'm more an enthusiast than an expert. I'm obsessed with how I can bring out my best self and manage the insecurities and blind spots that get in the way of success. My passion is then taking those lessons learned and sharing them with those who can benefit from them.

It was just shortly after coming up with this safety-to-helpful mind-set theory that I was put to the test with it. It was an early morning, and I was at the gym running on the treadmill — my least favorite way to spend my time, by the way. I saw an email come through from one of my bigger clients. I was working on getting a major contract for a class on collaborating I had recently designed. The email was from one of the trainers there, who had taken one of my classes before. He was relatively new, and he hadn't impressed me all that much in our initial introductions.

The first few times I met him he seemed obsessed with showing off how smart and qualified he was based on all his academic degrees. He was uber-polished and liked to throw around big words. I found it exhausting. It was clear he wanted to impress upon everyone how much smarter he was than me.

So when I got an email from him requesting a soft copy of my collaboration course materials, I was pretty irritated. Who did he think he was? While still on the treadmill, I replied it wasn't that simple, because the course would need to be purchased and his company was about to sign a contract to have me deliver the class. I sent the email and went back to running.

In no time at all, I received a response from him stating that he would use the handout he had from the class he attended and just change the content to the company's logo. I hopped off the treadmill immediately and went out to my car. I was fuming. I was petrified. I was ready to strangle the trainer. Who the fuck did he think he was?

I fired off another email explaining in my most professional passive-aggressive manner that there was such a thing called copyright laws that prevented him from doing what he proposed. I layered in that his boss, a good friend of mine, would not approve, but I'd be happy to speak with her. I sent the email with a smirk on my face.

I drove home. During the drive I started to imagine how my major contract was going to be lost. I had just left a well-paying corporate position a few months before this to go into business on my own, which meant I had no guarantees when or if I'd be making any money to pay my bills. I also worried that my decision to leave may have been foolish based on what people were saying about the economy. Safety mode was fully triggered.

Then my mind went to how smug the trainer had been when I first met him. Did he think he was smarter than me? How dare he. I had years of experience. I was great at my job. After all, I was the one who had recognized collaboration was going to be a hot topic for most businesses. I was the one who had designed the class. But then again, I was just a small-town girl with parents who never even graduated high school. I came from poverty. I never went to an Ivy League school. Looking good mode was fully triggered, as well.

Step One: Self-Awareness

Then a moment of clarity hit. This collaboration class was built on the safety-to-helpful mind-set. But here I was being completely reactive. My fear that I wouldn't book enough work was putting me in safety mode. The result: I didn't want to share. I wanted to hoard my class and cling to whatever work I could get. My ego was triggering my need to look good. I didn't want this person to get the better of me. And I was worried about looking good to this trainer who I supposedly didn't care about. So I engaged in this passive-aggressive battle to prove he was less intelligent and informed than me.

Step Two: Change Your Story

I tend not to try to one-up other people. I'm not a fan of competition. I don't enjoy it. So why was I competing with the trainer? Why was I going out of my way to put him in his place? Of course, I was trying to protect my safety and ego.

If I wanted to get back to my best self, I had to stop overvaluing my ego. I told myself I was guaranteed to be successful that year and I would book enough work and not have to worry about money. I didn't know if that was the truth or not. But I also didn't know I *wouldn't* make enough money. It was all fiction at this point, so I might as well write a story that reflected a happy existence instead of something that brought out the worst in me.

I also reassured myself that I was good at what I did. I didn't need to be better than someone else. There was room for everyone's greatness, including mine. I let myself off the hook of having to prove myself. At the end of the day, I reminded myself that I cared most about helping people.

Step Three: Focus on Helping vs. Judging

Now what? What should I do? What would I do if I were being strategically helpful? Well, I'd revisit what my ultimate goal was in the first place. The truth was I wanted the company to have access to the collaboration class. They needed it. They were struggling with teams that were operating in silos, not communicating with one another, and swimming in conflict. I loved this company. I'd worked for them before, and I cared about their success. Also, I loved its employees. And if I loved its employees, I must love this trainer too, even if I didn't care for his behavior or current approach.

What were mysteries to me was what this trainer's ultimate goal was, what his genuine talents were, and how we could authentically align. So I sent him another email. I apologized for coming across the way I had and let him know I'd help him find the best solution to this challenge. I asked if we could meet in person that day.

By the time we sat down together, my defensiveness had dissipated. I was focused on the greater good. That didn't mean I was ready to be a martyr and give up my stake in all this. But first I needed to understand his side of things.

At first he stayed guarded and competitive. Instead of being judgmental, I recognized he needed to feel his safety and looking good needs were protected. He explained his clients were expecting the class, and he didn't have to use my content if it was going to mean drama. I let him know if the content was the best-suited for the client, we'd find a way to make that happen with minimal drama.

Eventually, he began to feel safer. He came clean that he had committed to the client that they would get the class at no additional cost. He hadn't realized his company didn't own the content. He was new to his role, and this could become a major credibility issue for him. It took some brainstorming and collaborating between the two of us before we came up with a pretty fantastic solution.

He'd deliver the course content at no charge to the client. I'd train him so that he'd deliver it correctly. He'd track the data from the class, one of his unique talents, and we'd use the data to market this course across the larger organization. In the end, he solidified his credibility with the client and I got my major contract, which ended up being even larger than what I had originally anticipated.

Now, this is a happy ending. Things don't always play out so nicely. But when you speak to the greatness in others through the greatness in yourself, you almost always get better results. This is where creativity and synergy thrive. This is where innovation and strategic solutions are born.

This strategically helpful mind-set is the key to applying all the other tips and processes in this book. You could implement every best practice perfectly, but if you're coming from a place of fear and insecurity, you will end up burning bridges and damaging relationships.

And in this day and age of rapid change, relationships — both good and bad — will last longer than any work that is in front of you today.

CHAPTER 2:
Labor of Love

"Nowadays, people know the price of everything and the value of nothing."

—Oscar Wilde

I'm sure you've heard the saying, "If you love what you do, you'll never work a day in your life." There are two types of people who quote the adage. One pooh-poohs it because they're working their asses off and not making the money they think they should, and the other shouts it with glee after having found "success" in the form of money.

The truth is doing what you love doesn't guarantee you a fortune, nor does it give you a pass from hard labor. But it might just increase your odds of both.

The Value of Money

Based on most people's standards, I grew up poor. I know what it's like not to know if I was going to eat each day. Some would look at my childhood and be appalled, while others would envy its "luxuries." It depends a lot on what you have and how you look at it.

This has perplexed me. What equals suffering from having too little and what equals bliss from having just enough?

I'm not sure. And I'm way too early in my life's journey to solve that riddle. But I do know survival has something to do with suffering, and vice versa. And some—maybe even most—of the circumstances that get us into survival mode are way beyond our control. (I don't know about you, but I was not consulted on the choice of my particular parents, nor did I have input on being born in a town in the middle of the desert.) But there are some basics to survival that are universal: oxygen, food, shelter, and safety from attack. Money can have a direct impact on some of these, particularly food and shelter. We have not figured out how to charge for oxygen…yet. And sometimes all the money in the world can't keep you from being attacked.

What's interesting is money in and of itself has absolutely zero value. Now that's a crazy thought. When it occurred to me that my biggest fears were tied to something completely made up by long-dead people, I was seriously pissed off. This realization definitely shifted things for me, but it didn't solve all my challenges. After all, a girl still has to eat.

I won't pretend to have solved the magic money equation, but I'm on to something when it comes to moving from living in poverty to living a comfortable life—at least here in the United States. I get other political and economic systems work differently. And I definitely don't take for granted the freedoms a capitalist system affords. I'm not here to say any system is better. I'm just calling out that the US brand of capitalism is the particular system I have experience navigating.

Let's not forget one of the most obvious freedoms of capitalism—that is, if you can sell something that people want to buy, you can make money. And if you can sell something that lots of people place a high value on, you can make more money.

Personal History–"Who the Heck Is She to Tell Me?"

I'm going to share stories from my own history throughout this book to show how I've discovered the "best practices"

I'm recommending. The following paragraphs provide some background on me and how I came to be writing about this topic in the first place. Feel free to skip this section if you're not all that interested in my story. It's not necessary for this book to be of use to you. But if you're wondering, "Who the heck is she to talk about money and work, etc.?" read on.

I was born and raised in a small town — Barstow, California. It's the gas station stop in the middle of the desert between Los Angeles and Las Vegas. It's a small desert town that survives thanks to the nearby military training bases and the big rigs and trains constantly passing through. I was never a fan. It's the desert. Not my favorite environment.

My dad grew up in the gorgeous beach town of Dana Point, in Southern California. When I was young, we'd drive there to visit my grandmother. We'd spend cool days on the beach, water everywhere and beautiful palm trees decorating the sky. To me it was paradise. One time, on the way back to the desert after one of these trips, I asked my dad why we lived in the desert instead of the beach. His answer was, "Because we're poor." I remember saying, "But aren't there poor people at the beach? Where do all the poor people live? And can we move there?" Amused, my dad just smiled at me.

My mother was from Germany. She met my father when he was stationed there while serving in the US Army. She moved to sunny California with him and ended up in Barstow. From the green, parklike German countryside to the arid mountains of the high desert. I personally think that might be grounds for divorce. But she was a woman who didn't shirk from her commitments. I didn't know at the time, but my paternal grandmother wasn't a fan of my mother. Needless to say, when my grandmother died, the money that supported her beach living went to my father's *other* children, from his *first* marriage. My brother and I got nada, a fact my mom never stopped complaining about.

My father was diagnosed with Parkinson's disease when I was four, and he had to resign from his job as a fireman. Before that, we didn't live a lavish life by any means, but we knew there would be food on the table. We were lucky because my father had retired from the Army, so that meant his medical care costs were covered by the military, not that there was much medicine could do for a Parkinson's patient back then.

Quickly, my father became a vegetable of sorts. My mother did what she could to help us survive. She figured out what government assistance programs could help us get by. Even before the Internet, she was a master of research, and quite resourceful. But she also suffered from depression and mental illness.

So when my dad stopped working and my mom eventually had to care for him 24/7, the sense of "lack" was ever present in our house. We didn't know if we were going to have enough money to make ends meet month to month. My mother got us approved for government-issued food assistance, which came in the form of cheese, butter, the dreaded powdered milk, and school lunches. So yes, we were technically on welfare. The "good news" was so were many of the people I went to school with.

When my mother sat down at the kitchen table to do the bills every month, she would talk about how she might have to put my brother and I up for adoption. Now that may strike you as poor parenting, but for my mother it was just reality. She had been sent to work at a young age, and she had no idea if she was going to have to do something similar with us. As you can probably imagine, being exposed to that sort of talk at such an early age had some sort of effect on me. To this day, I feel a pang of anxiety when I pay my bills, no matter how much money I have or don't have. As a child I promised myself I wouldn't have a family of my own until I figured out the money equation.

Neither of my parents graduated from high school, and together they weren't exactly the best at setting my brother and I up for successful careers. Now, I can't exactly blame them. My dad had no idea a debilitating disease would rob him of his ability to work. He'd been a jack-of-all-trades, master of none, jumping from tank driver and boxer in the military to civilian barber, deep-sea diver, and fireman, with several odd jobs in between. My mother had been a restaurant cook, but she assumed, as did many women of that era, that if she stayed home to care for the kids, her husband would bring home the bacon. That didn't end up working out as planned.

I learned relying on the adults in my life to secure my well-being wasn't the best strategy. I knew there was power in work, and I wanted to earn my own money. Money had become the answer in my mind. I'd begged for a newspaper route for as long as I could remember. My mother didn't like the idea of a little girl riding around at the crack of dawn by herself. As an adult, I can understand. As a child, I was infuriated.

So as soon as I could, I was sneaking behind her back and working. I took my first job, illegally, at a fruit orchard. Some of my thirteen-year-old friends and I spent a summer slicing apricots so they could be dried. When I got that check for three months of working in the hot sun—I think it was around seventy-five dollars—I was sold. That check meant I could control my destiny. I could do something and bring in money. After that came a fast food job.

A friend of mine told me they were hiring at the local Foster's Freeze. At that time, it was legal to work at the age of fourteen with a work permit. This was my moment. My career would begin. I would be legit. I'd be working indoors at a business. I didn't know what it would lead to, but I knew I wanted that job.

My goal was to be able to pay for my food, clothing, and eventually my shelter. I wanted to be in control of me. I wanted to remove my mother's right to tell me what to do. I knew she and I were different in terms of how we saw the world. I knew my emotional well-being and survival wouldn't have a chance if I stayed under her roof for too long.

So I got a ride with my friend to Foster's Freeze for the interview. That's where I met my first and arguably best manager. I remember not knowing what to wear to a real interview. The apricot farm gig was so under the table, it didn't matter how you showed up. But this was different. To me, this was serious business. I wanted this job. I needed this job. Not only did I need the money to buy my freedom from a pretty tumultuous home, but I needed it for another reason: I sensed this was the beginning of my future.

Looking back, that day truly was a critical point in my life. There were about a dozen teenagers sitting in line in the dining room. When it was my turn, I was called back to the manager's office. He was a thin man with big glasses. He was friendly, but you knew he meant business. He offered me a seat in his small office, and the interview began.

He looked over my application and work permit. I don't remember what I wrote. I think he asked me a few basic interview questions. I don't recall what I said, but I was a painfully shy person at that point in my life.

At one point he asked me why I should get the job over all the other kids sitting outside waiting to be interviewed. I froze. My mind was reeling. On one hand, I wanted the job. On the other hand, some of those kids out there were good friends of mine. I didn't want to sell them out. And to top it off, I had no idea if I *should* get the job. After all, I had never had a job before. I didn't know if I would be any good at it. He leaned over, looked me square in the eye through those big glasses, and said, "Let me give you a hint. Now ain't the time to be humble."

Something clicked in me right then. I didn't say I was better than anyone, but I started selling, and I sold my little heart out. I don't remember what I said, but I'm sure it had to do with how quickly I learned, how hard I'd work, and how much I loved ice cream. Whatever I said, it worked.

What I learned in that moment was to value myself. To value what I brought to the table. That there is power in believing in yourself. That didn't mean I was better than anyone else, but I wasn't less than anyone else either. That seemingly insignificant moment has played out a thousand times in my life and was the seed to my growing sense of worth.

It was also the beginning of my love affair with work. I worked fast food for a while. If you've ever done it, you know how unpleasant it can be. I hear people talk about fast food jobs as simple. Let me tell you they are not. Working at that Foster's was one of the toughest things I've ever done, and if I have children, I plan to make a stint in fast food a mandatory part of their teens. I had to learn tons of info about the food we sold and all the ways it could be special-ordered. I learned about the value of money in each ketchup packet I put in someone's bag. And I learned how important ethics were when the manager entrusted me with the accuracy of the business's nightly deposit. Most of all, I learned to multitask and work with people.

The Value of Purpose

My people-navigating skills have turned out to be my most valuable asset. None of my fancy titles or annual merit increases have provided me with more negotiating power than that skill. At the time, there was no way I could have known how much working in the customer service business was going to pay off for me. I know now that the reason it paid off is because it ultimately aligned with my life's purpose.

Not to toot my own horn too loudly, but I know there are others who wouldn't make a dime doing what I do. It's not their purpose, and they don't possess the natural talents and instincts I have for it. They have a different purpose. Just like I didn't get one ounce of inspiration from playing basketball during PE in high school. But I'm sure Michael Jordan had a completely different experience. My point is there is potential value in everything. But the value is tied to knowing who we are and what we were meant to do.

So many people focus on how to make money and don't take the time to tune in to what their purpose is. When you know your purpose, your talents align. What you do ends up being of service to someone. The world benefits, whether on a small or large scale. Following your purpose doesn't necessarily mean making millions, but I believe if you are living your purpose, you will be provided for.

On my path to discovering my purpose, I've done some pretty unglamorous things. I've worked four jobs at a time just to pay the rent, lived all week on ten dollars worth of seafood-flavored Top Ramen, and had to drag a passed-out homeless dude from the restroom of a restaurant after he shat himself. The struggle is real, my friends. But what help could I be to you if I hadn't had all these experiences? What would I know about work if my parents had set me up with a trust fund that let me sip strawberry margaritas around the pool all day? Not that there's anything wrong with that, but it wouldn't have helped my purpose.

Learning your path involves realizing there is no job that is worthless or less than. The only job not good enough for you is the one that doesn't feed your purpose. From that perspective, the minimum-wage jobs I did in the beginning of my career were way more critical to my success than any later high-level executive jobs. But that corner-office gig may be the most important job to someone on a different path than I'm on.

One of my favorite TV personalities is Mike Rowe, who used to host *Dirty Jobs* on the Discovery Channel. He once gave a TED Talk where he discussed the "war on work" our country seems to be conducting. Since when did it become cool to criticize food workers and other minimum wage workers?

I remember a conversation I had with a coworker a few years ago. She was trying to decide what her son would do for a summer job. I mentioned my idea that working fast food is one of the most humbling, skill-building jobs a person can do. I emphasized how he could learn about customer service, sales, hustle, and business all in one place. She looked at me with conviction and said, "My son will be doing bigger things than that with his summer."

I shrugged. Truth is, who am I to say what her son should be doing with his summer? After all, I have no idea what his purpose is. What bothers me is minimum-wage jobs are viewed by society as being for losers only, as if it takes no brains to do them. I believe any job has the potential for dignified contribution. Any job can be critical to someone's success. Fine if it's not your cup of tea, but to view those who do that work as less than is not only deplorable in my book, it's ignorant.

We tend to view a job's worth based on how much money and power it produces. The day laborer's job is worth less than a pro ballplayer's. Yet the day laborer may be tending the home you live in, while you may never even meet the pro ballplayer.

This is not about fairness. I'm not saying it's unfair for the pro ballplayer to make a gazillion dollars a season. That's the beauty of capitalism. If you can find the demand for what you're supplying, then you can command money for it. I understand we also tend to value the rare.

I don't watch a lot of professional sports, so the value of that job is pretty low for me. But I get it. For centuries, humans have been obsessed with watching live competition, and sports is a major pastime for us. So if you are phenomenal at playing one of the big-time sports, you are going to make a nice living. Now, if you are a day laborer, your "product" may not be that unique. But if you have a unique way of delivering that product, if you put art into how you tend to landscaping or lay pavers, you might be able to turn that into something more marketable.

Of course, there are no guarantees or easy-to-follow instructions. But what I can say for sure is if you *don't* value your capabilities and unique talents, no one else will either. Many of you have spent so little time contemplating your purpose that you are completely disconnected from it. At the same time, you might be bitter that no one pays you more money for what you do...even though you may not value what you do either.

To know your value is a lifelong journey of discovery. But the first step is to remove judgment and shame. Some of us have unique talents that were embraced by the social circles we were born into, while others have been shamed, ridiculed, or belittled for our unique talents. We are leaving an age of few career options and entering one with room to be anything you want to be. We aren't fully in this new world yet, even with the bursts of creativity we see all around us (self-driving cars, anyone?). But we're getting there.

Most of us were raised by well-meaning parents who tried hard to turn us into productive adults. My mother was convinced the only jobs you could make money at were architect or doctor. I think she got the bug about being an architect from watching one too many episodes of *The Brady Bunch*. I mean Mike Brady managed to make enough money to provide a nice house for eight kids, a dog, and live-in Alice. I can't say it was a bad deduction on my mom's part, but it had nothing to do with my unique talents and passions.

I wanted to be a writer, an actress, a showgirl, and the first female POTUS. I was writing poems and short stories ever since I was old enough to put pen to paper. But as much as she embraced my interests, she told me every chance she got that only a few lucky ones made any money at it. She wasn't wrong. But she couldn't fathom a day when you could self-publish your own books on Amazon and then promote them online via social media. That's not the world she lived in.

As for being an actress or showgirl, let's just say she felt only women of a certain moral persuasion went into that line of work. Yet I loved the idea of entertaining audiences and changing people's lives through my art. After all, if it hadn't been for television shows such as *The Jeffersons*, I wouldn't have had the conviction that I could "move on up" through hustle and honest work.

What I do believe is there are clues in childhood fantasies and dreams, if you look for them. What you are attracted to contains information about your purpose. Like me, maybe you were also raised by parents who denied their own purpose. This doesn't make them bad parents, but it doesn't qualify them to help us find our purpose, either.

Get Acquainted with Yourself

Are you tuned into what ignites your passion? I do a lot of career coaching, and the first thing people want to know is how to climb a ladder. But hardly anyone knows why they're climbing the ladder or why they chose that particular ladder to climb.

Before I jump in with strategies on how to negotiate that ladder, I have to get them to realize — and care about — their own personal purpose. Typically, that starts with me asking a lot of "why" questions. Like a kid asking why the sky is blue, I'm relentless. And I usually frustrate the other people. They look at me like they've been sold a bill of goods. I must be a fraud and a waste of their time. If I'm such a great career coach, then shouldn't I know the right career path for them?

And just like that they've gotten to the heart of the issue, and one of the biggest challenges: people can only hear, and make use of, advice that is in sync with their level of self-awareness. So I refuse to move to the tactical stage of career coaching until they have a sense of what their calling is.

They used to call me the Employee Whisperer. At first, it was just for fun. But I take the sentiment behind that nickname seriously these days. I believe there is nothing more critical than a person tuning in to who they are at their core and being able to express that through the work they do. So for me, the most important aspect of coaching is helping others tune in to that. Everything else is just a math problem. Not to belittle the work, but the path that opens up for you once you know your purpose is a lot clearer and rewarding.

Get out There and Date, You Big Flirt

So where do we start? Well, the first thing I do is help the people I'm working with pay attention to their lives — to open themselves up to their longings and to trust what they are attracted to is meant for them. In a way, I encourage them to respond to their wants like a child would rather than an adult. In this case, "gimme gimme gimme" is better than denying, or not even noticing, what they're attracted to.

There are plenty of ways we become shut off from what excites us. We can grow numb to life because it hurts too much to hear something we know we are meant for is only for "other people." Or we can judge those who have what we desire. We tell ourselves a story about how the person driving that fancy car is probably super-materialistic. We assume the woman who lives in that nice house is some trophy wife who married rich. The truth is we have no idea.

Think about this time as an exploratory stage. What I tell people is to get out there and *date their lives*, flirt with their surroundings. Stop worrying about whether or not something is possible and just start to allow themselves to connect to those things in the universe that speak to them.

My job at this stage is to help people activate their brains and ignite their passions. What does dating one's life look like? I tell people to start tracking the things that make them curious, angry, jealous or, yes, lustful. Now is not the time to worry about whether we think we should go after any of it or whether any of it is for us.

This idea came to me when I was working in human resources at the Walt Disney Company. On the surface, I had a pretty sweet gig. I'd been promoted at a time when few people were moving up, thanks to the crappy economy. I loved the people I worked with and I felt appreciated and valued on the job. But something was missing.

I started noticing this woman as I'd pull into the parking garage at random times of the day. She was lean and in shape and always seemed to be returning from a jog. She looked so carefree and light. At the time, I had put on quite a bit of weight. So at first I felt shame when I saw her. I had let myself go. Then I felt anger. She had such a small build she probably never had to worry about putting on weight. I pictured her laughing with her friends at lunch while casually eating a juicy bacon burger. Her skin glowed, and she didn't have a care in the world. How could she? I mean she jogged whenever she wanted. Her thighs were tiny and her shorts didn't ride up. I couldn't even wear shorts at the time for fear of the thigh burn that would inevitably ensue.

As the days went on, I continued to bump into her. What stood out was she wasn't at work in the middle of the day. She wasn't wearing some polyester blend suit hoping to look professional. I was. I was working seven days a week, averaging fourteen-hour days. Not that anyone was making me do that; I'd always been a bit of a workaholic. But what I noticed was my health was deteriorating. Something wasn't aligned in my life.

Then I started to notice more people jogging during the day. There seemed to be a revolution of people not in the office during business hours. And they all seemed so much happier than I was. How dare they.

My mind started to tune in. If I was noticing this phenomenon and having such strong emotional reactions, I knew I needed to pay attention. So I examined what was calling to me. A few things came up, all related to the sense of freedom I imagined these afternoon joggers experienced. For all I knew, they were all out-of-work actors with nothing better to do. But their reality wasn't the point. Mine was. What mattered was what my reactions told me about what I wanted for my future.

Eventually, I realized it was time for me to venture back out on my own as a consultant. It was a yearlong journey of self-exploration, with several other factors playing into it, but the more I tuned in, the more I saw those breadcrumbs leading me down the path.

The crumbs weren't just about my work; they were about my life in general. I believe I was being called to a healthier lifestyle, with more time for myself and more control over how I spent that time. I still work seven days a week and clock a ton of hours every day, but now I'm investing my time in activities that give me a major return on my energy. My activities are in alignment with my purpose, and I feel satisfied.

I still haven't taken an afternoon jog, but the point is I could if I wanted to. I am in the driver's seat of my life's experience. And there is an indescribable power in that.

Past, Present, and Future

Another way to help identify your passions is with the Past, Present, and Future questionnaire. Your answers to these questions will help identify how much you know about yourself, how deeply you value your skills, and whether you are connected to your purpose or still running on the hamster wheel of success as defined by someone else.

Whatever it takes to help you identify what you love, you need to take the time to do it. Please note: it's perfectly acceptable for you to love something that you don't do for a living. In this case, you may choose work that supports you being able to do more of that. Either way, what's critical is for your life to align with your purpose. This is what helps us feel content, successful, and balanced. There is no better gift that you can give yourself than accepting and cherishing who you are and the unique role you play in this world.

Career Questionnaire

Fill out the following questionnaire to help you reflect on where you've been, where you want to go, and what you may need to help you get there. Feel free to discuss the exercise with those close to you to help you get a comprehensive view of your background

FOCUS AREA	EXPERIENCES
	What are the most important skills you've learned so far? Why?
	How would you describe your progress in your career thus far?
PAST / CURRENT CAREER	What have been the most impactful experiences for you? Why?
	What are your favorite and least favorite aspects of your current role?
	What is the one task or type of project you would like to do more frequently in future roles? Less frequently?

FOCUS AREA	CURRENT STRENGTHS
	What do you do really well?
	What are you recognized for most often?
	What are your unique experiences and capabilities?
CURRENT STRENGTHS	Which of your accomplishments are you proudest of?
	What kind of work gives you the most energy?
	What kind of work drains your energy?

FOCUS AREA	SKILL GAPS
SKILL GAPS	What experiences or capabilities do you lack that people on a similar career path have?
	What do others perceive as your greatest weakness?
	What development gaps do you need to address before you can pursue your career goals?
	What other experiences do you need to have in order to accomplish your career goals?
	How well do your career goals align with your current development opportunities?

FOCUS AREA	PERSONAL DRIVERS
PERSONAL DRIVERS	Describe a time that you felt extremely motivated to give 100% to a project / initiative.
	What do you value most in terms of your career?
	What do you consider a reward for a job well done?
	What role would ultimately position you to do what you've always wanted to do? Why?
	What tends to negatively affect your motivation?

CHAPTER 3:
Know What
Makes You Pop

*"Keep knocking and the joy inside will eventually
open a window and look out to see who's there."*

—Rumi

When I'm coaching people, after helping them start paying attention to their lives and igniting their passions, we move to filling out this diagram, which I use for aligning purpose with actions. This is what I call your Pyramid of Purpose, or POP.

I think of our purpose as that top stone of a pyramid. When you look at a pyramid, every stone is the same except for that top one. Everything else is a brick that helps make up the pyramid's base. But the top stone is unique. Our purpose is the same. No one else can necessarily see it; only we know if we're living our purpose.

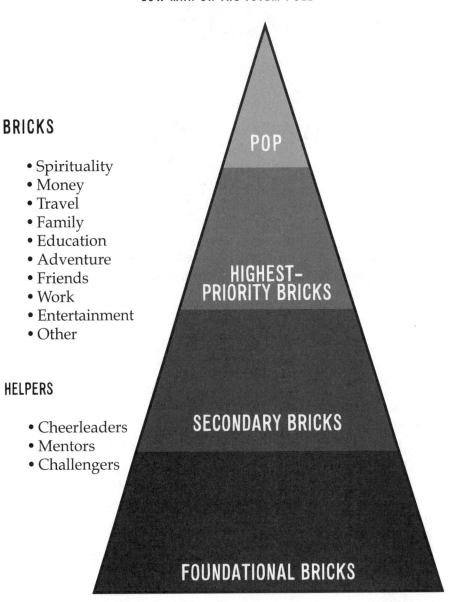

BRICKS

- Spirituality
- Money
- Travel
- Family
- Education
- Adventure
- Friends
- Work
- Entertainment
- Other

HELPERS

- Cheerleaders
- Mentors
- Challengers

POP

HIGHEST-PRIORITY BRICKS

SECONDARY BRICKS

FOUNDATIONAL BRICKS

Pyramid of Purpose Key

- **POP**—The top of your pyramid represents your purpose in life. This is always intangible and can only be measured by you. It can change throughout life. The bricks below should be lined up strategically to support you achieving your purpose. Without an awareness of your purpose, you may be stacking your bricks in a way that achieves a different purpose entirely and leaves you feeling less successful and content with life.

- **Bricks** — The bricks listed are general examples of the tools/resources people may use to achieve their purpose. It's a reminder that work or money is never the purpose. However, it's important to know how work and money serve to support your purpose.

  - **Highest-Priority Bricks** — These bricks are the most clearly connected to your purpose. This doesn't mean they are more important than the other bricks, but they will likely get most of your time and focus while you work toward your purpose.

  - **Secondary Bricks** — These bricks are important and get some time investment. However, they tend to work as support for the highest-priority bricks. If your purpose is to leave behind tools or products that help others live better lives, your highest-priority bricks may include Work, and a secondary brick may be Vacation/Travel as a way to keep you fueled for the work you do.

  - **Foundational Bricks** — These bricks serve a critical role of keeping things going. However, there will probably be less time invested in them. In the preceding example, the person may have Family as a foundational brick. This doesn't mean family isn't important to them, it just means it serves as the foundation that enables the person to go after his or her purpose. However, someone who sees his or her purpose as being a good provider for his or her family will put the Family brick in the highest-priority brick row.

- **Helpers** — This represents the key people to have in your life to support you achieving your purpose. One person may play all three roles. You may have several of one type of helper and zero of another. This just highlights the type of support you may want to bring into your circle.

  - **Cheerleaders** give you energy through support and unwavering belief in what you're capable of.

  - **Teachers and mentors** provide guidance and wisdom because they have traveled toward a similar purpose.

  - **Challengers and nemeses** can sometimes show up in difficult ways. But their purpose is to push you beyond what you're currently capable of. Sometimes that's done through intentional "tough love." Sometimes that occurs by them just behaving in ways that trigger you. Either way, they can be leveraged for valuable lessons and skill building.

Breaking Down the Pyramid: *Just Another Brick in the Wall*

When looking at the bricks that make up your Pyramid of Purpose, the bricks and/or their placement will change throughout your life. Sometimes the money brick is high up on the pyramid, and other times it may move to the bottom. Other bricks that may be on your pyramid include family, adventure, friends, school/education, travel, health/fitness, work, and just about anything else you can think of that supports what you are up to.

BRICKS

- Spirituality
- Money
- Travel

- Family
- Education
- Adventure
- Friends
- Work
- Entertainment
- Other

The key is to place your bricks thoughtfully or at least be aware of them and where they are on your pyramid. The higher up on the pyramid, the more time you will invest in those bricks. This usually means there is greater risk and sacrifice associated with those bricks.

In my twenties, for example, education was a priority. I spent most of my time studying. I took risks to make sure I could finish my schooling. But in my thirties, the money and work bricks were about equal near the top, and the education brick dropped toward the bottom. It became part of my foundation instead of my focus. As time went on, I had years that were mostly about travel and adventure. Now in my forties, the health and fitness brick has moved up. I'm noticing my work brick is sliding down, but the money brick is moving up. I'm looking for ways to invest and get money to work for me so I'm not constantly working.

Family and friends are important to me, but I see those bricks as part of my support system. It's not that they lack priority or value in my life; it's just that the time and risk taking associated with them has been minimal. I've chosen not to have children (at least so far). I've also spent many years single and not in a relationship because of my focus on education and work.

I'm always perplexed when people discuss work/life balance. By conventional thinking, my life is majorly out of whack when I'm in my flow, but I love what I do. For me it's not about balance; it's about alignment and knowing how to shift when necessary.

People Who Need People Are the Luckiest People

Now as much as family and friends are not my top bricks, the people in my life are critical to my satisfaction and progress. This includes my closest loved ones and — surprisingly — those I've sometimes seen as my nemeses.

There are at least three roles people can play on your Pyramid of Purpose. Some people play all three roles at different times. Others stay firmly in one role. Regardless of where they sit, they all serve to help you.

HELPERS

- Cheerleaders
- Teachers or Mentors
- Challengers or Nemeses

Cheerleaders

Cheerleaders energize your journey. They don't necessarily have to get what your purpose is about, but they believe in you. They are excited to see you succeed at what you love.

These people understand you won't always be available when you are going after your life's purpose. They accept you will sometimes do strange things to reach your goals. They seek to understand what you care about and do what they can to make your path easier. They tend not to question or critique you. As far as they're concerned, you are winning simply by going after your dreams.

These people are amazing and precious. They are the fuel in your gas tank for the long journey. It is imperative that you don't take these people for granted. While they love unconditionally, they will not demand your time. Don't overlook them.

Teachers or Mentors

Teachers and mentors hold valuable wisdom and experience directly related to your purpose. They don't need to be older or more advanced; I'm amazed at how many children serve as teachers to those willing to tune in to their unvarnished, natural wisdom.

Teachers or Mentors tend to push you out of your comfort zone. They may dish out tough love and a fair amount of criticism. The point isn't to make you feel good; it's about getting you to wake up to your purpose and to help you step out of your comfort zone. Their pushing tends to be deliberate and helpful. They consider how much you can handle and what you are truly ready for.

I hope this book serves as some form of teaching or mentoring for you. If what I write here ruffles your feathers, I'm quite all right with that. What I'm not okay with is you not knowing how to harness your best self. And I'm not okay with you telling yourself you are the victim of circumstances. Not on my watch, my friend.

Challengers or Nemeses

Challengers and nemeses possess qualities that trigger you. They're the people on the team who drive you nuts — the boss who intimidates you, or the client who infuriates you. They tend to bring out negative emotions in us, such as anger or fear, which points to something in ourselves that we must tackle to be prepared for the next level of our journey.

I see the journey as a video game of sorts. Imagine speeding through level one. You completed it, but you didn't master jumping over all its obstacles. Now you get to level two and find the same obstacles to jump over, but now fireballs are coming at you. If you didn't master the obstacle-navigation skill in level one, the fireballs of level two will surely turn you into toast.

When I'm coaching people who can't stand another person, I try to convince them that avoiding the person, hoping she or he goes away, or deciding to quit, is like guaranteeing they come across this same troubling behavior in an even higher-stakes situation.

Instead, I suggest gratitude might be a better response. The truth is this person just set them up to move to the next level, if only they are willing to listen to what their fear or anger is telling them. That doesn't always happen right away, of course. Many of us are busy casting ourselves as the heroes or victims of our stories and others as the villains. The problem with this narrative is it puts us in the passenger seat and not the driver's seat. Better to see these people as challengers who have something to teach us. That way, we stay in the driver's seat and focus on what we need to learn to get to the next level.

My Pyramid

As for my purpose, I look at it as helping people find *their* purpose. Granted, that's a bit intangible. How will I know when I've accomplished my purpose? Only I can be the judge of that. My instincts will tell me when I've arrived and when I have more work to do. Some might see their purpose as being a good father or experiencing the world or changing the world. There's no wrong purpose. And your purpose may shift throughout your lifetime.

I look back at all the different jobs I've held over my career. I can remember feeling disengaged and irritated with most of them. I can see now that my level of satisfaction or dissatisfaction was directly connected to how much I felt I was helping people find their purpose.

I remember coming up against this dilemma when I was in the United States Air Force. I was a Russian linguist, and this particular assignment had me working for the National Security Agency with a top-secret security clearance. Fancy, I know. But I was bored out of my mind. Truth be told, I spent most of my time on a computer as opposed to interacting directly with humans. I can't tell you how many times I got in trouble for distracting my team members with *Cosmopolitan* quizzes about their personalities and discussing their motivations and fears. Not stuff you would have found in my job description.

When it was time to decide whether I'd reenlist, the master sergeant sat me down like I was his daughter, not the best approach for someone like me. I've never been one to respond well to the wise old sage imparting wisdom to the naive youngster. He was surprised to find out I wasn't going to reenlist. When all his tactics failed to sway me, he resorted to the ultimate guilt play: "But what about your patriotic duty?"

Now that hit me hard. I grew up in a military family with a military last name, for crying out loud. I'd watched *G.I. Jane* more times than I want to admit. When I originally joined, I dreamed of changing gender norms and riding through the front lines, sacrificing my own safety to protect my country. Instead, I was tied to a desk job that I couldn't help think was a waste of government dollars. What was worse is the military owned me. I couldn't quit or apply for a job that better suited my talents.

To my mind, it would have taken nothing short of a constitutional amendment to change my career path. So I looked my master sergeant square in the eyes and said, "I don't trust the military to allow me to fulfill my patriotic duty. I'd rather gamble on my ability to find out what that is and deliver on it on my own."

Bold words for a twenty-something with no idea what she wanted to do with her life. But I sensed I wouldn't find out if I stayed in the military. So I finished my enlistment and reentered the civilian workforce. One decision led to another, and here you have me. Looking back, I can see that as much as my job involved helping others, it didn't specifically focus on *helping others find their purpose* (which I would later identify as *my* true purpose).

The Marine

Here's another example of how this plays out. Years ago I was doing some customer service training for the call center employees of a popular cruise company. This was about the time I first started using my pyramid theory. My concept was simple: If people were clear on their purpose, they would be more service-oriented. They'd see how choosing to work in customer service supported their ultimate purpose, even if only temporarily. The point was, customer service wasn't just about the customers—it was about the employees. The more employees viewed what they did as supporting their purpose, the better customer service they provided. That stellar service was a natural and inevitable outcome, or side effect, of their attitude.

So I asked the class if anyone there knew their "top of the pyramid." A large hand shot up, and a deep voice boomed from the back, "I do." Up stood a formidably sized young man. He explained he had been in the Marines.

He explained the top of his pyramid was to be the CEO of the company. A few people chuckled. I said there's nothing wrong with wanting to be the CEO. People become CEOs all the time. But I didn't believe that was the top of his pyramid. He got a bit argumentative and defiant. I asked him what he would do if the company went out of business. He said he'd go be the CEO of a different company. So I explained a title or job is always a brick in the pyramid. It may be an important brick, but it's still a brick. It can be exchanged for something else. It's not our ultimate purpose.

So then I asked why he wanted to be a CEO. He thought about it and then replied it was for, you guessed it, money. I shook my head again. Then I explained money is never the top of the pyramid. Money is always a brick as well. It helps fund our purpose, but it's never our purpose. If money is integral to the funding of your purpose, it will be toward the top of the pyramid. Think Wall Street banker. If money supports your purpose but it's not the closest thing to your purpose, it may be toward the bottom of your pyramid. Think Mother Teresa. Money wasn't her focus, but you can bet money enabled her to give more to the people she was trying to help.

My favorite quote on the topic is from Oprah, who asked: "Who do I help by being poor?" Oprah's money brick is up there, but you can bet she doesn't inspire millions because her purpose is money. She can reach millions because of the empire she's built. Her purpose is funded by money, but it's not money itself.

The marine looked skeptical, and so did most of the class, so I put it to a test. I asked them to raise their hands if they were willing to take $1 million from me, tax-free and 100 percent legal. Most raised their hands. Those who didn't said they were waiting to hear the catch.

Well, the first catch was this was make-believe. The second catch was they wouldn't be able to use or move the money. It had to stay in the room we were in. They couldn't buy anything with it, invest it, or borrow against it. Who wanted it now? Everyone dropped their hands. With those stipulations, money was nothing but paper taking up space.

I did have one guy say he'd invite his friends over and show them all the cash. They wouldn't know he couldn't spend it. As clever as that scheme seems, the reality is he would still be using the money to "buy" popularity. Money was still just a brick being used to build something else.

The moral of this little game was money is only of use to us for what it can buy. That means money by itself is worth nothing. This makes it a tool instead of a purpose. People who have money high on their list of priorities are usually using it as a brick to buy or build an intangible purpose—security, status, popularity, freedom, etc. If the million dollars is just sitting in a room and can't be spent, then the money itself is useless. That's how you know it's a brick.

Once I had the marine sold on the idea that money is a brick and not a purpose, I asked him why he wanted so much of it. What would he buy with all that money? He paused and then said he'd buy himself a new house, another for his mom, and also a new car for her. This, of course, won over every girl in the class. But I found this interesting. I continued with my questioning. Why did he want to buy a new house and car for his mom? Was she in a poor area or car-less?

He paused and slowly shook his head. No. He explained he wanted to give back to her for all the sacrifices she had made for him. I then asked if working in the call center had anything to do with his mom. He paused and shrugged. I took a stab and said it seemed that even though he had written his purpose was to "to be a CEO," his choices and values all seemed to align with wanting to be a good son.

I'd hit a chord. I could tell by the way his eyes watered up a bit. I asked if I might be on to something, and he nodded quietly. I let it go at this point and moved on. He had shared way more than he had planned, I could tell. I wasn't in the business of exposing people's soft underbellies. I just wanted to help them get to their truth.

After class he approached me. He said what I had observed was right on point but that he realized that what he really wanted to do is live a life of adventure.He explained he had joined the Marines to get out and see the world. He loved his time in the service. But his mother was constantly stressed about what harm may come to him. So at his first chance, he got out of the Marines and came back to be with his mom.

He took this job because it was at least with a travel company. But since he'd been back he'd been edgy and even picking fights with his mom. He missed the adventure he experienced in the Marines. I pointed out that he was *hovering* around a purpose of seeing the world but *living* the purpose of being a good son. Where he was, wasn't his mother's fault. He chose to make being a good son his purpose. If he wanted something different to be his purpose, such as experiencing the world, then he needed to make that choice. And if he wasn't going to do that, there was no point in blaming someone else.

When we aren't happy with the circumstances of our lives, we so often blame someone or something else. The reality is being dedicated and loyal to our Pyramid of

Purpose takes risk and sacrifice, and may not make everyone around us happy.

Somewhere we were told life was all about being happy. I disagree. There is plenty of beauty to be found in pain and suffering. Some of my most gorgeous lessons came packaged in trauma, loss, and disaster. People frequently use the analogy of a caterpillar changing into a butterfly to describe transformation. But what everyone leaves out is just how gnarly the process inside the cocoon is. There's a reason nature knows to hide it away from everyone. But think about it—that caterpillar is dropping serious weight, losing legs, and sprouting wings. Brutal. Nature is brutal. Life is brutal. There is beauty in that brutality if you understand what transformation is.

The marine was in the middle of a transformation, evolving into the next level of himself. And he had some tough decisions to make. Eventually he made peace with the fact that he was in a transition phase. His father had died the year before, and he wanted to be there for his mom. He got he needed to acknowledge he was, in effect, choosing to be a good son as his purpose, and therefore his job was perfectly suited to supporting that. But the job was also temporary. At the same time, he was slowly building toward his purpose of seeing and exploring the world, and when the time was right, he would have that conversation with his mother.

This little realization put his focus back in alignment. He stopped feeling so frustrated, lost, and bitter with his situation and the people he believed had put him there. As a side effect, he showed up fully committed to his current job, and the company benefited from that.

The IT Guy

Here's one more example of the Pyramid of Purpose in action. This also happened while I was doing work at the cruise company. I got a call from one of the leaders in their IT department. She had an employee who worked the night shift. His job was to help troubleshoot issues the ships may be having while out at sea. If he couldn't solve the problem, he would have to contact one of the leaders on call to help resolve the issue. People on the ships and in the office had complained about him being difficult and disrespectful. The IT leader let me know the employee needed customer service training.

I'm always cautious when people "prescribe" solutions for employee challenges. To me, it's a little like a patient telling a doctor what medication she or he needs. So I set up some time to meet meet with the employee after one of his night shifts.

The empllyee was none too thrilled about having to meet with one of the "suits," as he put it. I'm used to being seen as the enemy when I first start working with people. It's common, and often arises from people having been treated like problems instead of human beings.

As the employee described it, the "jerks" in the office and on the ship didn't know "their head from their ass." He said he'd been working this job for decades and knew his stuff but that people didn't like the answers, so they wanted to talk to somebody with a fancy title. That meant he had to call one of the on-call leaders, who were, of course, all in bed. They got irritated with him because they didn't want to climb out of bed and drive to the office. He shook his head.

After listening to the employee's side of things, I started to explain the Pyramid of Purpose concept. He stopped me right away and let me know he was not one of those self-help suckers. He didn't care one bit about all the touchy-feely guru stuff I was peddling. Fine. "Then tell me what matters to you," I said. He told me all he cared about was getting his boss off his back.

All right. I could work with that. But I called bullshit. The employee would have been making different decisions if he cared that much about his boss. So I pushed. I asked, "What if I could guarantee your boss loved everything you did. Would you feel like your life was complete?" He shook his head in disgust. He told me he could care less what the "suits" thought of him. I could tell that was the truth.

I pushed again. I asked what he'd wish for if he could change one thing about his job. He said he'd want everyone off his back. I called bullshit again. He'd perform differently if that were the case. He was a bright and clever guy. I didn't buy that was a priority for him.

The employee got pretty frustrated and angry with me. He shouted that he took the night shift to avoid dealing with jackasses and all he cared about was getting a paycheck. Dare I push him further? Yes, I dared. So I called bullshit for a third time. If he cared about getting a paycheck, then he should be fine, because the company had paychecks. But he kept making decisions that put him on write-ups, preventing him from being eligible for raises, promotions, and bonuses.

"Look," the employee said, "all I care about is getting off work and spending time with my son." Then he grew quiet and his body folded inward. Awwww…now we were on to something. We had gotten past his bravado and tapped into something that truly mattered to him.

I explained if his purpose was to be a good father, he'd have to make some different decisions while on the job. He got defensive again and exclaimed, "I am a good father." I assured him I was not about to critique his fathering skills. But I pointed out that his behavior had been aligned to a purpose that seemed more about being right and winning than about being a good father.

Working the night shift chipped into his energy reserves in a way that a regular day shift wouldn't. To ensure he had as much positive energy as possible for his son, he needed to make decisions that reduced rather than increased his stress levels. All that fighting and arguing was just adding negative energy instead of positive energy. Combined with the sleep challenges of a night shift, that drastically reduced the quality of energy he had left over for his son.

I had his attention. We started discussing how being patient with others and selling instead of pushing his solutions on people would help keep his stress levels low. He left the coaching session. I wasn't sure if he would change, but I knew he was much clearer on what purpose he was choosing.

A month later, I checked in with the employee's manager, and she explained she hadn't received any complaints regarding him since our coaching session. Interesting. I started coming in early, hoping I'd run into him. I did. When he saw me he immediately tried to turn the other way, but being the pushy little self-help guru I am, I chased him down.

Once I caught up to him, I asked how things were going. He shrugged and said "Fine," the people person in him shining brightly. I mentioned his manager had told me things seemed to be working well. He let out a long, irritated sigh and then said, "I did your whole Kumbaya pyramid thing." Oh, how I was falling for this prickly charmer. I asked what Kumbaya pyramid thing he did.

The employee told me he was bothered by how much energy he'd been wasting on people he didn't care about and that doing so was taking away from quality time with this son. So he took a picture of his son and stuck it on his office phone. Every time he got a call, he'd stare at his son's picture and ask himself what he needed to do to make sure his boy got the best of him once he was off the clock.

Now as great as this news was, the man still had a lot to learn about navigating conflict. What was great is he stopped investing in a purpose that wasn't bringing him any satisfaction — the purpose of being right at all costs. Instead, he was now investing his energy and time into something that truly meant something to him — lowering his stress levels so he had more to offer his son.

The moral of all these stories is simply to be clear as to what your purpose is. Align your priorities to that purpose. Don't blame others if your pyramid of purpose is out of whack. This is your pyramid to tend to.

CHAPTER 4:
The New Rules

"Adaptation is a profound process. Means you figure out how to thrive in the world."

—John Laroche, character from the film,
"Adaptation"

We've discussed how to get aligned with your purpose. Now let's prepare you for navigating the work world in pursuit of that purpose. Here are some of the new rules of the workplace that few people reference directly, even though they're pretty prevalent in all the work environments I've come across so far.

New Rule #1-Think Like a Businessperson Not a Student

No matter what generation we hail from, a lot of us show up like students in the workplace. We are waiting to be taken care of by the powers that be. In school, those in charge make all the decisions. They map out our entire future. Sure, we may get to choose an elective or two, but even those are curated for us. We spend eighteen to thirty years, sometimes more, in school and then are unleashed into the workplace completely ill-equipped to think like businesspeople.

Sometimes those who did the best in school are the ones who struggle the most. Think about it. If you get good grades in eleventh grade, what are you guaranteed? A spot in twelfth grade, of course. There's no, "Hey, it's tough out there. There's only a few twelfth-grade spots. The competition is stiff, so bring your best." No. Promotion is *guaranteed* to anyone who completes eleventh grade. So we get high performance ratings in the business place and then are offended when we don't get a promotion too.

But here's the thing: promotions are *not* rewards. A promotion is a new damn job. Get that through your head. We live in a world where an army of junior analysts scrutinizes every big company and how they use their funds, and that includes how they handle head count. If your company doesn't have a need for the position you are getting promoted into, you, my friend, are a prime candidate for getting axed in the next reorg. And let me tell you, your company will be doing reorganizations on the regular. It's the new way of staying nimble in an ever-changing economy. I can't tell you how many people I've seen promote themselves out of a job.

If you applied for a job with a higher title and pay at another company, they wouldn't look at your résumé and say, "Wow, look how hard and long you worked. We should reward you." Hell no! First, they need a strategic reason for the position in question to even exist. Next, you need to be the right fit. This is a combination of experience, style, and — increasingly in this social media–driven world — developed relationships.

Here's the deal: business is not like school. For starters, the people in charge at school get paid to guide you to success. But in business, *you* are getting paid to help the company succeed. That means they don't owe you a mapped-out career path. They don't owe you promotions and raises. They don't owe you anything other than the negotiated rate for your services.

Tough talk, I know. But I also get how it's not entirely employees' fault. For decades we've been working for highly structured organizations. These organizations were based off the same structure as factories. They needed employees to focus on doing the same thing over and over again. There weren't computers to do repetitive tasks or databases to hold all the knowledge and history. So long-term employees were the lifeblood for these businesses.

Because they needed a workforce that would hang around for as long as possible, they groomed us to do just that. Central to work was loyalty to the company, and we were often rewarded just for showing up, getting promotions for time in service. The idea being the longer you stay, the better it gets, with that gold watch dangling at the end of it all. Geez. Companies even paid for people's retirement. Anything to keep the employees obedient and loyal.

But the challenges businesses face today are different. It's no longer about producing the same reliable product year after year. It's about constantly coming up with innovative products or services. So businesses need a nimble, dynamic workforce instead of a steady-state one

On the other hand, we're not entirely off the hook for thinking like students in the workplace. You know how capitalism works, right? When I hear people complain companies just don't care about their employees anymore, I tell them that in business, it never was about "caring" for the employees in the first place. It was about ensuring a steady supply of labor and doing what was good for the bottom line. That doesn't sit well with a lot of people. They will call that greed. I simply see it as the way businesses need to operate to stay in existence.

I don't have an issue with companies being out for a profit. But the smartest CEOs understand investing in their employees can help their companies thrive. That investment includes retention strategies, development opportunities, and promoting from within. But it's not an obligation or duty. In fact, it's dangerous to treat investing in employees as anything other than a business strategy. Why do you think we saw that huge wave wipe out so many middle- and upper-management positions in the 1980s? When the purse strings got tightened, the people who were promoted as a reward as opposed to a business need were the first to go. And that trend has only increased in this century.

The good news is this phenomenon opens up a lot of opportunity. If you're not following a prescribed career path (because one basically doesn't exist), you can carve your own. As daunting as that may sound to those still thinking like students, the truth is you have a better chance than ever at doing work that feeds your soul when blazing your own path and thinking like a businessperson.

When it comes to anything you want from a company — whether a promotion, development opportunity, new assignment, or raise — you need to see what you're asking for as a business trade. You should have a solid rationale for what you're trying to get from the company, and you'd better make damn sure there's something in it for them. The old "I'm a hard worker and I deserve it" line needs to be permanently blotted from your vocabulary. Instead, you need to steep yourself in a "Here's how my idea can help you" kind of approach.

New Rule #2-Focus on Building Your Brand vs. Collecting Titles

When I teach a class, one of the first things people ask is how they can get a promotion. What do they want to do? Invariably, they spit out the title above their own. We've been taught to get as many letters behind our title as possible. What they aren't seeing is how all this title chasing is just part of getting lost in the hamster wheel community.

If I ask them what makes them unique, I get a blank stare. If I inquire about the service they are selling, they may regurgitate the title of their department or function. But they have no idea how to distinguish themselves in the marketplace.

Vice president, lead supervisor, senior manager, head mechanic…those are generic titles that a million other people hold. If you tell me that's your title, or if I see it on your résumé, it gives me a sense of what you do but no idea *how* you do it or, more important, how *well* you do it. That's the difference between building your brand and collecting titles.

Think about it. What creates a more lasting impression, "coffee" or "Starbucks"? "car" or "Ferrari"? "Talk show host" or "Oprah"? To stand out from the supposed competition, you need people to get your brand, whether you're an administrative assistant, plumber, or executive.

I remember one employee who had a strong reaction when he realized I expected him to define and build his brand. Here was this guy who was known as one of the nicest people in the company, sitting there clearly trying to lock down his anger. I had a great deal of respect for this guy, so I was a bit concerned at his reaction.

I asked what bothered him. He explained he hated the idea of doing stuff like this. That it felt like bragging and didn't feel authentic. He just wanted to do a good job, go where he was needed, and not have a fuss made about him.

But here's the truth of his situation: Our department had been reorganized. My manager was trying to figure out who belonged where and how best to protect our jobs. This was 2008, and they were cleaning house, especially in human resources. When she asked my employee, Salvador, what he ideally wanted to do, he essentially told her, "Whatever you need me to do." In his mind, he was being a team player. In his mind, he was being low maintenance. Actually, he was making her job difficult.

The reality of human resources is corporations use it to clean house and lay people off, then they lean out HR itself. Why? Because we are a cost center. We cost money; we don't make it. Also, most of our jobs are seen as nice-to-haves instead of need-to-haves. That's the nature of the beast. You can either bitch and moan about it or figure out how to deliver need-to-have services. I choose the latter.

My manager was trying to figure out how to place Salvador somewhere that wouldn't get picked apart or seen as not necessary to the mission. But she was doing that for a whole department. As great as Salvador was and as much as she liked him, what he used to do had been eliminated. So by not being able to define his own brand, he was creating more work for her at a time when jobs were getting cut left and right. Not a solid strategy. Little did he know she had come to me and said, "Find it. Find what he can be good at. I don't want to lose him, but he's not doing himself any favors."

So there I was looking at this wonderful, committed employee who had a lot going for him—everything but a business mind-set. Here's how I explained the purpose of branding to him. If he walked into a store and every product was in the same box with no labeling, how would he make decisions about what he would buy?

A little light came on for Salvador, but it was just a flicker. He was still struggling with the bragging piece. "So I have to label myself with 'new and improved'?" he laughed. Not exactly.

Then I said, "Think about what labels do. Ideally, a good label creates an emotional reaction. It makes clear what the product is, what its core attributes or benefits are, and what makes it unique. And it does all this within a second or two." I emphasized that a good brand for him would make it easy for his customers, peers, and managers to know how to get the best out of him, to know how and where to leverage his skills, and to know what not to expect from him. In the end, he should stop seeing branding as bragging and start seeing it as teaching. He was going to make it easy to learn how to work with him.

Now this hit home for Salvador. It wasn't about saying, "Look at me. I'm so special. I'm better than everyone else." It was about knowing what services you provide and making it easy for the end user to leverage them.

We also looked into the "why" behind the services and skills he brought to the table. Remember the Pyramid of

Purpose? What was driving how he approached his work? In the end, a large part of his brand was his ability to adapt to multiple situations, support the team, and implement strategy. The point was we didn't use branding to make him somebody he wasn't. We used branding to make it clearer exactly who he was and who he wasn't. From there, we could better determine the best position for him.

Titles have their place and probably never will go away. They are useful, after all, to show where you sit within an organization. But their importance is waning. They are only a small piece of what people use to get a sense of who you are. If you remember that you are running your own business no matter where you decide to work or set up shop, you'll realize that building your brand is part of the customer service you should be providing to every person you work with.

New Rule #3—Weave a Web vs. Climb a Ladder

This rule is about your career path and dovetails with the previous one about not getting too caught up in titles. Now here's the thing: I would never discourage anyone from going after their dreams. If you sense your path is meant for leadership, you need to follow that.

Can you guess the number one reason companies ask for my help? To coach employees who have promoted themselves into a position of incompetence. Just because you are awesome at making widgets doesn't mean you will be equally awesome at leading a bunch of widget makers. Leading people is a whole different ball of wax, as they say. Unfortunately, it's been treated as a part of the natural evolution of a successful employee. I may be a great people leader and business strategist and not know squat about fixing a car. And you may be a genius mechanic and not be talented in the least at leading people. One does not necessarily lead to the other, nor is one more important than the other.

I'm simplifying, of course, but the point is people management is an art and talent all its own. But most companies treat moving into management as the normal evolution for anyone who is good at their job and motivated for success. Then, to make it worse, they provide little training on how to be an effective people manager. So we've got employees everywhere who accept these critical roles for the extra pay and the symbolism of moving up a rung on the ladder, and they are simply winging it.

Now, some come to the table with a natural talent for leadership. We see these folks who seem to take to leadership like fish to water, and we mistakenly believe leadership just happens, or at least it should. But the truth is there are many more "leaders" who have absolutely no business being there. They're miserable, and often making everyone around them miserable too.

A couple things are shifting in organizations that make the old adage "People don't leave their jobs; they leave their leaders" a little less relevant. For one, people are changing jobs a lot more, and that includes managers. Gone are the days of working with one leader for decades.

Also, more and more work is getting done through projects. Project management used to be a specialized field. Large organizations would have tons of people with "project manager" in their title. Now, lots of employees get the majority of their work done via projects. And that can mean you are managing people who don't necessarily report to you. With project-based work and less hierarchical organizations, the ability to lead has become even more critical and less tied to title.

Here's what I recommend: Before accepting any leadership position, take a good, hard look at your Pyramid of Purpose and decide if it aligns with your purpose. Treat it like a new role and not as an add-on. If your company isn't training managers, take it upon yourself to study best practices and ask for different perspectives on how to get the best out of the people who report to you. Most of all, understand you will be in a position that affects others' careers and livelihoods.

No matter what your purpose, try not to get obsessed with the climb up the ladder. Even high-level executives get assessed for the totality of their career experience, which includes lateral moves and sometimes smaller roles that afford unique opportunities. In the end, it's the depth and variety of their experiences rather than how quickly they shot up the ladder that matters. In fact, climbing up the ladder too quickly can be a red flag—a sign a person may not be seasoned enough or is too interested in the title as a trophy.

New Rule #4—Perform Like a Consultant vs. an Employee

This little nugget was taught to me the hard way. It was 2001, and I was working in a small scientific staffing firm, training scientists to be salespeople and recruiters. Not exactly glamorous or easy. It was my third job since the military. I was on a mission. I didn't know for sure where I was going, but I had lots of hunches and opinions about how a workplace should run. In hindsight, I can see most of them were pretty on point.

My challenge was not everyone cared about my opinions, and most of the leaders didn't care for how I shared them. Don't get me wrong; I knew how to be professional. But if you thought the military would have taught me to keep my mouth shut, you'd be wrong; it did the opposite. I mean you can't get fired from the Air Force. Sure, they can discharge you, but you'd have to do something against their laws for that. So you can be a jerk, and there's no danger of losing your job. Same goes for most government jobs.

Now flash forward a few years. I was using the same approach as I did in the military, which went something like this: "With all due respect, sir or ma'am [*insert why they're idiots and offer my own solution*]." Whether you're right or wrong, you do that enough times and you're going to make some enemies.

My problem was I was thinking like an employee. Employees see hierarchy as either their parent or their enemy. They either ask for permission from authority or push against it. But consultants...well, consultants have to hunt for their food. Every meeting and every person equals potential work. A good consultant is always selling and partnering.

Consultants don't ask permission, and they don't fight their clients. Consultants can't just show up and be obedient. They have to provide some additional value. They're expected to elevate the conversation, partner with the business, and help them see or do something they wouldn't have on their own. If they don't, they don't get a call. Simple as that. End of story.

I got introduced to this concept after being laid off from the scientific staffing firm. Let's be clear—I got laid off because they couldn't fire me. I was good at my job. Really good. Well, I was good at the function of my job. But I was an asshole to those in charge. I felt they were major disappointments as leaders, and I didn't respect them, from the CEO at that time on down, minus my own manager, who was in the trenches with me. In a time when people were losing their jobs left and right, you'd think I'd play it safer. But I made sure they knew how I felt about their leadership every chance I got. So guess who was on the top of their list the minute they started to look at a layoff? Yeah, that would be me.

But that was just the first domino. I was lucky enough to have a manager who let me know I was on the chopping block. Thanks to her, I had a new job lined up the Monday after receiving my pink slip on Friday. The new gig was with a small online university.. Easy breezy.

So there I was at my new job still believing having the right answer was the best answer. I didn't think about how I was making anyone else look when I shared my awesome thoughts or showed what I could do. This was a small company, and the leaders had all grown up there, so they had little exposure to anything else. I had years of experience in a variety of environments. As an employee, I figured, show up and shine. And if they couldn't handle it, too bad for them.

That didn't go over so well. Two months into the job, I again found myself in a little office having paperwork handed to me. When I asked if I was being fired, they said, "No, you're good at your job. We're just eliminating the position." One week later, they had promoted someone from within and simply changed the title of my so-called "eliminated" position.

I could defend myself by describing some of the shady practices I called out at both these companies, and I'd be right. But in the end, whom did I help? My approach didn't influence any change, and all it got me was unemployed.

So I found myself an "involuntary consultant." I had to go hunt for my food. All of a sudden, everyone was on equal footing with me. Instead of seeing people above or beneath me, I saw every person as a potential client. Someone's title no longer pit me against them or automatically aligned me with them. Instead, titles simply gave me clues as to what problems I might be able to help people with. It was no longer me "fighting the power." It was my brain in a conversation with their brains, looking for how I might be of service. That went for the CEO as much as it did for the person working in a call center.

I could no longer shout out my ideas just because I thought they were good or hide out just because I thought something wasn't my job. I had to speak up, and I had to sell and influence people. Sometimes I had to influence five people to move something forward. And here's the kicker—I wasn't in charge of any of it, and they weren't beholden to me for one damn thing. If I wanted to get the gig, they had to *want* to work with me.

Also, I wouldn't last long if I just did whatever they asked. Trust me, after being laid off twice, I felt like a beaten dog. I had my tail between my legs. My bark and bite had definitely disappeared once I realized I couldn't afford my rent or car payment without an income.

So when I first started taking on work as a consultant, I was compliant and agreeable. I asked what they wanted and tried to serve up as ordered. That blew up in my face pretty quickly. The reality is they wouldn't need me if they knew exactly what to do. That meant I had to speak up, I had to sell, and I had to have good ideas. I had to figure out how to share all those opinions but in a way that connected with people instead of pushed them away. The more I engaged people as my equals and partners and focused on how to help elevate them, the better the results.

I get the word *consultant* may conjure up negative images for you: the person who bills a ton of hours but does nothing, companies that swoop in and craft solutions so complicated no one ever acts on them, or the person who mucks up the whole process because she or he doesn't get the culture.

But those are crappy consultants. I'm not saying be a crappy consultant. I'm saying be a phenomenal consultant. A phenomenal consultant will outperform a phenomenal employee every time. An employee is transactional. A consultant creates a holistic experience, addressing all the needs of clients, even if that means referring them to someone else. The goal is to get clients to a better place.

You'll be amazed how empowered you will feel when you take this approach, even if you're working as an employee inside a company. I dare you to start viewing your boss or manager as your client. They are paying your salary, after all. Say you were billing them for your services, what would you need to know and understand about your primary client in order to provide them with white glove service? You can take it the other direction as well. I double-dog dare you to view your direct reports as your clients. How much do you know about the customer base that you work with every day?

Doing this one mind-set-shift exercise can overhaul your whole approach. Often it will dissolve most of the issues you are experiencing on the job. Few people show up as their best selves when identifying as employees. But consultants are always partnering. They are equal players in the room, even if they aren't in charge of anything.

New Rule #5—Building Relationships vs. Networking

The last new rule is about relationships. That mushy topic no one likes to talk about. Sure, we talk around it. We publish book after book on teamwork, trust, and collaboration. And many of these books contain highly useful information. But for any of it to work, you have to give a shit about people. You have to be genuinely open to looking at how you affect others.

Reaching out and doing that dreaded thing called "networking" is critical. That seems easy to do in this world of social media and thousands of people "liking" that photo you just posted of yourself at the gym or of your kid hitting the neighbor guy in the crotch with his baseball bat. But the reality is networking by itself doesn't do anything for you. It doesn't automatically make things happen. That's true no matter who you are—whether you're running your own business, leading a corporation, or working the front line. For your network to work on your behalf, the relationships that make it up need to be strong, authentic, and well-fed.

This played out quite clearly when I was asked to help with an interview process. A department was looking to hire someone who could work across the company, training employees on new policies and procedures tied to a major change being implemented.

The topic wasn't sexy, nor was there much in the way of consequences or rewards tied to people doing what the training was telling them to do. The company was looking for someone who could train, make it engaging, and leverage relationships across the organization.

One of the candidates I interviewed was a dynamic, experienced technical trainer who had worked at the company for years, so she knew people in almost every corner of it. Perfect. That was easy. Not...so...fast.

The leader asked me to reach out to contacts in the different regions to feel out what they thought of the candidate. What I learned was she was popular and well-liked. But when I asked if they thought she could influence change, they typically paused then replied with some variation of, "I like her, and I don't want to be critical, but I don't think anyone would take her seriously."

Fascinating. Everyone knew her, and most even liked her, yet she didn't have relationships that would work on her behalf. And that's the issue with networking vs. building relationships. You want to build relationships that will *have your back*.

People are sometimes confused about what "having someone's back" means. This isn't about loyalty. This is a *skill set* first and foremost. Do you have relationships with people who are good at their jobs, command respect, and know how to take a stand without being divisive? If not, I don't care how loyal your friends are, they won't be able to help you.

The other aspect of having someone's back is connected to the *quality* of your relationship. Are you seen as someone who should be backed? Do you perform reliably? Do you help others look good? Can you be trusted to deliver in unpredictable situations? Can you handle juggling the various personalities involved in getting major change completed? If not, why would anyone with credibility hang their reputation on yours?

Now, there's a balance, of course. If nobody knows about you, how can they have your back? I remember getting out of the military and being desperate to find a job. I had my degree in hand and a few years at the National Security Agency on my résumé…and I had no idea if I could get a job. Worse, I had no idea where to start. I went to one of the military's transition meetings, but the main message simply seemed to be: "Go network."

Ugh. That just felt gross to me. I didn't want to push myself on people. I hated that. I had spent years in retail and hated having to sell things such as shoes and luggage to people who may or may not have needed what I was selling.

I felt like an all-out prostitute reaching out to people to see if they would get me a job.

But I needed an income, so I printed my résumé on fancy paper (someone said it would help me stand out) and went to the job fairs. At every one, I found myself sitting in a corner, munching on the free food, smiling at passersby, and not knowing what the hell to do. Networking sucked.

I know some people who absolutely love networking. More power to them. I can't stand it. I'd rather stab my eye out with one of those sporks they give you at fast food restaurants. But I love helping people. I love being of use, being of service. I'm a social butterfly when I know there is something I'm bringing to the table that people can use.

I've had people tell me what a good networker I am. I'm always shocked. What the hell are they talking about? What I realize is I've built a reputation working for years at various companies. That reputation is based on me treating others with kindness and going out of my way to help people whether doing so fit neatly into my job description or not. And yes, when I've needed it, I've been lucky enough that several people have had my back.

Now, don't get me wrong; there are a few people out there who didn't get the best version of me. They triggered me and probably embodied the challengers on my Pyramid of Purpose. So they may not have had my back the way I'd have liked. But I get that. The more defined your brand is, the more you have to expect you won't be everyone's cup of tea. That's okay too.

Once you understand business relationships last a lot longer than any of the work you might be doing with people, you'll be more thoughtful about connecting with others. You'll truly see the people who are working with you — their concerns, fears, hopes, and joys. When you understand you are surrounded with unique human beings, it's hard for genuine relationships not to naturally develop. And in the end, it's those real relationships that will help you fulfill your purpose.

PART 2:
Build Your Business

CHAPTER 5:
Practice
Your Greatness

*"The greatness of a man is not how much wealth he
acquires, but in his integrity and his ability to affect
those around him positively."*

—Bob Marley

At the beginning of this book, I told you that you are great.
The thing is you may not feel great. Or you may not think
what you do for a living is great. But you need to wake up.
I'm not trying to make you feel warm and cozy inside or fluff
your ego. Instead, I'm trying to help you recognize only by
living, breathing, and consistently *showing up as great* will
you fulfill your purpose.

No matter what you are currently doing for a living, you,
my friend, are a business owner. This is something you'll
hear me say a lot. *You are a business owner.* Are you unemployed? Good news. You're not unemployed. You're a business owner with no current customers. Are you in a job you
hate, working for people you can barely tolerate? Good news.
You are a business owner. You're just in the wrong business.
But that's not anyone's fault but your own.

Now, before you throw this book across the room, let me
tell you my goal isn't to make you feel bad. It's to remind

you that you are powerful, that you are in charge of your life. Sure, you may have obstacles, but you are still powerful. And the choice you always have, no matter what your situation, is to *practice your greatness.*

If you are washing dishes, do so with greatness. If you are cleaning someone's teeth, do so with greatness. If you are heading up a board meeting, do so with greatness. If you are folding shirts, fixing a faucet, painting a house, performing surgery...well, you get my drift. Too often we assume the job is what determines greatness. It is not. *We* determine the level of greatness we bring to what we do.

And what's one of the first things you need to run a successful business? Commitment to making it the best it can possibly be. Don't worry if this is not the business you want to run for the rest of your life. Maybe you don't want to be a bartender forever. Well, demonstrating your greatness at bartending doesn't prevent you from changing your line of business later on. What it does is wire your brain to be accustomed to experiencing greatness, success, and a sense of pride.

Growing up, working at my aforementioned job at the apricot orchard, I remember sitting in the hot sun and focusing intently on whether I was cutting each apricot to the specifications given to me. I don't know if any of my friends were all that concerned about the accuracy of their apricot slicing, but I was. I wanted to do my job well. Not because I wanted to retire as an apricot slicer but because I wanted to be great at anything someone paid me to do.

The thing is I valued the trade of goods and services at a young age. I remember reading in history books about the barter and trade system and thinking how absolutely brilliant it was. I loved anything that seemed to equalize opportunity for people.

I also wanted to do right by those who had toiled in the hot sun picking these apricots. The fruits can be fragile things, especially as they ripen. These people had seriously strong hands. The amount of attention required to delicately retrieve each fruit by hand from the branches did not go unnoticed by me. I was going to slice each one in a way that would build on their effort.

I know that sounds like pretty neurotic behavior for a thirteen-year-old. But my point is after a summer of working as an illegal apricot slicer, I didn't feel less than because my job wasn't glamorous or high-paying. No. Instead, I felt powerful and capable. I did that job well, and I knew it. Nobody had given me feedback or a trophy or even a raise. I didn't need someone else to validate me. I knew I had done an amazing apricot-slicing job because of my focus, effort, and passion. I took it seriously.

That elevated my sense of self-esteem. It gave me the confidence to apply for a job that fall, when I turned fourteen. I was old enough for a work permit. My father had passed away that year and money was tight, so my mother reluctantly signed the paperwork and I took the next step in my career. I became an ice cream server.

This may all seem silly to you, the musings of a child worker. But the reason these jobs are important — and the reason I include them when referring to my "career" — is this is where, through commitment and appreciation, I started to practice my greatness. This is what hundreds of companies are trying to figure out. They call it "employee engagement." How do they get employees to engage in their jobs as opposed to simply phoning it in?

My answer is it's up to the individual. Employees need to stop looking outside themselves for greatness. Stop looking for the promotion that will finally put enough letters in front of their title to make them feel successful. Stop looking for that end-of-year performance rating to tell them whether they are great. Stop begging for accolades from their bosses. Instead, they need to recognize whatever they choose as their line of business and career — this is where they will have the opportunity to practice greatness or mediocrity. But the choice and the honor are theirs. No one else is going to spell it out for them.

Pick a Business That Easily Brings Out Your Greatness

Don't get me wrong. I get that there are times in our lives when we take less-than-ideal jobs. Sometimes survival, convenience, or necessity dictates that we accept a position outside the business we want to be in at the moment.

If you take a job for survival, meaning that you need the paycheck more than anything else, treat this as a temporary fix. Trust me, you don't want to practice years of survival mode. Be determined to change jobs as soon as possible. Now, what that means depends on what your calling is. You might "change" your job just by changing how you look at it. All of a sudden, seen in a new light, the job of necessity can morph into your life's passion.

This happened to me. I had taken a job as a trainer in a call center partly for the weekends off and partly for the money, which I needed to afford my apartment. I had just been told that the FBI job I thought I was a shoo-in for, based on my military experience as a Russian linguist, was in fact not going to happen. I soon found myself resenting my call center job. I wanted to do something big. This was not it.

A few years later, I was working as a trainer, this time at a travel company. I still viewed my work as a had-to-have job to pay the bills. I still resented that it wasn't more glamorous or "hero" worthy. I was going to school full-time for screenwriting at the time. I had shifted my dream to becoming a moviemaker. I was going to change the world.

So when a coworker asked me, "But what if this is what you were meant to do? You're so good at it," I promptly replied, "Oh, hell no! I'm meant for bigger things." I'll never forget the look on his face. I had all at once insulted what he did for a living and belittled myself. But his expression wasn't sadness; it was pity. As if to say, "Oh, you poor lost soul." I interpreted the exchange as if he were saying this was all I would amount to. I remember feeling angry and defiant.

Many years later — too many to count — I am still a trainer. I'm not sure when the shift happened. At some point, the many tiny moments where someone in class said thank you for waking something up in them finally added up; the job I had resented had become my full-blown passion.

I've morphed the work into a bigger business that aligns with who I am and what I care about. I no longer work for a single company as an employee. Instead, I work for a multitude of companies as a consultant. What can I say? I've always had an independent streak.

I've also had times where I found it took entirely too much energy to show up and practice my greatness. That's a clue that gives me insight into which businesses I should be in and which ones I shouldn't. The feeling could arise from many situations. Maybe the environment is so negative that it drains and stresses you to exhaustion. Maybe you're not making enough money to feel safe and secure. Or perhaps the work just doesn't feed you anymore.

If this sounds like your current situation, then you must recognize you are the person who is responsible for changing it. You are practicing mediocrity in your business. This is dangerous. My first recommendation is to get back to doing your job with greatness. You need the feeling that comes from practicing greatness to make good decisions. Don't become drunk on misery and then start making decisions about your business, aka your career. That's basically just drunk-dialing the universe.

Seriously, I've seen plenty of people leave jobs they hate for ones they supposedly were going to love, and in less than a month they were back to being miserable. No doubt about it: greatness is a habit. Start practicing now.

CHAPTER 6:
Determine What Kind of Business Owner You Are

"Knowing yourself is the beginning of all wisdom."

— Aristotle

Once you have a sense of your Pyramid of Purpose, you naturally start being more strategic and helpful, and you practice your greatness in everything you do. That's why it's so important to get clear about what kind of business-person you are.

Knowing your purpose will give you useful insights as you choose what job market to enter. You might feel a need to work with animals, fly planes, make Christmas sweaters, or help the elderly. Your calling is something only you can identify. While going after your calling, though, you have to figure out what type of businessperson you are. Knowing this will make it much easier to decide what environment best sets you up to practice your greatness. This chapter talks about what to consider when picking your business.

LOW MAN ON THE TOTEM POLE

Are You a Long-Distance Runner or a Sprinter?

What's great about how business is evolving, with companies laying off employees more frequently than ever, is the freedom it gives you to move around. Job-hopping doesn't raise a red flag the way it used to. For some that's heaven. For others, that freedom is so unsettling it prevents them from focusing on what they were meant to do. But make no mistake about it: the day of having to carve out your own path is here. So even if it feels daunting, you need to start taking ownership of the business you're running.

While you endeavor in carving out your path, it's good to know what type of businessperson you are. If you are slow and steady like a long-distance runner, then you probably thrive in environments where you can see things through from beginning to end. You are good with managing the day-to-day tasks required to maintain a successful business.

Also, as a long-distance runner, you keep a steady pace but don't rush. For you, it's more about consistency and long-term impact. You tend to have patience and appreciate the work that goes into getting things done right the first time. You don't get discouraged with a lack of immediate change. You prefer things to evolve slowly.

As a long-distance runner, you have to guard against getting so set in your ways that you don't see the landscape is changing quickly. You may not recognize you need to find a different trail to run on or temporarily switch up running styles.

Then there are the sprinters. You show up with sudden bursts of productivity and then disappear to rest and refuel. You get things done quickly. In fact, you get more done in an hour than some people get done all week. The downside is once people get wind of your glorious spurts of productivity, they start expecting that level of output hour after hour, like a long-distance runner might do. But you need to refuel, step away, and disengage.

You thrive in new, different, and even chaotic situations. You like to start things explosively and create momentum. But once things settle and get into maintenance mode, your brain tends to disengage. If you're not in a business market that prioritizes fast and intermittent services or products, you may be seen as unreliable and flakey. However, if you work in an environment that requires on-the-spot problem solving and constant reinvention, you will be viewed as a star performer.

Back in the day, it was the long-distance runner who was likely to be seen as the golden employee—a loyal employee who shows up every day, works steadily, and produces consistent quality. But as technology advanced and change became the norm, the long-distance runner got—ironically—left behind. They are viewed as stuck in their ways, resistant to change, and not agile enough.

It's the sprinter who has gone from being unreliable and flakey to innovative, responsive, and driven. A résumé filled with several jobs now says "diverse background" and not "sketchy work history."

The truth is we all have to know what type of running we are ideally suited for. We have to seek out environments and roles that sync with our running style. And we have to pay attention so we aren't caught off guard and have time to adapt when our type of running is no longer needed.

Can you do that? Can you switch up styles? Can you go from long-distance running to sprinting? If so, for how long and how well? The answers to these questions will not only help you in making decisions about what job suits you best but also in deciding when a situation is worth working through and when it no longer serves your purpose.

While it might seem like sprinters are cooler and securely are in the lead, in reality the race is starting to even out. Companies are beginning to recognize they need a diverse team of talent that can handle the sprinting *and* the long-distance aspects of business.

LOW MAN ON THE TOTEM POLE

Are You an Inny or an Outy?

You may need to be completely independent and own your own business outright, or you may feel more comfortable setting up shop under the umbrella of another, larger company.

When you work for another company, *you are still a business owner*, but you are delegating some responsibilities, such as procuring work and handling benefits. In exchange, you get a certain level of stability with a predictable income.

When you work for yourself outright, *you are still an employee*, meaning you have to answer to customers just as you would if you were on the payroll of a company. But you have more autonomy to make strategic decisions about the business. In exchange, you increase the volatility by not having a predictable income. At least at the beginning, you will have to be okay with "hunting for your own food." (However, in today's climate of frequent layoffs and unpredictable job security, having your eggs in several baskets can also work in your favor.)

You may need to experiment with both strategies to get a sense of where you land on the independence-stability slider. A lot of people are compelled to figure that out when they lose a job. It's like getting thrown in the pool without knowing exactly how to swim. Some figure it out and make it back to the safety of dry land. Some find they love being in the pool. And a few drown. That is the nature of survival.

Ideally, you make choices based on what you want, not out of desperation. But we don't always get that luxury. But I will say this: It helps to know what brings out the best version of yourself. Then do all you can to secure your "market share" in that type of environment.

Are You a Details Person or into the Big Picture?

Everyone knows you gotta wear both hats in most jobs. But people usually lean one way or the other. Whether you're a naturally detail-oriented or big-picture person, know we tend to overvalue what we are best at. If your brain is wired for details, understand there is a great deal of work that is desperately in need of people like you. If your brain is wired for seeing the big picture, understand there is a great deal of work that is desperately in need of people like you. Just don't make the mistake of thinking that one orientation is better or more necessary than the other. You'll not only alienate a lot of people who can help you, but you'll also limit your capacity to flex from one skill to the other.

The danger comes in not reading your environment. When people primarily expect you to be a whiz at details and you excel at big-picture thinking — or visa versa — it can be exhausting for everyone. As important as it is to contribute in both areas, you want to position yourself in the type of environment best suited for how your brain works naturally. Trust me, it'll be easier on everyone.

Do You Need to Be at the Top, Middle, Back, or Front?

Too often we get obsessed with rising to the top. And why? Because somebody told us climbing the ladder was the only path to success. The truth is we're not all suited to the corner office. Just like not every football player is suited to be the quarterback, even though that position gets the most attention from fans and the media.

Some of you are especially skilled at playing middle positions. You're great at connecting the dots for others and translating messages between multiple stakeholders. Nothing excites you like getting to see a high-level view of the organization, but you can also dive deep into the day-to-day.

Or you may do your best work behind closed doors, away from the hubbub, where you can concentrate on the details. Maybe you prefer to fly under the radar, doing work that, if done well, is never even noticed. Your satisfaction comes from simply knowing you've left the world a better place for others through your work.

Maybe you need to be at the top so you can see the lay of the land at all times. You're adept at envisioning the direction of an organization and skilled at getting others committed to working for a common cause. You thrive when in charge and carrying the brunt of responsibility.

And there are those of you who need to be out in front. You need to have your eyes and ears connected to the action, your hands actively involved in whatever's being created. I've seen plenty of people go from a deep love for their work to complete apathy because they accepted promotions that pulled them away from what connected them to their purpose.

Do It for the Love

Don't take a job for the glamour; take it for how it will help you achieve your ultimate purpose. I can understand if you're concerned about how much money you can make. My advice? Separate what you do in pursuit of your purpose from how you manage your money. I'm not here to tell you how to manage your money, but I can tell you that this strategy has always worked for me.

First, I look at what I want to do, then—and only then—do I look at how I can make the money I need to actually do it. As I began to excel as a trainer and coach, I was tapped several times to take on higher-level positions. More often than not, I declined. Not because I wasn't fond of money. On the contrary, I had struggled financially most of my life, so more money definitely appealed to me. But I believed in my core that I could make the money I wanted doing something I loved.

More than once, I've had to make a gut call about whether to accept a promotion. Often, I was turning down more money. But I was playing a long-range game. I knew the more vertical I went in an organization, the further away I would get from what made me great, which was working with all levels of employees. As a trainer, I got to sit in meetings with some of the company's top executives while still working with frontline employees and hearing about their day-to-day challenges. This vantage point provided me with quite an intimate view of the company. My best position is the middle. Not the back and not the front, but smack-dab in the center of everything.

Something told me that playing the middle was what worked best for me. And I also sensed I needed a bigger playing field…and, yes, a bigger paycheck. Eventually, I figured out that becoming an external consultant would check off all these boxes for me. Sure, there was more risk in going out on my own but also greater reward than I would have inside a company, even as an executive.

Now that's just me. Someone else—maybe you—would thrive in some of the positions I turned down, while they might absolutely hate being a consultant. That's why it's so critical to know what works best for you. I was sure. But if you've just begun examining what works best for you, you may need to experiment with a few roles before you find the right fit.

Are You a Solo Act, Ensemble Member, or Nomad?

No one succeeds alone. It's critical to be—and be seen as—a team player. You absolutely need to know how to get along with others to leverage the talent, and goodwill, of those you work with. At the same time, you also need to have a sense of whether you tend to contribute best as a solo act, ensemble, or nomad.

If you excel as a solo act, you may still be an awesome team player, but you may need to contribute by working alone while you create and partnering with the team on how to use what you created. Maybe you're a programmer who codes alone in the confines of your own office. The product you produce certainly takes the needs of the customers and team members into consideration, but for it to come to fruition, you need to go off on your own to make it happen.

If you feed off the energy that comes from partnering with others, you probably shine in an ensemble. You contribute in many ways but especially as a connector. You help glue the different parts of the ensemble together. You also build off the work of others. You enjoy being part of something big and fighting for a collective cause together. You are most likely viewed as a team player in the traditional sense. But if thrown out on your own, you may have to fight the perception that you are unable to take the lead or lack a clear vision. If this sounds like you, make a point to let others know you do your best work as part of a team, but also build your flexibility, so you can contribute in a variety of situations.

Finally, you may do your best work as a nomad, traveling solo from one community to the next. You adapt well to change; in fact, you require it. You bring your unique perspective and talents to the table, and then move on to the next problem.

No matter your style, it's your job to educate others on how you work best, so they know what to expect from you. It's also your job to learn how to adapt and flex when needed. Doing a good job at both will make things easier on you and your colleagues. And let's face it — if you're going to practice your greatness, you may as well make it as easy on yourself as possible.

CHAPTER 7:
Getting Clients, Aka the Job Hunt

"Most men live lives of quiet desperation and go to the grave with their song still in them."

—Henry David Thoreau

This quote strikes a chord in me every time I read it. The idea that we could go to our grave never experiencing our calling, never realizing our fullest potential…well, it keeps me up at night. Because I know this quote is true.

I've walked both my parents to their graves. My mother's death and—more painfully—her life haunt me. I knew her to be wildly intelligent. She taught herself English after arriving in this country with my father, whom she had met in Germany while he was stationed there with the US Army.

She would make my brother and I do extra hours of schoolwork after we came home from school. She researched and learned about the healing properties of food long before *organic* became a household word.

My mom had a brilliant but troubled mind. She suffered from depression, anxiety, paranoia, and an overall sense that the world was an ugly, ugly place. She also lived her life as a victim. Don't get me wrong: she had plenty of things that legitimately kicked her down. Being a woman in war-torn

Germany, for one. Being a woman at a time when women were expected to marry, have kids, and unquestioningly support their men, for another.

I'm sure there were all kinds of things my mother wanted to see and do, but she consistently made decisions to protect herself. She was a fighter, for sure. But she didn't believe good things were ever in store for her, so she played small. I was there the day she died. I know for a fact that she died with her song still in her.

I think of these things when I'm starting something new or embarking on working with a client. Whether as an external consultant or an internal employee, I consider whether I'm going to decide to go to the grave with my song still in me or whether I'm going to make decisions, take risks, and gamble on myself. And every time I've gambled on myself, it's paid off in a way that has set me up for greater success. And more than that, it's made me feel alive, capable, and ready for more.

You need to go into your client meetings with your own spirit, determined to make sure you don't leave your own song trapped inside. This doesn't mean you just talk the whole time. It's about being true to yourself and that inner guidance system of yours. Look, there's a ton of books, articles, and classes out there that go into great detail about what to say and do to land a job. It's not rocket science, and there's no sure formula. But I'd like to share a few tips that I have found personally useful and effective for those I've coached.

Now, I know some of you already are independent business owners, or you are looking to become self-employed. Some of what I'm about to say may not apply to you, because I'm primarily speaking to those who are working for companies and organizations in the traditional employee sense. And even you will need to "interview" for work on a regular basis. It might be with the potential customer deciding whether to sign on with you or buy your product, but believe me, we are all interviewing on a regular basis.

How Do You Get in the Door?

I won't waste your time with a ton of details about how to network, build relationships, etc. There are plenty of articles and books online for that. Find some good ones, do your research, and prep yourself as best you can for getting in the door.

What I'm going to share with you is what those articles don't. I learned about these critical missing details firsthand. When I was leaving the military, they sent us through a transition office that was supposed to help veterans make the big leap into the civilian world. The problem? Most of the counselors were either government employees, meaning they'd never worked in the private sector, or people who were not particularly skilled at getting work.

So I left with a semi-decent résumé but with no real strategy. My résumé captured what I'd done so far, but it wasn't targeted to a particular job or client, and it did a crappy job of showing what was unique about me.

I got tossed in the pool and, luckily, figured out how to swim pretty well. Now I've spent the last fifteen years or so coaching others to speak for themselves and market who they are and what they can do. Following are the topics that I cover with my career-coaching clients. But trust me, these are real-world-tested techniques that I've seen work over and over with my clients...and myself.

Résumés Need to Tell Your Story, not Your History

If your résumé is like most, it reads like a job description. It tells me what your responsibilities were but leaves me with scant idea what it will be like to work with you. What happens when you come on the scene? Not only that, it probably doesn't tell the story about why you went from one position to the next. I have no idea if you were strategic about changing positions or if you're just bobbing around letting the waves of life take you where they may.

Here are my top ten tips for writing an effective résumé.

1. **Speak the language.** I usually have my clients send me four job postings that appeal to them. Then I have them describe what they find attractive about the positions. I scan the postings for common themes in terms of language, hot words, anything that should clearly be represented in their résumés in order to catch a recruiter's eye or, increasingly, the electronic eye of a résumé-scanning system.

2. **Drop the mission statements. Seriously.** It makes you sound corny and completely outdated. Instead, use the top space of your résumé to tell a bit of your story in bullet point format. I prefer a personal quote, a few bullet points about your key strengths/talents, and a few highlights that describe what happens when you are brought into the mix.

It could look something like this:

Retail Store Manager

"I believe the success of any store starts and ends with the customer. But the glue that makes that a worthwhile experience is the love for and integrity of the brand, along with the engaged passion of each team member."

Team Leader who is focused on finding an opportunity to evolve own experience and capabilities within my retail career.

- **Successful in both start-up and turnaround management roles** — have helped drive the launching of and revamping through creative problem solving, focus on team management and partnership, and passion for connecting to the customer through a holistic merchandise and service experience.
- Versatile leader who partners with team members to create a **collaborative workplace** that focuses on efficiency and profitability, via **tailored and engaged customer service**.

- Leads teams and known for **participative leadership style** that focuses on leveraging unique talents and experiences of a diverse workforce.

3. **Use your real estate.** Because your most recent job is probably the most relevant to the job you're applying for, you want to give a bit more space for that description. I tend to give four to five bullets for the most recent job, three for the previous, and just a brief two- to three-sentence summary for any older jobs.

    That's the general approach. If you have certain jobs that are more relevant, be sure to give them the appropriate real estate.

4. **Describe your context, not just your responsibilities.** Under each job title, you want to write one to two sentences that describe the unique circumstances of that position. This is your chance to let recruiters know a little about the environments you thrive in. You might emphasize that you supported multiple leaders or client groups at one time. Or you may talk about how you worked in an ever-changing start-up environment that required high levels of resilience and constant communication. Whatever the circumstances, take this opportunity to make sure your audience knows not only what you do but in what setting you do it.

5. **Write mini-stories.** When assembling your bullets for each job, don't just say what you did; tell little short stories in one sentence. Follow the formula of (Context + Actions + Timeframe = Results). *Context* is simply the opportunity or challenge you spotted, *Actions* is what you did about it, *Timeframe* is when you did it, and *Results* is the impact you had on the team, department, or company you worked for.

Example:

- Revised inventory, merchandising, and restocking procedures, leading the department from worst-performing to first in department rankings within the district, also top five in the western territory within one year of being on the job.

Context = worst-performing

Action = Revised inventory, merchandising, and re-stocking procedures, leading the department

Timeframe = within one year of being on the job

Result(s) = first in department rankings within the district, also top five in the western territory

6. **Don't write your whole autobiography.** No matter your experience, nobody needs to hear your life story. Figure out what's relevant. Be concise, and move on. Two to three pages max. And I'm not talking about two jam-packed pages. Instead, cover the most critical points on the first page but make sure you leave enough white space to make it easy on the eyes to scan.

   Leave the nice-to-know info for the second page. This may be where you highlight your education, technical skills, or certifications. I call these the qualifiers. They don't signify whether you can do the job or not, but they may be necessary to get in the door.

7. **Make it easy to scan.** Nobody reads like they used to. Thanks to the Internet, our brains are more accustomed to scanning than reading. I've already mentioned the importance of white space on your résumé. Next, you need to master bullets, **bolding**, and ALL-CAPS to guide the reader's eyes to where you want them to go.

8. **Consider ditching your cover letter.** Lots of companies have stopped asking for, or expecting, them. If there's an option to attach a cover letter, go ahead and use it. But don't make it boring. The key is to write something that isn't already on your résumé. Ideally, you link what is unique about the company with what is unique about you. Chances are, nobody is going to read it, but if they do, you want it to be good.

9. **Beggars can't be choosers. So don't beg.** The unspoken rule for producing a great résumé is knowing what the hell you're good at and explaining why companies would be lucky to have you. Even if you have an eviction notice on your door, nothing but four packets of Top Ramen in your kitchen, and you're recycling bottles to get enough money to do your laundry, don't beg. In fact, if you're that in need of a job, the worst thing you can do is come at it with a lack of confidence.

10. **Don't be a jackass.** The flipside of not begging is not bragging. I'm all for putting your best self out there. In fact, get good at knowing what you're fantastic at and making sure people hire you for that. But remember this: being fantastic at what you do doesn't make you better than anyone else. One of the most soul-sucking, time-wasting, and money-burning moves a company can make is bringing in someone who makes everyone else miserable.

   The old-school idea that if you're good at what you do and make the company tons of money, it doesn't matter how you treat others, was never true. And there's a ton of data out there to support that. So know what you're worth when you write your résumé, but don't concoct a story that comes off like someone trying to look good. Write the truest story you can, focusing on how strategic and helpful you are.

The résumé has been around for a while, and even though it's morphed over the years, it's probably not going anywhere soon. But it shouldn't be treated like some big, mysterious thing. It's a marketing piece. When you look at it like that, you realize you wouldn't buy a car simply because someone handed you a flyer with the timeline of how it was built. You want to know how it will perform for you when you drive it off the lot. And you want to know how it will feel to drive the car. So your résumé needs to create an emotional connection for those who are scanning it.

Full Example:

Store Manager

"I believe the success of any store starts and ends with the customer. But the glue that makes that a worthwhile experience is the love for and integrity of the brand, along with the engaged passion of each team member."

Team Leader who is focused on finding an opportunity to evolve own experience and capabilities within my retail career.

- **Successful in both start-up and turnaround management roles—** have helped drive the launching of and revamping through creative problem solving, focus on team management and partnership, and passion for connecting to the customer through a holistic merchandise and service experience.
- Versatile leader who partners with team members to create a **collaborative workplace** that focuses on efficiency and profitability via **tailored and engaged customer service**.
- Leads teams and known for **participative leadership style** that focuses on leveraging unique talents and experiences of a diverse workforce.

Career Experience Highlights
Asked to step in for an underperforming store with high inventory loss and low sales. Within first year **overhauled store operations**, performance expectations, and made

strategic hiring decisions that enabled us to pass a surprise store audit, earning the highest score in the district.

Trained store staff to move **from transactional to a consultative customer service** approach that involved enhancing their sales skills, as well as **personally learning Chinese** to connect with the primary customer demographic.

From beginning of employment, was promoted rapidly from frontline staff into leadership roles due to **ability to handle changing environments**, while driving productivity across multiple teams.

Professional Background

Store Manager Super Store, Inc., Anywhere, USA   08/15–Present
Responsible for store management that includes team performance management and development, merchandise inventory and sales, customer relations, annual budget strategy, and profitability for a multimillion-dollar store.

- Revising inventory, merchandising, and restocking procedures, leading the department from worst-performing to first in department rankings within the district, also top five in the western territory
- Helped improve our store's overall customer service survey scores by partnering with team to foster a customer experience that was service-driven in a timely manner
- Elevated store's overall focus on customer engagement, delivering a full-service approach that goes beyond greeting and responding to requests/complaints. This includes leveraging Chinese language and cultural understanding, as well as training on add-on selling in a way that compliments the unique needs of the customer
- Established reputation for operational excellence for back of house / front of house demonstrated through quarterly audit inventory reports

Assistant Store Manager Friendly Place, Inc. Anywhere, USA 2012–2015
Responsible for sales floor and staff management for a high-volume annual-sales store, while ensuring sales goals were met and exceeded via a connected customer experience.

- Recognizing that sales and customer experience would be positively affected by teaching Chinese to the staff regarding basic hospitality and cultural nuances to build loyalty with our primary customer base.

- Partnered with District Manager to increase vital product that was critical to the store's location. By studying reports on sales trends with the bus tourist purchases, was able to double the flow from the DCs, which increased sales by 35 percent.

- Through training, mentoring, and working hands-on with associates, was able to be part of promoting seven direct reports to leadership roles within store.

- Within one month on the job, revised merchandising color and product flow, increasing "full outfit" purchases across the store vs. single-item sales.

Assistant Store Manager Happy Times, Inc., Anywhere, USA 2009–2012

Actively recruited and trained to help store with sales during a turnaround performance strategy. Partnered with store manager to supervise staff, exceed customer needs, and create and implement strategies for sales, merchandising, and budgeting.

- Known for working well under pressure, being called upon as point liaison between HR, executive leadership, and store personnel during the opening and closing of outlet stores across California

- Helped crack an international counterfeiting crew with the help of local store partnerships, enabling police to make arrests, recovering more than $200K in fake $100 bills

Education / Personal Background

- **BA, Business Relations** University of Cool, 2005

What About Social Media?

More and more, social media is becoming the way people connect. As little as ten years ago it was viewed as a place for losers and tweens. But now, if you don't have a certain online presence, you may be seen as out of touch. Of course, that depends on the industry you are targeting. Here are a few things to consider when it comes to social media.

1. **Reputation is king.** Consider whether your online presence is helping or hindering your reputation. With just one search, recruiters and hiring managers can get a pretty good sense of who's applying for a job. If your résumé grabs their attention, you should assume they are Googling you. It's up to you to assess how much and what kind of exposure will help your business goals.

2. **Know where you need to have a presence.** Most white-collar professionals are expected to have an online presence. Depending on how you use it, something such as a LinkedIn profile can be great for networking and raising your visibility with recruiters.

   On the other hand, if you provide a service that's considered more blue-collar — if you are a tattoo artist, hairdresser, or construction worker — you'd better be on something such as Yelp or an industry site. And you don't have to have a brick-and-mortar location.

   No matter the situation, a well-managed online presence on sites such as LinkedIn can't hurt you. On a side note, there is some debate around whether to post your picture on sites like this. I recommend you do. I know there's a risk some recruiters could inappropriately use a photo to screen out candidates based on physical appearance, but that's outweighed by the human connection a photo can help make. Plus, recruiters may view profiles without a photo as fake or old. Just something to consider.

   You will also want to tune in to your industry. Search for professional organizations where key players have a presence, and consider whether contributing by sharing articles, blogging, etc. can help your visibility and reputation.

3. **Remember that nothing is private.** When you publish a play-by-play of your personal life online, your

footprint is out there, somewhere. Even if you're diligent about your "privacy" settings, tuning them so only close friends or family can view your material, it only takes one glitch for your personal life, with all its dirty laundry, to become visible to the world. Consider what profession you're in, or are striving to be in, and who your clients are. Always assume what you post could end up being more public than you expect. My golden rule is this: Don't post anything that could make your clients — aka boss, peers, direct reports, etc. — feel unsafe or uncomfortable when working with you. The last thing you want is that pic from Cabo (you know the one) making your coworkers question your judgment.

4. **Leverage that access.** Done thoughtfully, social media is pretty awesome. It creates an opportunity to make yourself visible to people who may not know you exist otherwise. Also, if you're not big on in-person networking, you can create reasons to attract the clients you're looking for without having to go hunt them down.

   Back in the day there were the newspaper classified ads, then Monster.com; now there are a ton of general and targeted job search engines out there. Most of them do the work for you once you fill out your profile. When I was looking for a job, I had a routine every morning where I'd search for new postings and tailor my application to each one. I erred on the side of applying for everything that seemed remotely in line with what I was looking to do. I call it the glitter against glue approach. I threw a bunch of glitter out there in the form of my résumé and waited to see what stuck.

   Never before have we had so many ways to find and connect with those we were meant to work with. A plumber can post videos of how to fix a sink to demonstrate his skill and demeanor before anyone hires him. A legal professional can host a blog where she gives out tips for the general public or shares information that helps keep her peer group up to date. No matter your profession, you can find — or create your own — bridge to clients online that goes beyond what a résumé can do for you.

5. **Always align with your brand.** People tend to trust others more when they have a sense of how they live, think, and engage interpersonally, which are all components of your brand. Everyone's brand is unique, and your social media presence should highlight what makes you different. To keep myself "on brand" without going too far, before I hit "Post" on anything, I ask myself: "How would I feel if someone decided they didn't want to work with me because of this?"

   So...I'm a cat lover through and through. I tend to share quite a few cat-related pictures and jokes on my personal profiles. That's a big part of who I am. And if someone thought I was too much of a crazy cat lady to work with me, I'd be okay with that.

   But I also balance my posts with articles that reflect the views I bring to my work. This shows anyone who's looking, these topics aren't just what I talk about when I'm paid to; I think this way all the time. In that way, my online presence shows who I am and helps support my brand.

   By the way, when it comes to humor, I don't post anything that demeans another person in any way. Part of my brand is I create a safe space to learn. If someone stumbles on a post of mine that undermines that, I've immediately lost trust. Plus I just don't believe in putting that kind of negative energy out in the world, whether through conversation or online posts.

Relationships, Relationships, Relationships...Relationships

How many times have you heard someone talk about the importance of relationships? "It's who you know." I hate that phrase. Mainly because when I was in my twenties and in a new town, I didn't know anybody, but I still needed a damn job. Also, doesn't that phrase just make you think of nepotism and ass kissers? It does for me.

As my career progressed and I moved from company to company, I started to understand the world is a small place. If not small, definitely connected in strange ways. People I had assumed I'd never see again would pop up in random situations where they could influence my career. But I still don't think it's as simple as "who you know." So let me elaborate.

1. **Who knows about you?** For someone to want to hire you, they have to know you exist. Plain and simple. There's a boatload of highly qualified people. And there's also a boatload of companies in need of their qualifications. But neither knows about the other. That's the beauty of social media, like we just discussed. But that's also the best case for in-person networking events.

   If you're adept at in-person networking, it can work in tandem with your social media presence. In-person networking is especially powerful if you give something of yourself while there, such as a speech or some type of knowledge sharing. Maybe you can have a booth where you can offer free samples of something you produce. At minimum, bring a flyer that highlights what you do, tailor it to your audience, and don't be afraid to make it more visual and catchy than just a résumé.

2. **How do people feel about knowing you?** It's not just who you know anymore. Now, it's also how those people *feel* about knowing you. Slowly but surely, the

days of being a jerk to people and still progressing in your career are coming to an end. People talk…a lot. When they feel like you are fake, mean, rude, or unreliable, they talk. On the other hand, if they love working with you, they also talk. And not only do they talk; they tend to sell on your behalf. Of course, having people say nice things about you is not the core reason for treating people well; that's gotta come from somewhere inside. If treating people well isn't connected to your value system, trust me, people will smell a fake. And guess what they'll do? They'll talk.

3. **Do people respect you in your role?** So people know you exist. They also like you. But would they rely on your expertise? Would they respect your decisions? And especially, would they listen to your input? I've sat on several interview panels where the candidate had all the right connections and was considered "popular." This seems to be a big thing now, thanks to social media. But inevitably the question comes up: "Sure, people like the candidate, but would anyone *listen* to her or him? Do people respect this person?" If the answer is no, there will be an apologetic decline to the oh-so-popular person.

4. **Are you building or destroying relationships?** Every interaction you have with another person is a relationship-building moment. That person you ignored in the elevator? You just took a withdrawal out of the relationship bank. The person to whom you gave a polite smile and said "Good morning" as they passed you in the hall? *Ka-ching.* You just made a little deposit.

   Maybe you'll never see that person again. Maybe that person will never be in a position to influence whether you get hired, promoted, or included in critical work. Doesn't matter. As you go through your day, you are either fine-tuning your relationship skills and expanding on a positive presence or you're wasting those skills and diminishing your presence. You see it's not just about other people. It's about how you're wiring your brain. It's about the kind of energy you're putting out toward others and the habits you're building every day.

Get in the habit of greeting even strangers in a genuine, polite, noninvasive manner. This might be uncomfortable at first, but you'll be surprised at how quickly it starts to feel natural to you. Because it is. You will instantly be seen as approachable. I have gotten legit job offers because I struck up a polite conversation with someone in a grocery line.

Of course, if a person gives you the heebie-jeebies, then use your better judgment. But I see so many people who regularly don't acknowledge the majority of humans who are in their workspace. People remember how you make them feel. Golden rule: make people feel safe *and* welcome.

5. **Are you treating even that "difficult person" as an important relationship?** Way too many times to count, people reach out to me for help with dealing with a difficult person. We sit down and talk about what's blocking them and what's triggering them. I give them advice. They express relief. Then when I reach out to them a week or so later, they tell me they didn't go through with the planned conversation because the person quit or moved. As far as they're concerned, problem solved.

But it isn't. The problem was never the other people. The problem was how the other people's behaviors triggered the fears or insecurities of those seeking my guidance. It's the trigger that we want to focus on. It's the trigger that's the gift the other person is pointing out to us. And you can be certain that if you pass up the opportunity to work with this person on your trigger, someone else will show up soon enough exhibiting the same behaviors and pressing on that trigger even harder. And each time that happens, you will struggle a bit more with it. Why? Because the brain is building a memory pattern of not being able to solve the challenge. Your frustration gets triggered easier and easier each time, because you don't have the memory of engaging differently or addressing the issue.

I often see this pattern repeat itself. This time the trigger is coming from a customer, now from a peer, then a boss…then a high-level executive, and so on. The first time we're presented with a chance to work toward a better relationship is the best time to do it. You put it off, and you start building negative patterns. The next time, the stakes may be higher, but your patterns will have stacked the deck against you rather than for you.

For example, the head of an HR department once reached out to me to discuss the challenges she was experiencing with one of her direct reports. Her employee was cutting her off in meetings and arguing with her in front of others. We went over some ways to approach the issue and practiced having a conversation with the employee.

When the day came to have the conversation, it turned out the employee had given notice and was moving on to another company at the end of the week. The HR executive sighed with relief when she recounted this turn of events during our meeting to catch up, telling me she was relieved not to have an uncomfortable conversation. I surprised her when I advised her to take advantage of the low-risk opportunity to tackle this dynamic once and for all by having an honest conversation with the employee. She said she didn't see the point.

A few months later, I got a call from the same head of HR. This time she was having issues with a peer with whom she needed to co-present at a big conference. Her colleague was talking over her in meetings and shooting down her ideas. We discussed why this was triggering her. I helped her connect being triggered by the dismissive behavior of her colleague with how she had been triggered by the behavior of the earlier employee. She acknowledged this behavior brought her right back to her childhood. She was the youngest of three and never felt heard. Eureka.

After we role-played a bit, she said she felt comfortable and would definitely give it a try at the next meeting. When I touched base with her again, she told me she and her peer seemed to be getting along better and she didn't want to rock the boat.

We fell out of contact. I don't think she was interested in hearing about how I thought she needed to have a conversation she didn't want to have. I get it. Changing our approach to life and relationships isn't easy. It's usually simple but rarely easy. If it were easy, we'd just do it.

A year or so later I got a call. It was the head of HR again. She had quit her job. The company had brought in a new senior executive. Within the first week, she was asked to present an overview of her team's activities. The new leader, who was also her new boss, cut her off and explained the majority of their work was going to change. She snapped. She threw her presentation down on the table and stormed out.

My former client saw her actions as finally standing up for herself. She failed to recognize the less dramatic opportunities she had had to do just that in less high-stakes situations. This was in 2008, and the job market had taken a nosedive. It took her some time before she was able to find work again.

It's natural for us to wait to get dislodged from our comfort zone. But just because it's human nature doesn't mean you can't override that inertia and be proactive. In fact, I recommend it. Instead of avoiding them, view the people who trigger you as prime learning opportunities to advance your relationship-building skills. If you can work through why and how certain behaviors trigger you, then you're one step closer to determining a more effective response.

There's no exact science to getting clients. But determination and a little strategy go a long way. So does resiliency. If you fear rejection, you're less likely to put yourself out there. Instead, I recommend embracing that rejection as the universe telling you where to turn. There's a roadblock to your left? Then turn right. But keep moving. Keep putting yourself out there.

After a while, you'll hone your approach and build the client-finding muscle. How great would it feel not to worry about getting work because you have confidence in your ability to generate interest and attract clients? (Great. Great is how it feels.)

Sample Before Résumé

EXPERIENCE
OD / L&D Consultant
ABC Consulting, Inc., Sherman Oaks, CA   **June 2104–Present**
Identify client needs that focuses on building bridges between the unemployed and corporate businesses

- Design and deliver strategies for onboarding non-traditional candidates that include military veterans, domestic abuse survivors, and individuals making major career changes
- Coach managers and executives on how to develop for talent and leadership bench-strength

- Conduct needs assessment with clients, focused on building org structures and processes that enable higher levels of efficiency and collaboration
- Manage office administrative and logistic planning, to include budget, staff, and travel

L&D Consultant

Squares Company, Fairfax County, VA   **September 2012–July 2014**

Designed and delivered financial literacy training, increasing the retention of content and capabilities demonstrated by students

- Facilitated hands-on practical application financial training, customizing experience of Finance Park participants
- Partnered with internal clients to identify key business goals, building a reputation for quick-turn around times and creative tailoring of content that engaged participants and delivered results

Instructional Designer & Facilitator

Big University, Herndon, VA   **December 2011–July 2012**

Developed and facilitated Federal Financial Aid (Title IV) policy training to keep Strayer Student Financial Services in compliance with Department of Education regulations

- Collaborated with Student Financial Services Ombudsman to address and solve students' Title IV Financial Aid issues, and to identify and assess training opportunities to minimize future issues
- Trained new hires and existing SFS agents regarding system advancements to Strayer's in-house Title IV federal aid management programs, as well as annual changes to Financial Aid policy

Instructional Designer & Training Lead

TravelerUSA, Santa Clarita CA   **September 2002–February 2011**

Designed and delivered training presentations, including new hire foundation skills, leadership development and technical applications

- Developed individual courses and comprehensive programs to train shoreside and shipboard employees in customer service skills, practices, and motivational matrices
- Provided one-on-one coaching tailored to address unique department needs

EDUCATION AND ACCREDITATIONS

- B.A. Degree, Sociology — CSUM 2001
- Train the Trainer Certification — CEU accredited program 2003
- American Society of Training and Development Member 2002 – 2007
- Certified Financial Aid Administrator (FAA) 2012

EXTRACURRICULARS

Currently serving as a Director on the Board of Project Be Kind, a nonprofit organization providing charitable service and grants to mothers and children affected by homelessness and domestic violence

https://www.linkedin.com/pub/june-smith/36/502/52b

References available upon request.

Sample After Résumé

Learning & Development Manager

"I believe we're always learning, whether we like it or not, sometimes simply from the cultural norms within our workplace. The trick is making sure that the learning companies invest in enables employees to perform vs. distracts or disempowers them."

Recently relocated and focused on finding an opportunity to evolve own experience and capabilities within my learning & development career.

- **Successful in both start-up and turnaround management roles —** have helped drive the launching of and revamping of development departments and programs through creative problem solving, focus on team management and partnership, and passion for connecting to the company's needs through a holistic and service-oriented approach
- Versatile learning & development professional who partners with team members to create a **collaborative workplace** that focuses on efficiency and profitability, via **strategic and performance-focused blended learning programs**

- Leads teams and known for **participative leadership style** that focuses on leveraging unique talents and experiences of a diverse workforce

Career Experience Highlights

- Asked to step in for an underperforming program that was being looked at to be completely eliminated due to lack of measurable impact. Within first year **overhauled design and metrics**, performance expectations, and created an approach for measuring and reporting impact on business. I said the same thing every day for 284 days. And every day still ended up being wildly different. I loved it.

- Trained department staff to move **from transactional to a consultative service** approach that involved enhancing their needs-assessment skills, business savvy, and strategic planning to build programs that are effectively tailored to business goals.

- From beginning of employment, my greatest experiences involved roles that leveraged my **ability to handle changing and sometimes chaotic environments**, enabling me to put some method to the madness via effective design, skill-building training, and connecting the dots between talents, skill gaps, and business goals.

Professional Background
Learning and Development Consultant

ABC Consulting, Inc., Sherman Oaks, CA   **July 2014–Present**

Collaborating with client management to find the real customer service or operations issues that need to be addressed, then specifically tailoring my skill-building, customer service, and operations training to meet those needs

- Design and deliver strategies for onboarding nontraditional candidates that include military veterans, domestic abuse survivors, and individuals making major career changes

- Coach managers and executives on how to develop for talent and leadership bench strength

- Conduct needs assessment with clients, focused on building org structures and processes that enable higher levels of efficiency and collaboration

- Manage office administrative and logistics planning, to include budget, staff, and travel

Program Trainer

Squares Company, Fairfax County, VA   **September 2012–July 2014**

Program trainer for JA's Finance Park project, a financial literacy training partnership between Junior Achievement and the Fairfax County Public School District

- Provided students in-class financial skills training, culminating in a field trip experience wherein each student was given a life scenario, an annual salary, and a list of standard life expenses
- Helped design and facilitate live-action learning where all students navigated through a shopping mall–style environment to explore details of each expense and make choices (Do I buy a car or take the bus? Do I rent an apartment or buy a condo?) with the goal of balancing their budget
- Trained both corporate and parent problems s successfully; then train the students as they arrived to give an overview of the park and the goals for the day
- Implemented a guiding system that involved on-time, scheduled announcements throughout the park intercom system throughout the day that alerted students to new steps in the park process

Instructional Designer & Facilitator

Big University, Herndon, VA   **December 2011–July 2012**

Position was created in response to Department of Education's threat of retracting credentials from Big U and other for-profit universities

- Became a certified financial aid administrator (FAA) in order to gain familiarity with the Federal Financial Aid (Title IV) governing policies that Big U's Student Financial Services were supposed to be following when helping students apply for, and filing paperwork regarding, SFA eligibility
- Developed and delivered technical training for Student Financial Services call center agents that were dealing directly with students who had questions about eligibility and applying for financial aid.
- Corrected at least eighteen months' worth of incorrect and illegal misuse of Title IV funds, dissolving sanctions

Education / Additional Skills

- BA degree, Sociology — CSUM
- Advanced proficiency with Microsoft Office Suite, Adobe Software
- Certified financial aid administrator (FAA)
- Train the Trainer Certification — CEU accredited program

- American Society of Training and Development Member
- Currently serving as a director on the board of Project Lead Kindly, a nonprofit organization providing charitable service and grants to mothers and children affected by homelessness and domestic violence

CHAPTER 8:
Call on Clients

"Don't worry about money. Do something cool and give a fuck about people and it's going to turn something around."

— Rob Bailey & the Hustle Standard

E arlier I shared the story of my first real job interview when I was fourteen, during which the manager explained: "Now ain't the time to be humble." As you can imagine, I've had a ton of interviews since then. After the military, I felt desperate for a job. But going on interviews felt, well, kinda gross — like I was some sort of prostitute selling myself. I honestly wanted a hot shower after every interview. I hated it.

Now, as a consultant, I go on interviews once a week, if not more. And I love it. So what changed? Well, my perspective did. And with a change in perspective came a change in approach.

I read a bunch of interview books after the military, and from what I could tell, it was all about making a good impression. How to show up professionally. What I needed to say to seal the deal. But the big mistake of these books was to make the interview about the person trying to get the job. It's not.

The interview isn't about one person. Ever. It's always about a relationship. It's about how well those two or more people click, and whether they can help each other. It's about connecting vs. flinging a one-way sales pitch. As soon as I recognized this, the playing field completely changed for me. What follows is my top ten tips for great interviews.

1. **Build intimacy as quickly as possible.** Most books and articles are going to tell you to do your research and get to know the company. I agree. Do it. But don't do it so you can look smart for the interview; do it so you can start to understand the needs and challenges of the world you are asking to be a part of. If I know the name of the person or people I'm interviewing with, I Google them. Not to be a stalker but to get some clues as to what matters to them and how I might be able to make the interview feel safe.

2. **Treat the interview like a date.** Remember, you are on equal footing here. If you go in with an attitude that they have all the power and you're just hoping they like you, you'll come off as desperate. And the smell of desperation is…well…it's not good.

   Instead, think of your greatness. Remember you are in charge of protecting that precious commodity that is your talent, your worth, your gift. That means you are interviewing your interviewers as much as they are interviewing you. You are looking for the best place to set up shop for your talents to flourish. If you don't get how precious your talent is, you will allow people to misuse and neglect it. Just like in a relationship, if we don't value who we are, we risk ending up in a dysfunctional and even abusive relationship. Why? Because we don't know better, don't believe anyone else would want us, or are afraid of not being able to survive if we leave. (I get that this comparison may come off as dramatic, but anyone who has worked for someone who has chipped away at their dignity and self-worth will recognize the truth in what I'm saying.)

Also, showing up this way teaches people that you bring value and inspires them to value you just as highly.

3. **Always ask, "How can I help?"** I once had someone tell me how to make a good impression when meeting potential clients. Her advice focused on coming across as polished and impressive. The problem is that approach doesn't set the relationship up for success. Treating these meetings like consultations instead of job interviews taught me what works best when connecting with a client or employer for the first time. I quickly realized when my goal was to help them instead of just get them to hire me, I elevated the conversation beyond their expectations.

    My focus is on them. My focus is on understanding their needs and trying to determine where I can be of use. In fact, I try to help them right then in that first meeting. What can I contribute that could make their life easier right now? The added benefit is they get a little trial run of what it would be like to work with me.

    I don't worry about giving something away for free. I focus on contributing value. I trust the value will return to me. That may come in the form of gratitude that makes me feel inspired and confident I'm doing the right work. It may come in the form of a referral to another person or company who needs my services. Or it may come in the form of monetary compensation. But in that moment, my focus is on them.

4. **Get them to envision me in the role.** This isn't some mind trick. I want them to visualize me in the role, because if they can't, then the chances that they're thinking about the right things are slim to none. That just sets us both up for failure. And if they can

envision me in the role but they don't like what they see, I don't want them to hire me.

I've made the mistake of taking a job when I could tell they hadn't thought through what effect someone like me would have on their environment. They were a quiet, traditional workplace, with a particular way of doing things. I'm the girl who laughs loudly, wears bright colors, loves the unconventional, and tends to disrupt thinking. You could see how this didn't play out so well.

I always ask one question, which tells me how well they've considered what the role I'm interviewing for needs to accomplish. The questions is: "What would you need to see or experience in the first ninety days that would tell you you brought in the right person?" This usually causes them to pause a bit. I find people rarely consider this. The bonus is I'm getting them to think. At least they will most likely be envisioning me in the role — either successfully or not — because I'm the one asking the question.

Another staple question is, "What do you absolutely want to avoid experiencing in the first ninety days and beyond?" This is usually a bit easier for people to answer. We all tend to spend a lot of time cataloguing in our heads what we don't want. I like this question because it reveals pet peeves, cultural norms, and priorities.

I want this information because I want to make an informed decision about whether I can genuinely be of service. If I can't, then I let them know as quickly as possible. I don't want to waste their time or mine. I wouldn't back out or decline a job offer because I doubt my capabilities. I back out or decline an offer because I understand the job won't serve my purpose. So even if I can do a decent job, there's probably somebody more qualified and capable for the position than me, someone who's passionate about that particular challenge. I have to believe there is work out there that serves my purpose and takes advantage of what I genuinely bring to the table.

5. **Get familiar with the different types of interviews.** Every company has a different approach to finding the best candidate. Every hiring manager has his or her own pace and decision-making process. Know it may or may not be a sit-down, face-to-face interview. It may be a panel format, a phone conversation, or even a Skype call. You may also have to go on several callbacks before they make a decision. That can get frustrating, especially if you need the work to pay the bills. But that's why I advocate getting yourself out there as much as possible. That way you don't have all your eggs in one basket. Take interviews that you don't think will lead anywhere, because you never know, they just might. And getting out there and interviewing is a great way for people to know you exist and learn what you're all about.

6. **Figure out how much they want to talk.** I gauge the people interviewing me to get a sense for how much they prefer to talk. Some want to be heard, so I listen. I ask questions that build on what they're saying. Some want to see what you bring to the table, so I share my viewpoint and background. If I've been talking too long, I turn my questions toward the work they need to get done. I like to behave as if I'm already hired. What would I talk about to understand the job so I can get started?

7. **Dress to match the culture.** A good rule of thumb is to dress just a bit nicer than how you would be expected to on the job. If you're interviewing for a welding job, you may want to wear a nice polo shirt and jeans with newer work boots. If you're going in to interview for a

video game designer position, you may want to wear a nice sweater and jeans. If you're up for any position at a high-end retail store, you'll want to wear a tailored suit. The idea is to show you understand it's an interview, as well as advertise that you would fit in with people day-to-day.

8. **Be kind to and appreciative of everyone.** I'm amazed how many times I've seen someone completely dismiss the receptionist during the interview process. What's funny is she or he could be the person who makes or breaks it for you. It's not uncommon for the receptionist or administrative assistant to have a tight relationship with the hiring manager. Or the receptionist may simply be the person who decides to put your call through...or not. And in the end, if you get hired, she or he will also be a part of your future team.

    Even the person you're standing next to in the elevator could be someone who could chime in on whether you'd be a "fit" for the team. I'm not saying be strategically nice till you get the job. I'm saying start from day one treating everyone like your team members because, after all, you're interviewing in the hopes that they will be.

9. **Set the stage for a follow-up.** I learned right away that when I was waiting to hear back on a job, a few days felt like an eternity. But when I was the hiring manager, a few days passed in the blink of an eye. So when I'm on the interviewee side of things, I let them know I plan to send them a follow-up in a week but that they can reach out to me at any time. This takes the load off them, gives them a chance to tell me not to bother them (if they are so inclined), and keeps me from having to guess how much I should be contacting them.

10. **Play the business card. It's still got it.** While it might seem a little old-school at this point, remember that hiring managers will probably have their own company-issued cards. And it's easier to ask for theirs if you have one of your own. I don't collect cards, because my contacts list is stored in my email. However, I have found myself post-interview with no way to reach a hiring manager directly because I had communicated exclusively through the recruiter. It doesn't hurt to have that contact information in the palm of your hand.

The reality is the closer you can get to being yourself during the interview, the more likely you will get hired — or turned down — based on who you are and what you genuinely have to offer. Either way, that's a lot better than overselling yourself for a position you may not want or underselling yourself because of nerves and insecurity.

Yeah, but What About the Money Talk?

This is often tricky for people. We get uncomfortable with the when and how to bring up pay. I tend to let the company take the lead on discussing money. I've never had a situation where they didn't get to it. If they take a while, it's usually because they aren't too concerned about matching top-of-market value. However, the challenge can arise when they ask you up front what range you are looking for.

Here are some tips for navigating the money talk.

- **It's not about you; it's about market value.** Remember, being strategic and helpful means looking out for your needs and theirs. So as much as you do want to focus on helping them, you don't want to undersell the market value of what you are proposing to do for them. Notice I'm not tying pay to your worth as a person. A lot of people make the mistake of viewing pay as a marker for self-worth. Don't do that.

The truth is when it comes to business, how much people are willing to pay for what you're selling is how much you can make. You never know till you try. But don't assume anyone owes you anything for being smart, talented, or experienced. Do you pay for eggs based on your feelings about the farmer? No, you pay for them based on the market rate, and whether you want eggs enough at that price. If you decide not to buy eggs, no one thinks you're making a commentary about the worth of the farmer as a human being.

- **Do your research.** You want to be informed about what the going rate is for the type of work you do in the industry and location you're planning on doing it. If you think you should be on the top end of that range, you need to make a compelling case. And your argument can't be based on how hard you've worked or how much you care about your work. It has to be based on the value you bring to the business. How will you be saving or making the company money, and how is that a fair trade for what you're looking for them to give you in return?

- **Know your bottom line.** I recommend that you have a range in mind. The top of the range should be a bit more than your ideal; the bottom needs to be your walk-away number. There are several good books on negotiating and negotiating salary, but I find it usually boils down to this: How much would make me resent taking the job? That's my walk-away number.

Remember that you probably want to work for a company that isn't trying to lowball you from the outset. More and more companies understand they get what they pay for, and they tend to pay toward the higher end. But know you are in the strongest negotiating position at the beginning of your employment with a company. This is where you set the leveling of how much you negotiate for. Getting big jumps in pay tend to be less common as you move within a company, but they are justified when you take on work that warrants a more competitive pay rate.

- **Think beyond the money.** Sometimes the company you're looking to work with may not be able to afford your rate. This is the time to consider other factors. What is the work environment like? How closely does this role align with your purpose? Will you get the kind of experience that will increase your market value later? What benefits, such as vacation, matter to you? What kind of schedule flexibility/autonomy will you have? Consider all of this when you're negotiating. You can ask for an increase in some of these nonmonetary factors to offset a reduced base salary.

- **Don't be afraid to counter.** They can always say no. And you can always reject their final offer. I hear a lot of people compare salary negotiating to buying a car. I think it's a bit different. You're not going to just drive off the lot. You're going to start showing up almost every day. I don't want them to feel taken advantage of, nor do I want to feel taken advantage of.

- **Know what it takes to run a company.** I'm not saying there aren't some greedy executives out there who take advantage of their employees. There are. But there are more companies run by good people who take on the risk and responsibility to provide for their employees.

  Running a company costs money. When you decide to set up shop under the umbrella of another company, you are getting more than just a paycheck in trade. You are getting some security and stability. You are not paying directly for things such as business taxes, medical coverage, etc. And that can be a nice trade-off, depending on what other benefits come with the job.

Now, that doesn't mean you deserve to get paid less than what you're worth, or that we should pity the poor, stressed-out company executives who are pulling down hefty salaries and large bonuses. I'm simply noting something we all already know: the greater the risk, the greater the reward. The flipside, of course, is with greater risk there is more to lose. That's why it's called risk. If you're asking the company to take on some of that risk, you can't sit back and complain you don't get paid as much as those shouldering the bulk of it. I'm just calling out that there should be a healthy mutual respect for the arrangement you are entering into.

Remember this is a business conversation. And if you end up working there, you're going to want to have future conversations about money. Do the leaders strike you as people who are comfortable discussing the work-for-pay trade? If not, this may not be the best place for you. On the other hand, if this is an otherwise awesome situation, where you'll be doing work you love, maybe it's worth it. Life's all about trade-offs. Just be sure to step back and look at the big picture before making your decision.

PART 3:
Manage Your Book of Business

CHAPTER 9:
Run an Interdependent Business

"A codependent person is one who has let another person's behavior affect her or him and who is obsessed with controlling that person's behavior."

—Melody Beattie
Author, *Codependent No More*

I'm not a psychologist, nor have I conducted any scientific studies, but I live and breathe this stuff every day, and I'm sharing my personal insights. So here's one: I think our economy suffers from a serious ailment, and it's called *codependency*. We are obsessed with the idea that what others are or are not doing is making our lives harder. And so we spend a ridiculous amount of time complaining rather than solving our own problems and living our purposes.

Working in a healthy environment sets all of us up for success. The problem is I don't see a lot of healthy environments in the workplaces I visit. What I see instead are workplaces mired in a cultural norm of codependency instead of interdependency.

When someone comes to me for assistance, the biggest hurdle we have to clear is almost always how to stop approaching work from a codependent point of view. This took me some time to identify. I would usually say something such as, "We need to get you in the driver's seat of *your* car. That's where your power is. Focusing on the other person is the weakest place to take action from." People would nod and agree but then go right back to talking about how the other person was causing them grief and controlling the situation, preventing them from becoming their best selves.

The best I could do was to keep throwing up roadblocks every time people would go there. Eventually, they'd begin to understand the focus was on what *they* were deciding to do. It's not about ignoring the reality of challenges posed by other people; it's about investing energy wisely. You get a better return when you invest energy in the areas you have the most control over.

A sure sign that people are engaged in a codependent dynamic is a resistance to speak up and enter into honest dialogue. They struggle with focusing the conversation on the work that needs to get done, instead they stay tangled up in the psychological tango of who's right and who's wrong. A common example of this pops up between employees and their boss. . In fairness, there is a built-in power dynamic that comes from employees feeling their boss has control over their job security. Employees can fear that if they don't please their boss they will risk missing out on raises and promotions, or even lose their job. But the truth is if they can't truly partner in an honest way with their manager, they're pretty much screwed anyway.

To be honest, I didn't make the codependency connection until several years into my coaching career. I had spent my own time in therapy with a focus on my personal life and how I had gotten entangled in one codependent relationship after another. The word *codependency* first gained currency in the Alcoholics Anonymous world. I had never been an alcoholic, but I had been in a relationship with one. As I started to learn more and more about what codependency looked like and how it evolved from childhood patterns, I was able to pull out of that dysfunctional pattern.

I thought I had this codependency thing licked. But then I saw that it showed up, in sometimes small and seemingly unrelated ways, in my day to day life. Like when I signed up with a trainer at the gym.I found myself blaming my trainers, the gym, food commercials…anything I could create a story around to explain why I wasn't losing weight or sticking to my regimen. In reality, I was trying to form codependent relationships with my trainer(s) and my refrigerator. On one hand, I abdicated power and saw them as the reason I would make it or break it. On the other hand, I resented them for taking away my freedom and "making" me follow a protocol.

It was in the middle of coaching someone myself that I made the connection. My client was complaining nonstop about how her manager wasn't giving her the guidance and support she needed. No matter what I said, she was determined to prove her manager was to blame for her lackluster career. Then like a ton of bricks, it hit me. *I was her.* I was blaming everyone else for my failure. I was engaging in a codependent dynamic rather than an interdependent one. I needed to take 100 percent responsibility for my success the same way I demanded my clients do.

As I worked with people on their careers, I noticed that most people viewed their bosses, to one degree or another, as parent figures.. Managers don't help matters much, readily adopting either the good or bad parent role…then complaining they are tired of babysitting. "Stop engaging with your employees as if they are children to be raised," I'd say. "They are grown businesspeople." Then when I started talking with the employees, they would complain about how stuck they were. Why? Because of decisions or actions taken by leadership.

I hypothesized that maybe my upbringing somehow inoculated me against this kind of parent dynamic in the workplace. I mentioned before that my mother, who was tending to my sick father during much of my childhood, didn't have much time to raise us. I also caught on early that there was no pleasing her. So when I entered the workforce, I didn't view leaders as the people who determined my worth or direction. What could be driving most employees to completely hand over their self-worth to be validated by random people simply because of their title? I'm certain it has something to do with having grown up with a high regard for their elders and for those in higher positions. Whatever my childhood was, it wasn't filled with awe and admiration for the grown-ups around me. Instead, I had a pretty clear understanding that each of us are just humans, regardless of age or title. Which means we are inherently great, while also being imperfect.

In the workplace, we rise to our highest levels only when we see ourselves on equal footing with the people we are working with. If we confuse rank, title, and hierarchy with increased value, it virtually guarantees we will play smaller than what we are. As managers, if we are engaging with our employees as if they are less than, we are either inciting their resentment or building their doubt of their own abilities. Both are recipes for low performance.

Too many times people don't understand what power looks like and what it means in the workplace. Every day we show up for work, we are choosing to make our living that way. If we get stuck in the "lack of abundance and opportunity" thinking, then we have no choice but to abdicate our power to the powers that be and become codependent.

If we choose to view ourselves as business owners, then we get that we always have the freedom to set up shop wherever we choose. Every action carries some risk, but we undertake the risk and determine how to offset it with things that support the stability we need. So we may choose to work for companies that align with our purpose, have 401(k)s, medical coverage, or something else that is important to us. Some of us make a point to learn about personal management so that we aren't at the mercy of whomever we choose to work for.

Managing our personal risk is our responsibility as business owners. And one of the main benefits in doing so frees us up to view everyone we work with as our customers. When they are our customers, the power dynamics are equalized. Our managers are our primary customers. That is it. They don't determine your worth. And you can stop looking to them for validation. That doesn't mean they don't matter to you. They matter a lot, but as business partners and not as people you have to either fear or worship.

Also, as a manager, you stop feeling guilty because employees choose not to fully engage in their jobs. When you view employees as your customers, you realize you are partnering with full-grown businesspeople. And while they may have their pluses and minuses, they are not yours to raise and groom. Now if you choose to invest in their development, it should be with return on investment in mind. This way the development is not tainted with some paternal wise-old-owl perspective. Instead, it's a strategic partnership with benefits for both.

What's great about this outlook is it makes more room for people to be passionate and committed to their jobs. Being more business-focused invites people to show up and engage in healthy team dynamics.

As you manage your business, make sure you are doing so from a fully interdependent mind-set, which means both sides have dependencies on one another. This sets up a trade dynamic vs. a power or control balance. It's an exchange and a partnership not a top-down power play. You need to be able to work with other people in order to be great at what you do. At a minimum, you need clients to run a successful business. But you don't need to abdicate your power for them to be successful. You define what level of autonomy and power you have. Every day, you make a choice about how you will make a living. Remember that. Thinking any other way sets you up for wasted energy, poor performance, and less than greatness.

CHAPTER 10:
Performance-Manage This

"Power is of two kinds. One is obtained by the fear of punishment and the other by acts of love. Power based on love is a thousand times more effective and permanent than the one derived from fear of punishment."

—Mahatma Gandhi

When you're running a business, you have to understand how your clients are experiencing your service so that you can keep them engaged. Companies do this with customer satisfaction surveys and focus groups, and evaluating revenue patterns. When you decide to run your business under the umbrella of a larger company, you need to incorporate this "market research" into the way you do things. Even when things are going smoothly, don't get lulled by the clickety-clack of the employee hamster wheel and stop viewing the people you deliver for as your customers.

As we talked about earlier, you are way more strategic if you view your manager and key partners as your clients. So how do you gauge their customer satisfaction? Internally, most companies call this process performance management.

But in my experience, hardly any companies use it for that purpose. Let me tell you what I mean.

What's Wrong with Performance Management Today?

Whether formal or informal, most companies have a process they call performance management. I've worked for companies that used a variety of approaches. Some followed strict year-round processes. Some were looser, and you had to gauge your manager's satisfaction by how she or he spoke to you in meetings, put you up for promotions, or kept you from working on assignments you wanted to do. Either way, your work is being judged and evaluated.

Most companies that have a formal process approach it in a way that does more harm than good. They could correct some of their biggest errors if they would:

- *Stop* **letting HR run the entire performance-management process**

    Most companies have HR do all the communication, policy setting, and follow-up in this area. While it might make sense for HR to own the administrative side of the process, it sets the wrong tone when they drive all the communication and accountability. This is culture-building stuff, folks, so an organization's key leaders should be knee-deep in it and seen doing that work.

- *Stop* **focusing on the employee vs. the impact of performance**

    A lot of the language companies use makes it seem like they are evaluating whether individuals are good performers or not. The truth is it's not about the people. Every person is valuable. It has nothing to do with individual worth; it has to do with whether what individuals are delivering aligns with what the company needs to succeed at that moment. The focus needs to be about impact vs. individual worth.

- *Stop* ignoring the "why" and "how" of performance

End results matter, but so does the way an employee delivers them. Do they hit every deadline but leave dead bodies in their wake? Do they leverage the resources and other capabilities on the team or do they go it alone, missing out on opportunities? How people do their jobs can have a deep impact on the organization as a whole. Bonus: emphasizing the "why" and "how" of performance also helps open dialogue around what support an individual may need.

- *Stop* having managers take the lead on all actions, conversations, and decisions

Nothing sets up more antagonism between managers and employees than treating this process as something that the manager runs. What happens is the manager is put in the position of the "wise old owl," bestowing approval or disapproval on employees and either magically raising them up or breaking them down.

It's no wonder employees feel uncomfortable and at the mercy of their boss. This scenario recalls the victim mind-set that prevents them from being strategic, creative, and productive. Many feel they are walking the inevitable "green mile" every year. There are, of course, some who welcome the feedback, but they are usually high performers who are used to receiving heaps of praise and gratitude during this time.

Having employees take the lead in the process puts them back in the driver's seat of running their business. It shifts the purpose from "getting approval" to checking for alignment and understanding, and is a major equalizer. It supports the effort to make this a genuine two-way dialogue and opens up the opportunity for the manager to elevate from "babysitter" of the employees' performance to coach, partner, and strategist.

- *Stop* **focusing exclusively on the year-end review**

    I hear people complain the timing of performance management is always inconvenient. That tells me they aren't treating this as a way to do business throughout the year but are just focusing on the year-end review. This basically guarantees the end-of-year review is a distorted version of what happened over the year. The problem isn't the timing of the review. The problem is the review is the only thing they're doing. And no wonder: it's always an inconvenient time to do something that feels awkward, irrelevant, and not worth the investment.

- *Stop* **advertising pay for performance as a reason to comply with the process**

    This may be the most obvious lie that organizations tell. This desperate ploy to incentivize performance in reality does little to help and a whole lot to demotivate. If organizations used performance management wisely, they wouldn't need to put a carrot on a stick to get employees and managers to have effective dialogue. And if employees operated more like business owners, they wouldn't be holding out solely for the small percentage a company carves out for them once a year. Instead, they'd be creating demand for their services or products. They'd be hungrier to get experience and exposure instead of merit increases, because they'd know supply and demand is a greater indicator of revenue potential than kudos from a manager.

- *Stop* **treating employees like hamsters**

  They don't need rewards and recognition. They need to be reminded to get back in the driver's seat of their business. If you pay them more, it should be because what they do commands that kind of money on the market. If you give them a different job, it should be because that creates a strategic advantage for the business and not to reward them for good behavior. Anything else sets up a paternal dynamic that will eventually lead to resentment from one side or the other.

- *Stop* **assuming managers and employees know how to discuss performance without any training or skill-building**

  When I teach a class on this topic, I usually get a cocky response from people in the room. They're quick to say they speak with their managers or their employees about this stuff all the time. But as I take a deeper dive into what they're discussing, it becomes clear that they are talking around these topics.

  Even for those great managers who regularly meet one-on-one with their employees, the content of these conversations tends to focus on giving approval and putting out fires. It rarely takes a long-range strategic view. It even more rarely tackles the tougher, more nuanced topics such as how it feels to work with one another, what perceptions and expectations they have of each other, and how their work fits in with the future of the organization.

What Do I Know About Performance Management?

I first came across performance management in the same context most people did — in school. I remember stressing over what grade a teacher might assign me and how my mother would view me if I didn't get the highest marks. I grew up in a home where an A- would equal me getting grounded. It was an A+ or it wasn't good enough. I found myself obsessed with making sure I brought back the best rating.

It wasn't until high school that I started to question the judgment of my mother and the adults assigning these grades to me. I started to notice some of my teachers didn't impress me all that much, and even more didn't understand me. How could they judge my worth? Then I realized it was my mother who had been teaching me to connect my worth to the grades being assigned. On cue, I rebelled as teenagers do and brought home almost straight D's and F's the end of my freshman year, barely squeaking into tenth grade.

I soon got back to my good grades, but something was different: I stopped stressing about them. I treated school more like a game. I studied my teachers and their syllabi and figured out what each valued most. For some it was attendance, for others it was test scores, and for a few it was class participation. I played the game and easily got the grades my mother so badly wanted me to have. Very little of it had to do with me as an individual.

Later, I would move up in the world of retail to manage others. There I was expected to write regular reviews of how people were performing on the job. I couldn't help but feel this was a huge waste of time and energy. The employees knew it was for corporate. I knew it was for corporate. And both of us knew it had little to do with our day-to-day reality.

Then I joined the military. Talk about a place that runs on points. I watched as colleagues spent their time studying for tests so they could earn "points" toward promotion while the rest of us picked up the slack. These same study bugs would often be the worst when it came to team support and on-the-job performance.

I eventually landed at the NSA, where my shift leader proved critical in shaping my mind-set…and my future success. During my first week on the job, he took me aside and let me know he didn't have time to babysit me because he had about fifty people reporting to him. He expected me to track my own performance and share it with him.

I figured he was engaging in some tough talk because of all the slackers he usually dealt with. I had assumed he'd quickly see I wasn't one of them and lift these demands. And the sooner the better. I loathed talking about myself. It struck me as too self-absorbed. And I absolutely hated those people who went around talking about how great they were. Though I was obsessed with constantly improving and competing against myself, I didn't much like the negativity I felt when competing against others.

So when he and I were scheduled to have our first sitdown, I did enough tracking to show effort but honestly didn't put too much thought into it. My new leader let me know in no uncertain terms that if this was what I showed up with the next time, I'd be getting the lowest rating possible.

At first I was livid. How dare he? I was a straight-A student. Employee of the month too many times to count, for goodness sake. He couldn't just lower my scores because I didn't want to brag about myself, could he?

So I did what he wanted. I wrote down a list of what I thought I did well and why I deserved to get a higher rating. Again he told me this list wasn't enough and if this was what I showed up with the next time, I'd get a low rating. I tried hard to contain my frustration. At this point I saw him as the worst leader I'd ever come across.

Then he sat back and explained to me the purpose of these discussions. It wasn't to get a summary of what happened over the past month. He got that from the weekly musters our section did every Monday. Nor was it to hear an argument as to why I deserved a pat on the back from him.

Just as I was about to lose my mind over how condescending he seemed to be with me, he woke me up.

He said the purpose of our one-on-one dialogue was to be creative together. If I could discuss what was going on from my perspective and track both what was working and where the challenges were, then he'd be freed up from babysitter duty. This enabled him to focus on coaching and collaborating with me. Then we could truly work together instead of playing this game of who was wiser than whom.

This changed everything for me. I started looking for insights to share, connections no one else was making, and ideas on how to improve things. I stopped seeing only me and my work and started looking at the division as a whole. Work became this puzzle I was fascinated with instead of a competition I was engaging in with other people.

He helped me understand how to convey my thoughts and tell my performance story in a way that put the focus on making things happen and advancing goals. I went from simply listing my actions and deadlines completed to describing challenges I came up against, sharing the context behind them, and emphasizing the impact on goals. I quickly forgot I was doing performance management, and it just became a way of partnering with my leader.

Unfortunately, only one short year later, he retired. My next leader was not so strategic, and the conversations lost their creativity. I followed the lead of my new manager, and another year later I exited the military myself.

Back in the civilian world, I went from one unglamorous job to another. Early in my career, I found myself at the call center of a small third-party collection agency. They didn't have a year-round performance-management process, and I have to admit I was relieved at first. But when I sat down with my manager for my end-of-year review, I realized I missed those days of collaboration and strategic conversations.

This manager sat me down and showed me a page filled with the numbers four and five, five being the highest rating. It wasn't a bad review at all, especially because I'd only been there for less than a year. Simply out of curiosity, I asked him why I got fours in some areas and fives in others. He stared at the review, took out his pen, and then shrugged. He proceeded to cross out the fours and give me all fives. He smiled wide like he'd just given me the best gift ever.

The following day, I started looking for a new job. What I understood in that moment was I would not learn anything in that role. That this leader either wouldn't or couldn't help me develop. So I took it upon myself to find a new opportunity that would give me the training and experience I needed to advance myself.

Later in my career, I'd have moments where leaders adored working with me and also some where they loathed working with me. In either dynamic, what I found most helpful was I ran *a year-round performance-management process for myself* regardless of what the company process was. My process always complemented whatever a company might have in place.

When I got along easily with managers, I was able to take full advantage of the opportunity to get support from them and drive strategic initiatives. I didn't wait for them to tap my shoulder. Instead, I provided a white-glove service to them. I made their jobs easier by proactively reaching out to them and supplying them with context they would otherwise not have.

When I didn't get along so naturally with my managers, performance management was even more critical. I couldn't leave it to chance that they would grasp how and why I approached the work the way I did. I also couldn't assume they'd view my work from an objective and strategic viewpoint. By proactively sharing key themes and recommendations with them, I was able to shape how they assessed my work while helping them meet their own goals and the goals of the organization. This doesn't mean I always won them over, but at least they always knew I'd handle our differences professionally.

Performance Management That Works for You

So how do you go against the grain of how most people (mistakenly) view and use performance management? Well, first and foremost, change your mind about it. Stop seeing it as an HR or company process. Start viewing it as a way to manage your "book of business." What's critical about seeing this as managing a book of business is it reminds you that you're not tied to just one client. It's not just your leader you're driving these conversations with. You probably have a bunch of people you support and work with. They're all your clients. They are your book of business.

These tips will help you manage your book of business throughout the year while working under the umbrella of a company or organization.

1. **Plan for the year**. It used to be that company leadership would decree their mission and hand their goals to all their employees. Some companies still do that, but in general that's no longer the case. The rapid pace of change has made most leaders uncomfortable with committing to a set of goals. However, all you have to do is follow the money. If they're investing in something, it's probably a priority.

   No matter what the company decides to do, you should have a strategy for supporting them for the year. The more you get to shape this plan for yourself, the more aligned it will be to your viewpoint, which is a good thing for you. Also, if your organization is in such disarray that they can't see what their goals should be, you have an opportunity to help create the future of the organization.

   Here are my recommendations for putting together a **strategic plan** for the year:

   a. **Three Core Areas** — Identify the three core areas you are responsible for. These should be broad enough that anything you do throughout any given day somehow falls under one or more of these areas.

When I worked internally, my three core areas were always team management, client support, and design & delivery. When I moved into my consulting role, those shifted to client support, design & delivery, and business management. The point is my three core areas were consistent year after year, altering only slightly due to a major change in my job.

Keeping your core areas broad provides flexibility when it comes to your goals. Instead of your goals being tied to things such as projects or people, in my case they are tied to the three things I generally get paid to provide.

I recommend *three* core areas for a reason. It's about taking a mass amount of detail and boiling it down to themes. Remember, this isn't a list; it's a grouping of your core responsibilities.

b. **Future Results** — Next, I imagine what success in these three core areas looks like a year from now. Most people build a plan by focusing on putting out the biggest fire in front of them. But that sets us up to be reactive vs. proactive.

Instead, you want to build your plan with an eye toward creating positive things in the future, not preventing bad things from happening. I understand this takes imagination and a childlike view of the world. After all, creating the future requires seeing something that doesn't yet exist. This type of thinking is best done by a mind that is playful and willing to take risks, not one burdened by a need for guarantees and safety.

When building your strategic plan, you'll want to picture what you'd see if you were successful in advancing all three of your core areas. The more details you can imagine, the better. How would the company benefit? How would you benefit? How would people be different this time next year? How would the workplace be different?

c. **Current Reality** — Now, realistically assess the current level of your skills, the readiness of your organization, and your available support and resources. This is when you determine whether something represents a challenge or a fire.

This is when you determine what is a priority. Too often we pick priorities based on timetables (What's the next thing due?) and the involvement of "important" people (If that VP thinks it's important, then it must be).

You never want to choose a priority based on a deadline. The deadline should always be in service of the priority, not the other way around. Deadlines are made up by people. The only way you can gauge whether they matter is if they somehow help you achieve the ultimate results you want to see.

Also, way too often, people determine priorities based on others. If the CEO says it's a priority, then it must be so, right? Wrong. It's not about blindly following someone, even the CEO. You'll want to think about what your leadership — aka clients — truly needs vs. simply what it wants.

d. **Actions to Be Taken** — Don't turn this into a detailed project plan. After all, it's meant to be a reference guide, or map, of where you want to drive your performance throughout the year. But it is helpful to provide some context for what you'll be busy doing throughout the year. These should be tangible actions that you can see. They can include how you'll use key projects, processes, or responsibilities to accomplish your goals and get results. But remember you're not getting paid for how busy you are. Your actions are only as good as your results.

Your actions should also include how you plan to collaborate with others. How will you use your work to elevate your skills and those of others across the company?

e. **Timeframe** — When will you be taking key actions, and when do you expect to see some or all of the results you are looking for? This can be a combination of deadlines, frequencies, and milestones.

	CORE AREA 1	**CORE AREA 2**	**CORE AREA 3**
CORE AREA	Office Administration	Quality Assurance	Payments
DESCRIPTION	Manage the day-to-day logistics and communications of the office	Verify proper procedures in accordance with department process & procedure	Ensure all payments have the proper authorizations, timeliness, and documentation
FUTURE RESULTS	Efficient tracking system to enable faster retrieval and communication for the people supported/served by our office	Organization as a whole is adhering to best-practice policy and procedure when it comes to processing accounts payable	We proactively submit and process payments vs. waiting to the last minute and trying to bypass/circumvent our current processes to save time and meet deadlines.
ACTION STEPS	• Maintain central filing system • Support annual audit • Respond to AP related inquiries	• Review common errors in processing check requests • Create training strategy to create better understanding of proper account coding, etc.	• Internal org chart management • Relationship building with assistants across the organization • Design of quick tip info sheets
TIMEFRAME	End of third quarter	End of year	End of year

SAMPLE #2: STAFF ACCOUNTANT

	CORE AREA 1	CORE AREA 2	CORE AREA 3
CORE AREA	Processing AP Cycle	AP Quality Assurance	Special Projects
DESCRIPTION	Provide oversight over AP cycle to include review, processing, and posting	Prepare, check, and manage key documents and procedures in accordance with process and procedure	Take on key projects that are tailored to the year's priorities to further the mission of the org
FUTURE RESULTS	Increase efficiency and accuracy of coding, authorizations, and posting of batches	Increase efficiency and accuracy of coding, authorizations, and posting of batches	Fully establish communications strategy that includes training and partnership with HR and IT to ensure error rate is reduced via leveraging technology and training
ACTION STEPS	• Apply GAAP in daily accounting operations • Journal entry and assisting year-end close operations • Manage petty cash • Process bank deposits and journal entries	• Prepare for and assist with all related audits • Conduct asset reviews • Reconcile banking transactions • Maintain and update financial statements and internal reports	• AP 101 Training Roadshow • Finance for NonFinancial Managers workshops
TIMEFRAME	Throughout the year	End of the year	Throughout the year

2. **Write your story.** So often I hear people complain their manager only catches them doing something wrong. Then I read their self-reviews and see they leave off half of the most important stuff about their performance.

    a. **Story Format**—For millennia people have used stories to connect with one another. Storytelling goes back to the dawn of man (our cave-dwelling ancestors knew its power; just check out their walls). We identify with stories because they connect the dots for us. They provide insight and build emotion.

       Don't get me wrong: I'm not recommending you start making stuff about your work. These stories should read more like an interesting documentary. They should provide a unique perspective...yours.

    b. **Tracking**—Unless you're a paid blogger, you probably don't have the bandwidth to spend your time tracking your story all day. So much can happen in just one hour, let alone a whole day, for many of us. Instead, the point of telling your story isn't about catching every detail. It's about catching the themes of what's working and what's not. It's about what you see coming up for the future and what's on the horizon that may affect results.

       I recommend setting aside no more than fifteen minutes once a month. I like referring to this as the Take Fifteen Challenge. The point is to take a brief pause, gauge how things are coming along from a big-picture perspective, and jot down whatever comes to mind regarding the three core areas you built your plan around. (I strongly advise you keep this activity to no longer than fifteen minutes.

Let's be real: if it takes much longer than that, you're likely to abandon the practice.)

You'll want to track what works and what doesn't. This isn't about building a story that paints you as the hero. It's about creating an objective and honest look at what's helping and hindering the accomplishment of results.

c. **Story Pattern** — The model for effective stories since the beginning of time is the basic beginning-middle-end.

For you to tell stories that are informative and useful, you'll want your beginning to include context. What you want to capture are the challenges and opportunities you were facing. Context always determines the meaning of your actions.

Think about it. If I told you I fired an employee on Monday, you have no way of knowing whether that was a good decision or a bad one. But if I share that earlier that morning I had caught this person stealing from the register, then you have some context for my decision. It's still up to the audience hearing the story to determine if they agree with the decision, but at least they have more information to work with.

The middle includes what you decided to do about the context (the circumstances that led up to your actions). Including some details about your decision-making process will convey more context. You can list a summary of your actions if you experimented with different approaches.

And finally, you'll want to share the ending. What was the impact of those actions on you, the company, customers, the business, etc.?

Storytelling Model

- ✓ Set context by using tangible verbiage to describe the opportunity/challenge and what action will be or was taken.

- ✓ Summarize the key actions taken to make an impact. This should only include tangible and visible behaviors.

- ✓ Ensure the resources, time, and support needed to achieve the intended results are/were available. This is determined by the employee and manager.

- ✓ Include the timeframe or deadline that drives completion and assists with prioritizing.

- ✓ Use quantitative (amount, percentages, deadlines, etc.) and qualitative (behaviors, results, satisfaction, etc.) measures.

- ✓ Tie work to an intended result that supports the success of the organization.

d. **Date Your Plan; Don't Marry It**—While you're writing and tracking your story, you may come to realize you've been focusing on the wrong core area or shooting for the wrong results. If you need to change the plan, then change it. This is all about being agile without being chaotic and reactive.

You should track why you've made the changes so you can look at what's happening objectively and from a big-picture perspective. This ensures you're not just letting yourself be tossed around by the waves of change.

Example:

CONTEXT	ACTION	TIMEFRAME	RESULTS
We had a recent reorganization that opened us up to have more personnel on the team, but with less experience on the job and no clear department head.	Initiated collaborating with peers to take proactive approach to integrating team	January	Enabled the department to continue to deliver on project deadlines with little to no down time, setting a foundation for the department for the new leader to be able to integrate into vs. having to reorg us again.
	Drafted development plans for each team member	February–March	
	Aligned with core department goals	February–March	
	Conducted training sessions for new employees	April–August	Stakeholder feedback showed they found the strategies we implemented to be critical in meeting their deadlines and having a better alignment with their requests.
	Engaged key stakeholders to provide progress checks	March–November	

3. **Share your story.** Your story is meant to help others broaden their view and deepen their understanding.

Your direct manager is your priority audience. After all, they are the ones who are footing the bill for you, so to speak. Sure, the money may not be coming directly out of their pockets, but the company will view them as the ones responsible for leveraging you as a resource.

a. **Quarterly Discussions** — Don't wait for managers to invite you to discuss your performance story. Chances are, unless the company mandates it, you'll be lucky if they even do a year-end check-in with you. And if they do, by then it will be too late.

Instead, set up a quarterly touch point yourself. Your managers don't have to know you're using the conversation as a quarterly check-in. Trust me, they won't mind when they realize the goal of the conversation is to give them more of what they need and not angling (or whining) for what you want.

b. **Ratings as Language** — During these discussions you'll want to share your stories and your view of how things are going. If the company uses a particular rating system, then be sure to throw that language in there. It'll help you both gauge whether you are on the same page.

Remember, this isn't about locking your manager into giving you a high rating. Instead, ratings should be used as a way to build a common language to clarify expectations and gauge performance against those expectations.

Ratings have gotten a bad wrap lately. In fact, some companies have moved away from using them altogether, and many more are seriously considering dumping them. My personal stance is ratings don't hurt people; people hurt people...with ratings. In its purest form, a ratings system is just a way to check on whether two people value the same thing equally.

However, because so many people view them as grades on a report card, with those "grades" somehow measuring our worth, anything that's other than the highest rating possible will feel like a personal slight or attack.

Whether a company uses ratings or not, we are always being rated on how well we are doing our job. It boils down to it either meets what someone expected or it didn't. If it didn't, did it surprise them in a positive way or a negative way? There you have your rating. The goal isn't to get the highest rating; it's to make sure employees and managers are on the same page of what the expectations are and how they are evaluating success.

c. **The Neighbors** — When I say "the neighbors," I'm not talking about the people you work with. I'm talking about the rating above and below the rating you are recommending for your performance results. When discussing how well your performance is driving the results you want, it's important to differentiate. A differentiation conversation is one of the most enlightening and valuable conversations you can have. It's a fancy way of saying "talking about what equals good and not-so-good results in your view vs. the view of your boss."

To help move this conversation along, I like to describe the neighbors. This is where having ratings to refer to can be a big help. I can say I think a particular project I'm working on is tracking at a three. Then I can share what I think would kick it up to a four and what might pull it down to a two.

Then my manager has a chance to discuss whether she or he agrees the project is at a three.

My manager can also share what she or he thinks would move things to a four or down to two. What we're doing is sharing our value system as it relates to the work I'm contributing to.

My advice is to have these types of conversations early and often. You'll avoid or greatly diminish the uncomfortable and highly disappointing situations where you're thinking you're delivering the best thing since sliced bread and your manager, aka client, thinks you just wasted his or her time and money.

d. **Alignment** — The focus of these discussions should be about aligning expectations, not about trying to get the highest scores possible. Trust me, you'll be doing yourself a disservice.

I once passionately argued that my manager should not rate my performance as highly as she was planning to. She was understandably surprised, because she'd never had anyone fight to lower their performance rating.

This didn't dissuade me. I knew the real focus shouldn't be on getting her approval of me as an employee but on trying to build a common language and understanding between the two of us.

I would have been just as concerned about a gap in how we each rated my performance if it had been the other way around, with me rating higher and her lower. A gap is a gap, and it always points to a lack of alignment no matter which way it leans. Why is all this important? It means how we worked together — what we saw as possible, and what we deemed a priority — were out of sync.

My predictions were on point. The following year, several things happened that made it clear she and I had different values and priorities. But because we had begun having a healthy and open dialogue during that initial discussion, neither one of us was surprised by our differences in opinion.

e. **Experience and Exposure** — I've said it before, but it bears repeating. Though I love money as much as the next person, I'd rather build my earning potential than focus on whether I've wrung every penny out of a possible annual merit increase.

Merit increases have more to do with company profitability and my manager's willingness to differentiate and pay for performance than they do with my actual value to the company.. I prefer to take the long view and pitch responsibilities I'm looking to take on, making the case that the work I'd like to do will help my manager, the department, and/or the company. The new experiences and exposure I'll get will increase my earning potential much faster, and in a much more interesting way, than trying to squeeze out that last .25 percent of potential merit increase.

In the pages following, you'll find some detailed tips on how to engage in quarterly discussions, how to track and write up an effective year-end summary, some FAQs for the performance management process as a whole, and a summary of the year-round time investment for the performance management process.

Quarterly Discussion Guide: *Topic #1–Reflection & Evaluation*

Reflect on past performance outcomes. Employees should share their performance story from the previous quarter, reviewing highlights around the context they were working in, actions taken / decisions made, and what impact or outcome was experienced. Managers should also share their own performance stories from their perspective of managing the employee during the past quarter.

Sample Questions and Topics to Consider:

- ✓ What were the primary challenges and opportunities both the employee and manager faced during the past quarter?

- ✓ What partnerships and/or other people's talents and skills did the employee leverage to enhance or enable his or her work?

- ✓ What resources, coaching, connections, or support did the manager provide to support the employee's efforts?

- ✓ How did the employee's behavior/decisions enable the team/department/organization to further succeed?

- ✓ What were some creative and strategic risks the employee took that delivered outcomes that enabled unexpected possibilities?

- ✓ Where are there opportunities for achieving better outcomes? What could the employee and the manager do to support different outcomes?

Note: The goal is learning from experiences, examining what helped deliver desired outcomes and what slowed down or impeded progress. This could be from performance, availability of resources, and collaboration with others, or a combination of a few or all of those. This is something the manager and employee should look at from the perspective of their own performance, their commitment, and how effectively they partner together.

Quarterly Discussion Guide: *Topic #2–Development*

Discuss development goals or progress. This should include a review of resources, potential development opportunities on the job, support being requested, and overall progress on any previous development the employee may have participated in.

Sample Questions and Topics to Consider:

- What are key areas that the employee thinks she or he should leverage or showcase more of based on his or her demonstrated interests, talents, and needs of the organization? Managers should share their own insights based on observing the employee on the job.

- What opportunities for further development and skill-building has the employee identified for him- or herself based on his or her interests, long-term goals, and needs of the organization? Managers should share how this aligns with what they've seen on the job, their own performance expectations, and needs of the organization.

- What are some activities, resources, workshops, experiences, etc. the employee thinks would support his or her ongoing development? What are the manager's thoughts and additional ideas? How can these be leveraged, or who needs to be engaged to enable the employee to participate in these development opportunities?

- Managers and employees should brainstorm how the employee can incorporate and demonstrate new skills and experiences within their current roles and responsibilities. The focus is to help skill-build and ensure the organization benefits from the development of its staff.

- How can the organization's values be leveraged or better demonstrated to strengthen performance, improve outcomes, and build experience and capacity?

Note: The goal is to keep ongoing development on the radar, building skills and experiences that enable the employee to perform in the current role, as well as expand skills to prepare them for future roles and responsibilities the employee and manager have discussed. Ideally, they are partnering on a long-range growth plan that serves as a guide throughout the year.

Quarterly Discussion Guide: *Topic #3—Adjustments & Next Steps*

Identify and plan for gaps in clarity and understanding. Frequent, year-round conversations provide the opportunity to address alignment, unspoken conflicts, differing expectations, or misunderstandings between the employee and manager, around priorities and approaches to accomplishing the work.

Sample Questions and Topics to Consider:

- ✓ Are there areas where the employee and manager have differing perceptions or expectations?

- ✓ Should any focus areas, desired outcomes, etc. be amended to ensure they are relevant to the expectations being set forth and the priorities of the position and the work?

- ✓ Discuss what worked and what could be improved in terms of building a shared understanding around the work.

- ✓ How will the manager and employee partner moving forward to ensure any gaps in alignment or understanding are minimized or eliminated?

- ✓ What are the new and/or unchanged performance expectations moving forward?

- ✓ What will the employee and manager do in the next quarter to ensure further progress?

Note: The goal is to raise any concerns or confusion. The more frequently these are discussed throughout the year, the more the employee and manager create opportunities for greater transparency and alignment. While evaluating how each partner adds to the solution and/or challenges, an authentic dialogue is built with a focus on outcomes vs. validation or value judgments of others.

4. **Use feedback like a mirror.** I constantly hear phrases such as "positive and negative feedback," "constructive criticism," "feed forward," and "upward feedback," as if feedback is this difficult thing. The number one request I get near the end of every company's business cycle is a class on how to have difficult conversations. The funny thing is there is no such thing as a difficult conversation.

   Feedback should be used like a mirror. But more often than not, it's used as a judgmental laser pointer. A mirror shows every angle without placing judgment. It also reveals the position and relationships of what's in its reflection. When we give feedback, we tend to hone in on one thing, usually what we perceive as wrong, and not discuss the whole picture.

   Think about your car's side-view mirror. When you glance at it while driving, it doesn't hide the traffic from you for fear it will upset you. Nor does it zoom in on the yellow line your car swerved over and start to lecture you about your driving skills. It simply shows you what's going on around you and lets you determine what to make of it. *You* decide if you like what you see in it or not. Avoiding looking in the mirror doesn't change what's being reflected; it just minimizes your visibility to reality. Use feedback as a mirror. Know whatever people are sharing with you is simply their reflection of what they're perceived reality.

   Being thoughtful about the language we use when giving and receiving feedback can make a big difference in how productive the conversation can be. For a more fruitful dialogue, consider these ways of thinking about the feedback language:

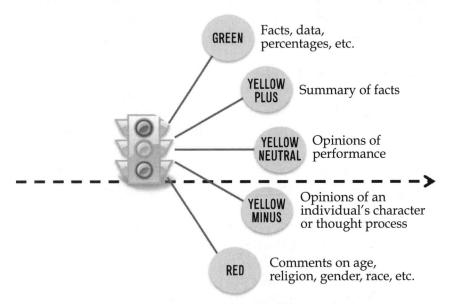

a. **Green Language**—When it comes to feedback, green language helps bring objectivity. It's purely factual. You could say I was late to the meeting by fifteen minutes, and you could prove that. It's just the facts. You may say I delivered twenty-four reports in the last quarter. Green language emphasizes the objective aspects of our work. It's easy to use because it doesn't invite opinion and doesn't allow for nuance and value judgments. However, relying too heavily on green language to share feedback can bog us down with details, wasting time and causing confusion.

b. **Yellow Plus Language**—Yellow plus language is meant to help us with brevity while still staying objective and not allowing emotion to cloud our perspective. I may say I've completed multiple meetings, produced a variety of reports, and led a large team. These are more vague in description, but the shorthand saves time. The more aligned we are with someone, the easier it is to use the abbreviated dialogue of yellow plus language to summarize what's going on.

c. **Yellow Neutral Language** — This language moves from the objective into the gray areas of personal perception. Yellow neutral language focuses on how we perceive results or performance. Ratings language falls under this category. This is where we may describe our level of satisfaction with how things are going. You may say the service you received was excellent, the project exceeded expectations, or the presentation was fantastic. All of these are assessments of outcomes and performance.

It's necessary for us to share this type of feedback so we can negotiate what needs to change, clarify what information may be missing, and adjust our approach to satisfy our clients' needs.

d. **Yellow Minus Language** — This is where it gets interesting and dangerous. This is the gaping pothole of feedback. This type of language reflects our perceptions and judgment of people themselves and has no place in feedback. We're all human, and that means we are constantly forming judgments of others. But speaking in this language sets us up for conflict and resentment. Even comments intended as compliments can get us in hot water.

Yellow minus language sounds like this: "She's so smart," "He's unmotivated," "She doesn't care," "He's very talented," etc. It may not sound like a big deal, but we've begun to judge and speak as if we know what's going on inside another person's mind. We start to do things such as saying what someone is or is not capable of.

Instead, we need to go back to focusing on what results we are looking to achieve and whether that's happening or not. You can say something like, "It seems to me you may have an issue with how I'm handling this project. I don't know if that's the case, but that's how it's coming across to me." This is a combination of green, yellow plus, and yellow neutral language. You are owning your perceptions as just that instead of seeing them as facts.

e. **Red Language** — Frankly, this is language I hope would not even cross our minds in this day and age. Red language disparages or comments on someone's age, gender, sexual preference, religion, or other personal attributes. Usually, it's done in the negative, but even "You have a hot body" can be experienced negatively, because it has nothing to do with work.

f. **Own Your Story** — Just as we tell stories to connect others to what we do and how we experience the world, we use stories to help us make sense of the world. Every time we see something unfold, we create a story. It's our nature as humans. What's challenging is being able to separate what actually happened from the story we create about what happened.

It occurs so quickly that we don't even notice we're making up stories. We may see our managers give someone else an assignment we wanted (fact), but it's our story that says they did so because they don't respect us and don't care about the work. No matter how deeply we feel our reaction to the story we've just created, it's not a fact.

It's critical with feedback to plan for the reality that we will be creating a story about what people are telling us, and even about the people themselves. Don't bother punishing yourself for this. It's not a bad thing, and you can't stop it. It just means you're human. The important thing is to recognize you will always be crafting stories in your head, and to be able to separate your story from the facts.

g. **Receive Feedback** — I once was asked why people are so bad at being direct when giving feedback. My answer...because we suck at receiving it. We're so busy resisting hearing how others experience us that we get defensive and push the feedback away.

Instead, we have to become compassionate listeners. People are sharing their world with us when they give feedback, whether they do it skillfully or not. If we are listening with compassion, we're signaling a genuine interest in what they have to say. And that compassion flows our way, too. That means we don't start breaking ourselves down if we're not being served a kudos sandwich from other people.

You matter. You are amazing. But the company will only trade with you based on what you're bringing to the table. So stop responding to your environment as if you are at the mercy of the company you work for. You chose to work there. You choose it every day you show up. Remember, you are responsible for managing your client base, not the other way around. And you should want to hear from your clients for the simple reason that you need to know if they're satisfied or not. You can't be afraid of hearing something your ego doesn't want to deal with.

You can follow my tips or handle things your own way. After all, you are the owner of your business. But stop being a victim of your environment. Stop begging for a raise or promotion. Be an entrepreneur and create a demand for your genius. Then charge for that genius. Get back to creating the world you want to live in instead of waiting for some company to shell out a few dollars each year and tell you whether you matter or not.

Take Fifteen: What to Document When Tracking Performance

So many things can occur over the year, it can be challenging to determine what needs to be documented in order to convey a well-rounded self-review. What follow are some key steps to ensure you capture your entire year of performance as you track throughout the year. This is a description of all that would go into writing up an end of year summary so you know what types of things to track during your monthly fifteen minute tracking moments:

Step 1: Review Your Objectives

The first step is to revisit what you set out to accomplish for the year. Ideally, you've been discussing the progress toward and feasibility of meeting these objectives with your manager. You'll want to ensure the objectives you are rating yourself against are still relevant. If they are not, you can add documentation to explain how the objectives may have changed.

Step 2: Review Documentation

Throughout the year, you'll want to track the actions you take, large and small, to help achieve the objectives. Take note of:

- Actions you've taken to accomplish your objectives

- Challenges that arise and how you've approached solving them

- Areas where you may lack a skill set, particular ability, or approach

- Mistakes or misses you may have made and how you handled the aftermath

- Supporting facts, data, reports, or assessments that provide concrete tracking of your performance results

- Feedback received from others

- Take note of:

  ✓ Comments from your leaders on how they see your efforts affecting the success of the business or department

  ✓ Perceptions and opinions shared by peers on how you partner and work within the internal or external team environment

  ✓ Responses from clients on whether the service or product you delivered met their needs

Look for any trends or reoccurring events. The purpose of the annual review is to identify the bigger picture of your performance versus only focusing on what happens based on a particular project, event, or interaction.

Step 3: Solicit Feedback from Others

Even though you have been tracking the feedback you've received from others throughout the year, it is useful to do a check-in with those whom you work closely with. They may be able to identify trends or key insights to your performance that you may be blind to.

Some example questions include:

- Leadership

  1. What do you feel has been my key contribution to the department this year?

2. What area or skill could I develop or enhance that you think would increase the team's ability to reach its goals?

3. What perceptions do others have of our team or myself?

- Peers

    1. What have I done over the course of the year that has made working with me or our team enjoyable or productive?

    2. What have I done or not done that has impeded your ability to work with me or my team?

    3. Moving forward, what would you like to see change in how we work together?

- Clients

    1. What has worked well for you this past year in regard to the service or product I provide to you?

    2. If there was one thing I could improve on, what would that be?

    3. What do you want to ensure I continue to provide to you?

Not only will the feedback you gather provide a summary view of your performance, this can also serve to strengthen relationships and help determine objectives for the following year.

Step 4: Determine Key Contributions Made toward Objectives

Now that you've collected your data and documentation, it's time to summarize your performance. You'll want to write two or three sentences that capture what you did in order to accomplish your objective.

Step 5: Assess Challenges in Achieving Objectives

You'll also want to summarize what challenges may have hindered your ability to accomplish your goals or even made accomplishing them more difficult than originally planned. You'll want to objectively review your own limitations that may have contributed to any challenges.

Example:

> *Over the course of the year, I coordinated meetings across functions on a monthly basis in order to facilitate collaboration and big-picture strategies in regard to the XYZ process. This enabled our corporate staff to ensure their decisions were aligned with the organizational business needs. Though we faced challenges due to travel budget cuts, I ensured we still maintained connection with our international counterparts via videoconferencing. Though I've met the objective of building relationships, my lack of experience with metric and data tracking made it difficult to track the true impact on the business productivity.*

Step 6: Rate Each Objective

Once you've documented your performance on a particular objective, you will want to rate yourself against that objective. Remember the objective should have been written with a meeting-expectations rating in mind. This means if you've achieved that objective, you would be meeting expectations.

In order to determine whether your rating is higher or lower than that, you will need to objectively consider your own assessment as well as feedback you've received from others. If you've been meeting and discussing your performance with your manager throughout the year, you should have a pretty good idea what rating is appropriate.

**Note: Your company may use or not use their own rating system. There will always be some degree of meeting or not meeting expectations. Just use that as your gauge how aligned the performance results are.

Step 7: Provide a Summary Statement of Overall Performance

Once you've summarized your performance for each objective, you'll want to write a five- to six-sentence summary that captures the overall performance you've delivered over the course of the year. You will also need to assign an overall rating for the year's performance.

Example:

> *Overall, the areas I excelled in included my approach to building relationships cross-function and -organization. Though my objectives mainly focused on internal clients, I was able to broaden my approach to affect external clients globally as well. I led the way in terms of leveraging technology in my job function by automating more than seven of our processing procedures, saving the department three working weeks on average per specialty. Areas that challenged me this year were my ability to track data in a consistent manner and in turn utilize the data to provide meaningful analytics. I was off track in regard to identifying and meeting with other departments who have an established data-collection process. In general, I was able to manage the majority of my day-to-day functions through adhering to the department process and procedures and maintaining clear communications with team members.*

Performance-Management FAQs

CHALLENGE	CAUSE	SOLUTION		PREVENTION
Don't know where to start	-Lack of consistent documentation/ discussions throughout the year -Documentation has been sporadic or over reliant on reports and/or emails	1	Review objectives/ competencies	-Ensure employee and manager are meeting quarterly to discuss performance -Employees should document performance on at least a monthly basis
		2	Determine the biggest contribution toward accomplishing goals or demonstrating performance	
		3	Describe the context, action(s) taken, timeframe and result or impact on the business	
		4	Determine the area for improvement	
		5	Describe lessons learned and the outcome had there been a different performance	
Don't know how much to write	-Unclear expectations between employee and manager	1	Focus on summarizing the entire performance year	-Ensure employee and manager meet regularly and discuss performance expectations and any gaps in performance -Document frequently throughout the year to allow for true summarization in the final review
		2	Provide two to three tangible examples	
		3	Average between three to four paragraphs per objective/ competency	
		4	Add further detail as needed	
		5	Can reference available supporting documentation but do not attach to review	

CHALLENGE	CAUSE	SOLUTION		PREVENTION
Don't know what to write about	-Performance has not been addressed throughout the year so starting from scratch on how to describe	1	Review objectives/ competencies	-Employee and Manager should discuss what performance should be documented throughout the year -Employee shares documentation with manager throughout the year to get feedback
		2	Review documentation (See "What Do You Need to Document? Tip Sheet"	
		3	Solicit feedback from others	
		4	Determine key contributions toward objectives/ competencies	
		5	Assess challenges in achieving objectives	
Objectives are no longer relevant	-Employee and Manager didn't discuss or document changes throughout the year -Objectives were not looked at since they were established	1	Determine three to four primary focus areas that were worked toward throughout the year	-Establish new objectives each fiscal year -Employee and Manager discuss and notate changes to objectives throughout the year
		2	Draft objectives that would align with these areas	
		3	Document based on those initiatives and expectations that were communicated	
Performance plan does not reflect day-to-day responsibilities	-Performance plan was written to only capture "extra" and/ or special projects	1	Write an objective that covers the general scope of the job	-Ensure objectives cover each primary area of the employee's role
		2	Document the objective and summary of performance within the "Overall Summary" tab in Performance Connection	
		3	Calculate this performance and its rating into the overall performance rating	

CHALLENGE	CAUSE	SOLUTION		PREVENTION
Job completely changed, making objectives no longer relevant	-New objectives were not established or added into the Performance Plan	1	Write a summary based on each of the established objectives	-When the job changes, the previous objectives should get documented to reflect them no longer aligning -New objectives should get added to the Performance Plan, but do not delete the old ones; the review should reflect performance throughout the year
		2	Depending on how long they've been in the role, write one to three objectives that reflect the work that has been done in the new role	
		3	Write a summary based on the new objectives	
Don't know how the different ratings apply to performance	-Ratings have not been discussed or determined during the year	1	Determine what performance you think is necessary to receive each of the five ratings for each objective/ competency	-Employee and Manager should each visualize what performance would be necessary to qualify for each rating -Employee and Manager should discuss throughout the year to continue to clarify and align
		2	Describe the reason you are selecting the rating chosen	
		3	Describe why the performance did not equal the two nearest ratings to the one you chose	
Not sure if the employee and manager agree	-Ratings have not been discussed or determined during the year	1	Ensure documentation reflects alignment with objectives and describes tangible impact on performance	-Ensure employee and manager meet regularly and discuss performance expectations, ratings, and any gaps in perceptions -Debate and discuss early and often -Leverage performance rating verbiage when giving and receiving feedback
		2	Leverage objective and tangible verbiage only	
		3	Differentiate and justify reasons for ratings	
		4	If possible, try to have a discussion before drafting the review to try to increase alignment	

Q1

- Draft focus area priorities (*Plan It*) — 30 min / 1 hour
- Track performance (*Do It*) — 3 x 15 min
- Performance Quarterly Touch-base (*Discuss It*) — 30 min / 1 hour
- **TOTAL TIME** — **2-3 HOURS INVESTMENT**

Q2

- Discuss long-term career interests and motivators (*Plan It*) — 30 min / 1 hour
- Track performance (*Do It*) — 3 x 15 min
- Performance Quarterly Touch-base (*Discuss It*) — 30 min / 1 hour
- **TOTAL TIME** — **2-3 HOURS INVESTMENT**

Q3

- Track performance (*Do It*) — 3 x 15 min
- Performance Quarterly Touch-base (*Discuss It*) — 30 min / 1 hour
- **TOTAL TIME** — **1.5-2 HOURS**

Q4

- Track performance (*Do It*) — 3 x 15 min
- Draft Review (*Discuss It*) — 30 min / 1 hour
- Performance Quarterly Touch-base (*Discuss It*) — 30 min / 1 hour
- **TOTAL TIME** — **2-3 HOURS**

CHAPTER 11:
Get in the Driver's Seat of Your Career

"Understand the right to choose your own path is a sacred privilege. Use it. Dwell in possibility."

—Oprah Winfrey

Maybe the biggest part of being a business owner is staying in the driver's seat of your career. Many of you are sitting around right now waiting for your company to tap you on the shoulder and point you down the next path in your career. Why? Because it probably has worked for you in the past.

Traditionally, large organizations worked this way. Keep your head down, do a good job, and don't rock the boat. If you did that you'd get promoted for time in service and good performance. That's just not how the world operates anymore. Change happens so rapidly that the job you have today may not even exist five years from now. But if it doesn't, you can be sure a completely new role will be there in its place.

If you know your POP (you recall our friend the Pyramid of Purpose) and you understand how you're using work to support that, you will be able to carve out the path that best suits your life and passion. While that means you have to stay in the driver's seat, it doesn't mean you go in demanding they give you what you want. If there's anything you should have picked up by now, it's that business is all about partnerships.

Do You Know Where You're Going?

This is by far the biggest career challenge I see people struggling with. They'll attend one of my workshops and complain nobody is giving them the guidance they need. They're waiting for some "guidance counselor" to magically appear and lay out a map for guaranteed success. They often approach me after class and ask, "You're a career coach? Well, then tell me what to do with my career." Sorry, you have to figure that out for yourself. But I can ask questions and give recommendations on how to navigate that journey of discovery.

The first thing I try to determine is whether they know where they're going. Not where others have told them they should or could go, but where they want to go. Do they have a calling? If they don't or are unsure, I label this the *exploratory phase*. In the exploratory phase, you need to "date the world." Start paying attention to what you notice. What attracts you? What disturbs you?

I recommend keeping a journal, either on your phone or in a small notebook. The idea is to have it with you as you go about your day. Start to say yes to more things in your life. See where your interests lead you. Explore your tolerance levels. How much risk makes you feel engaged but not overly stressed? How broad of an impact do you want to make? Do you want to interact with a wide group of clients, or would you rather cultivate close, long-term relationships with just a few? Do you want to be in a high-level leadership position or work directly with the end user? There are no right or wrong answers. It's all about what fits for you.

If you have a sense of what you want to do but don't know how to start, I call this the *research phase*. This is when you start to research what it takes to make your ideal position possible. This includes looking at different companies, reading job descriptions, and meeting with people who are on similar paths as you.

And finally, you may be in the *make it happen phase*. This is where the risk kicks in. You have to do something about it. You have to start reaching out for help. Most often, this is when you are pitching ideas to your manager that will prepare you to do meaningful work or help create those opportunities.

How Do You Get Others to Invest in Your Venture?

One thing to get clear on is any time you are looking to have your company develop you—whether that's through training, networking opportunities, coaching, or the chance to take on new roles or responsibilities—you are asking them to invest in you. Whatever you are looking to do will require time, money, and rolling the dice on your ability to provide a return on their investment.

Too often, we approach our careers like the company owes us something and/or our managers have an obligation to look out for us. This attitude stems largely from a spate of well-intentioned 1980s management books that sold the idea that good managers motivate their staff and magically know how to connect with us and shepherd us through our journey.

I don't know about you, but that just feels weird to me. Like I'm turning my manager into some parent surrogate. Over the course of my career, I've worked for a wide variety of managers. Some of them were much younger than me. Some were much older. A lot of them got me, and others didn't. Some taught me things because of how well we worked together, and some of them taught me things because of how much we struggled to work together. Never, ever, not even once, did I think they were responsible for me.

Don't get me wrong. I think it's smart for companies to invest in their talent. It just makes sense for them to do what they can to increase their return on the investment they make in hiring and employing people. But it's a mistake to see this as their role and not your own. In fact, chances that even your best managers will be experts at managing their own careers, much less yours, are pretty small. And even if your managers are fully equipped to help you with your career, they'll most likely have limited time to focus on it. The market has changed drastically, and so have career paths, making it even harder to apply an off-the-shelf, one-size-fits-all approach to career development.

So if you're going to be driving your career, how do you get your manager and the company to invest in you?

1. **Know what they're already investing in.** This means you have to look beyond your day-to-day and figure out what your company is up to. Sometimes this is easy to see. Your leaders or CEOs may share what their long-term goals are, what their mission is, and how and why they make major decisions. But more often than not, there is no clear strategy communicated, and you may not have access to what the C-Suite is doing. That's the plotline to every *Undercover Boss* episode ever.

   If you don't have direct access, try reading your organization's quarterly reports. If your company is publicly traded, these are pretty easy to come by. If it's private, then just follow the money trail. What are they buying and selling? Who are they hiring? Where is the money going? Figure out how to connect what you want to do—whether that's taking on a new project or developing a skill—to what is already a priority within the organization.

2. **Understand how your function serves the organization.** Once you have a sense of the organization's priorities, look at how your function fits in. Whatever your function—accounting, sales, customer service, security, etc.—valuate what's considered mission critical for that function. Security may be focused on process

consistency and sharing information. For accounting, it might be efficiencies and accurate reporting.

The leader of your function should be communicating what she or he wants the department to concentrate on and, if she or he is good, where the function fits into the broader organization's goals. Don't be afraid to research how other groups like yours are organized in different companies. This information can help you generate ideas that help you better serve your team and potentially take on work that aligns with your goals. (Don't forget your POP.)

3. **Know what your leader is up to in life and in business.** Remember, your bosses are your primary customers. If you're thinking of them that way, you have to be curious about what their pain points are, what they care about, what their priorities are. And here's why thinking of them as customers is so critical: we tend to judge our leaders, but we tend to embrace our customers.

What does this mean? Well, if you view people as your managers or leaders, you have all these ideas about what they are supposed to be doing. Are they measuring up as leaders? If they are, we put them on a pedestal. We idealize them and don't even consider ways they could do better. We're too busy letting them do all the heavy lifting when it comes to strategy and taking care of the department.

If, on the other hand, we see them as not measuring up as leaders, we will focus on their flaws and dismiss the idea that we should be helping them. Sure, your work ethic may demand that you show up and do a good job, but you won't necessarily be thinking strategically and trying to figure out how to get the most out of your partnership with them. All your energy will go toward tolerating them, at best.

By viewing our leaders as customers, we don't judge if they seem focused on looking good to their managers. Nor do we assume they are fine and don't need anything from us. Instead, we are looking for how we can be of service and trying to trade with them. Maybe you trade for more autonomy, different opportunities, support and guidance...whatever is important to you. (On some level, you are already doing this: we are all trading based on the paychecks we get for the work we do.) When we view our leaders as customers, we are paying attention to them as individuals, not just as owners of a title.

Whether we realize it or not, most of us have expectations about what a manager at "that level" should be doing. But what if you just looked at the person? What does John care about? What are Julie's concerns? Notice the difference. The first is focused on judging based on what we think a person in a certain position should be doing. The latter focuses on understanding the person, whether we agree with his or her choices or not. This perspective allows us to deal with the reality without feeling conflicted or tuning out.

4. **Determine what you can do that supports your own goals and aligns with your leaders' interests, departmental priorities, and organizational mission.** This is where you start to build the connection with your leaders. Ideally, you can brainstorm about this with your managers. They may have insight about ways to leverage your skills and passion that may not be obvious to you. But the reality is you may not have that kind of support or established relationship with them.

Either way, you need to show up with an idea of how you see yourself evolving, why you're a worthwhile investment, and how what you propose to do aligns with the goals of the people from whom you're asking for time, money, or resources.

Aligning Goals Is a Balancing Act

Get a Game Plan

Don't just walk into the room empty-handed. Your proposal doesn't have to be super-formal, but it should show that you've thought through what needs to happen to make it a reality.

Most of us just walk in and ask our managers for approval to take a class or take on new work. But we leave it up to them to figure out how to fund our request, how to make any necessary accommodations, and how to get their own managers to approve it. If you want your proposal green-lighted, you'd better make it as easy as possible for your leadership. The better you anticipate the obstacles and come up with solutions, the more likely your proposal will be put into action, and therefore the more influence you will have over how your time and talent are leveraged.

A few companies are starting to have their employees fill out individual development plans or IDPs. Companies that use them typically have their own way of naming, formatting, and handling their IDPs.

The good news is it doesn't matter whether your company has a formal IDP process or not. As long as you grasp how to think about the core ingredients of your development plan and how to discuss them, you can adapt your approach to the prevailing situation at your work.

You may be a top executive at a large company where they are investing in you and want to help you build your career growth. You may be a fry cook at a diner where no one is discussing your goals, but make no mistake: you're spending time there and you are still running your own business. No matter your circumstances, you need to get clear on how you're using your job and how you can build a strategic partnership with your managers.

Here are the core ingredients to consider when proposing development for yourself or pitching different work you'd like to take on. You can also view a sample at the end of this chapter.

1. **Determine the work you are proposing to do.** Development and growth is all about what you're *doing*. It's not a class. The class may help you, but the essence of what you'll gain comes from how you get to apply new skills and take on new responsibilities.

   My Example: During one of my stints at a large company, I wanted to train the leadership how to become coaches to their employees. I loved the topic. It connected to what I was looking to do long-term in my career. And the company had received quite a bit of feedback that employees didn't feel supported by their leadership. Even with all that, I still needed to put a proposal together. I was trying to get them to do things my way, let me lead it, and have them foot the bill for the time and costs involved.

2. **Identify your greatest strength.** You want to identify your greatest strength and show how it ties to what you are trying to get approved. What's that talent you are gifted with? What would you like to do more of because it's your passion? How could you use that to elevate what you do and what the group is capable of?

   My Example: For me, I was already pretty well experienced in coaching and program design. But building a program from scratch would challenge me to fine-tune those skills. I'd also need to get certified. This would give my experience the "stamp of approval," but it would also provide me another perspective on coaching.

3. **Identify your greatest gaps.** What do you need to get better at or learn to support what you're proposing? You may have gotten feedback from others that you need to improve in this area, or it may be a brand-new skill that you need to acquire. It's not about "fixing" what's wrong with you; it's about improving your capability and setting yourself up to execute on this new endeavor.

   My Example: Based on what I was proposing, I was pretty well cut out to do the work. However, I would be pitching that each department would foot the bill for the cost of training, including travel and any additional facilitators. Though the program would still be relatively inexpensive for them, it was a chance to start getting them to include employee development in their annual budget planning. But I had a problem: I could barely manage my own personal budget, much less maneuver the nuances of corporate finance. So for me, I would benefit greatly from development in this area, even though it wasn't my passion.

4. **Apply the 10-20-70 Rule.** This is a fairly well-established development principle. It breaks down like

this: The 10 percent stands for the level of impact traditional learning has on your skills. Think classroom learning, reading a book, getting a certification, etc. Trust me, I'm largely in the business of teaching classes, and it breaks my heart to see such a small percentage assigned to this type of development, but I know it to be true. No matter how good your memory, the brain can only do so much with just data and facts.

The 20 percent stands for what I like to call the "glue." This is you practicing and getting feedback on how you're doing. I'd also include watching people model something for you here. Repetition plays a big part in this. Without practice, it's easy to forget what you learned in class or for your brain to recall a warped version of it.

And the 70 percent refers to you incorporating the new skill or capability into your actual job. This is my favorite part. Because this is what you're pitching when you're asking for development. This is the thing that broadens what you can do, how others see you, and what shows up on your résumé. Getting the company to cover the cost of a class is all fine and dandy. But getting them to buy into you doing new and different work is what truly elevates you and adds to your cachet.

So when putting together your proposal, you should:

a. **Determine the 10 percent.** If you are looking to upgrade your skills, classes, certifications, online learning, books, etc. are a great place to start. But they are just the start. Remember, this type of learning affects your capabilities only by about 10 percent.

   My Example: I knew I needed a certification in executive coaching. And I also wanted to get some formal training in corporate financial planning and budgeting. So I researched a few options for both, to include costs and time investment.

b. **Determine the 20 percent.** Here's your chance to create a reason for you to get exposure to other leaders or people in the company you may not get to work with regularly. It can help you network. You can also create a reason to get more one-on-one time with your manager. This helps build relationships and also expand your awareness of the organization as a whole.

   My Example: I pitched that I be allowed to "shop" the coaching program to other leaders in our HR function, as well as meet with key executives across the company to get their buy-in for paying for the program. In the meantime, I asked to sit with my manager and get insight into how she managed the department's budget.

c. **Determine the 70 percent.** This is where you pitch the work you want to eventually take on. What could you be doing for the company with the right development? Now's not the time to be concerned with titles. Right now you want the chance to do new things, expand your skills, and stoke your reputation. If you are interested in getting a promotion, you'll want to create the demand for what you do first.

   My Example: I proposed to design the program and roll it out. This would significantly add to my workload, so I also shared how I planned to tackle the extra work, which involved redistributing and streamlining some of my current responsibilities. This didn't mean I just pawned off the crappy work to others on the team. I was thoughtful about how the work could be portioned out, considering the interests of team members and how their own workloads would be affected. The point is I did some of the heavy lifting for my manager instead of just plopping my proposal in her lap and expecting her to figure everything out. Of course, I was making recommendations; she would have the final say.

d. **Estimate the total investment.** You will want to do some research on what all this will cost. Include fees for classes, time away from your current role, any materials or new supplies, etc. Your manager may be able to find better pricing through the company's vendor relationships, but once again, you should do some of the heavy lifting.

   My Example: I researched the cost for the classes I was looking to take. Where possible, I tried to offer an ideal option and a budget-friendly option. I also estimated the time I'd be unavailable and how I'd cover my desk while in classes.

e. **Describe the impact on the business.** How will all this development benefit the company? How will you be saving or making the company money? How will you be improving efficiencies, customer relationships, employee retention, product integrity, brand reputation, etc.? This isn't about how *you* will be better. This is about how the company will be better off because of its investment in you.

   My Example: I highlighted how my plan would save the company money on external coaches, improve employee retention, develop leadership capacity, and polish the firm's overall brand as a "Best Place to Work." These were all things I knew were on the to-do lists of both my manager and her manager.

SAMPLE IDP

Priority	Development Area		Development Activities	Date & Desired Outcome
(Strength)	Strengthen leadership skills (managing a larger team and lateral leadership/ managing peer executive relationships across the enterprise associated with new role)	Education (10%)	Attend leadership courses. Estimated cost: $1,000. Resources needed: time away from office, support from leader to gain assignment on project	Mid-year — Enhance collaboration, strategy setting, and communication skills that will facilitate bridging silos across the leadership team
		Exchange/ Exposure (20%)	Discuss newly learned skills with manager and direct reports. Receive feedback from manager and direct reports on quality of skills	Throughout the year — Help drive efficiency of corporate processes that will result in an enterprise agreed-upon process for contracts.
		Experience (70%)	Integrate skill application into Performance Plan's Development Objectives. Participate in cross-segment project team.	ASAP Starting in Q2
(Challenge)	Increase ability to accomplish work through staff by leveraging their talents/experience and setting clear direction and strategy	Education (10%)	Attend communication and influencing classes. Resources needed: time away from office, support leader to apply new approach with team	Mid-Year — Build capability to adapt leadership approach to the various styles of the team members, identify unique talents, and communicate in a way that provides clarity and enhances team cohesiveness
		Exchange/ Exposure (20%)	Discuss newly learned skills with manager and direct reports. Receive feedback from manager and direct reports on quality of skills	Throughout the year — Demonstrated ability to strategically develop internal talent to meet expectations of the organization's goal
		Experience (70%)	Implement Performance Plan business objective around driving results through team, elevating the capacity and effectiveness of the team	ASAP Starting in Q1

Are You Ready to Pitch?

Next up is scheduling a conversation with your manager. Some managers regularly ask employees about their career goals. But in my experience, few leaders do this, and even fewer do it well. Often managers worry that talking about employees' career goals will be like opening Pandora's box — with employees reaching for the pitchforks and torches if they don't get a promotion. Nothing could be further from the truth. In fact, just knowing their manager is thinking about their career is sometimes enough to make employees want to stay and grow with a company.

But why wait on your managers anyway? Remember, they are your customers. Instead of viewing your pitch meeting as a career discussion, try treating it like a sales call. You're going in to discuss how you can be of service, and you've got some well-thought-out ideas to lay out.

If your managers are open to discussing your development, start the conversation there. They will probably appreciate how much thought you've put into it and that they didn't have to do all the work or promise you a raise.

If you get the sense that your managers aren't open to discussing your development, start with the problem you're looking to solve. Connect it to something you know is a priority for them. Get their buy-in on your proposed solution, then back into talking about your role in that solution.

Be ready to discuss:

✓ Your interests and long-term goals

✓ Your view of the big-picture needs of the organization

✓ How you see your function supporting the larger organization

✓ Which roles you believe position you to do your best work

✓ Ideas for how you can better support the organization

✓ Thoughts on how that can benefit other members of the team

But What About Your Promotion?

Right now, you might be thinking, "This is all well and good, but what about a promotion and a raise? I don't want to be doing more work for the same money." If this is you, I highly recommend you drop this old-school way of thinking about promotions. Few companies are promoting for things such as good performance and time in service anymore. Instead, they're demanding a valid business reason to justify the positions they have, and the people who fill them.

I'll go further: I highly recommend you *turn down* promotions that are presented as "rewards." If there is not a clear business reason for your new role or new title, and a clear business case for why you're the right person for the job, you are setting yourself up to be the first person on the chopping block during a layoff.. And with the clip of reorganizations on the rise, this scenario is more common than you might think. Also, the higher up you go, the more "attractive" it is to lay you off. If they can lay off one highly compensated executive but keep four frontline workers, trust me, the executive is boxing up his or her office.

I don't say any of this to discourage you from going after an executive positions if that's your path. I'm simply saying, stop swimming in the "employee" lane. Business owners don't need a title; they need business...repeat business...new business...ongoing business. Nothing is more important than creating demand for your services.

I've always prioritized doing interesting work over getting a bigger title. If I get to do the work, then my managers can experience what their world is like with me performing in the role, whether I have the title or not. And by driving my own development, I get to have a say in the work I do as opposed to relying on whether someone could guess I'd be good at something. Maybe it comes from being routinely underestimated, but I just don't buy that anyone else is going to understand what I can do until they see me in action.

Once I've created the demand for what I do, if the work would benefit from me sitting in a different position, then I pitch that. Notice I'm never asking for a promotion because "I deserve it" or "I'm qualified." I'm making my pitch based on the work. (I've sometimes created such a demand for the work I do that I need more hands on deck. That means asking for a team and uttering maybe the most dreaded phrase in corporate America: "increased head count." But as long as I can make the business case for more staff, and why my role should be elevated, then I'm on solid ground.) But it's never about getting some "gift" from the company. Promoting me should benefit the company, and if that's not the case, they absolutely shouldn't do it.

And if it turns out they don't have the ability or will to fund what I'm pitching at this time, then as a business owner I can make a decision. I can keep providing what I'm providing to them or I can let them know I'll be working with someone else but am open to coming back when the timing is right for them.

Remember, gone are the days when you have to be eternally committed to a company. We've finally returned to the glory days of entrepreneurial business. If you can't find or create the kind of opportunities you need at your current company, then either bide your time and continue to build demand or sell your services to a different company…but always let them know you're open to coming back when the time is right.

This isn't me saying, "The heck with them. I'm gonna take care of me." What I'm saying is timing is everything. There have been moments when I've needed to move to a different company to grow my "business" at the pace I wanted it to grow. But I never burned bridges, and when the timing was right, I often came back or partnered as a consultant. My point is: stop thinking you don't have options. You do.

Don't assume the manager should be doing all this for you. And above all, stay in the driver's seat. If you sit in the passenger seat of your career, then don't bitch about the way someone else is driving it.

Career Development Dialogue Guide

Below is a quick reference guide to having a development discussion with your manager.

PART 1: Share Development Interests and Needs	PART 2: Link Development with Business Needs	PART 3: Discuss Impact on Business
What is your long-term goal for your Career Web?	How do your career goals align with the goals of the organization?	How will investing in your development affect the way work is done?
What's your "Why" that drives and motivates you in your job?	How do your unique talents/skills support or elevate the function or department in which you work?	How will investing in your development increase efficiency or increase client satisfaction?
What key areas do you want to develop in? (strength and challenge)	What are the goals of our department?	What challenges do you foresee?
What resources/support are you asking for? (include cost)	How can the development you are looking to gain support the team?	What support do you need from leadership?

Development Capabilities Self-Assessment

Below is a brief assessment to help you determine the skills you need to better manage your own career.

Rate your capability and follow-through in the following areas as a 1 (unskilled at or never practice), 2 (somewhat skilled or practice at times, or 3 (highly skilled and practice consistently).

Managing Self

- Build and maintain a positive self-image, demonstrating a sense of confidence

- Interact positively and effectively with others

- Change and grow throughout life to proactively adapt to the environment

Learning and Work Exploration

- Participate in lifelong learning, supportive of career goals

- Locate and effectively use career information

- Understand the relationship between your work, the industry you're in, and the economy as a whole

Managing Career

- Secure and/or create work

- Make career-enhancing decisions

- Maintain balanced work and life roles

- Understand, engage in, and manage the career-building process

Identify the areas that have the lowest scores. These are the areas where you'll want to focus on skill-building. Use this book as well as your own network to develop yourself.

PART 4:
Grow and Feed
Your Business

CHAPTER 12:
Whatever You Do, Deliver It as White Glove Service

"Quality in service or product is not what you put into it. It is what the customer gets out of it."

—Peter Drucker

It's a great feeling when you can just relax and trust people will take care of their end of things. These people are almost always the ones who listen intently to your requests or concerns, the people who make the kind of eye contact that signals your needs are their priorities. It's easy to assume this type of experience happens only in traditional customer service industries such as restaurants or retail. The reality is everybody needs to figure out what their version of "white glove" service is. Then they have to make sure their customers feel that experience.

This goes for the service you provide to your manager, your employees, your colleagues, etc. If you're working, then you're exchanging services with another human in some way. The trick for you is to figure out what this level of service looks like for the business you're in.

The benefits for delivering first-class service go beyond repeat business; it builds credibility, and in today's world of flatter organizations and social media, credibility is powerful currency. In other words, people talk, and what they say gets amplified by how quickly and broadly the word gets around. If people trust you to take care of their needs, they are more likely to hear you, follow your lead, and allow you to do what you do best. They are more likely to spread the word that you are the right person to go to for help in your field of expertise.

Your version of white glove service may look different than mine, but there are some key things that universally convey to people that they can trust you to take care of their needs. Following are some common things people consider when deciding whether to trust you and take in your recommendations or recommend you to others:

1. **Sense of Urgency** — Do you convey that you will take this work seriously and make it a priority? Often your pace of speech, body language, and response time via email or phone will tell people you are on this for them. When you move or speak slowly, it can send the message that their needs will be taking a back seat to whatever inevitably pops up next. Sure, you may think you're being meticulous on their behalf, but they will see a lack of focus and urgency. If you're a slow speaker by nature, let people know ahead of time. But follow up quickly to demonstrate that doesn't impede your pace of progress.

2. **Assessing Needs vs. Wants** — Of course, some work does require time, deep attention to detail, and a slow and steady pace to complete. There's nothing wrong with that if it's done in service of the customer's needs. We often are so focused on delivering the end result that we forget to assess what the customer needs.

There's an art to balancing what you believe your customers need with what customers say they want from you. The challenge comes when what customers want is not in their best interest.

When this happens, you'll usually find customers are focusing more on *how* something gets done for them vs. *what* they are ultimately after. A great question to ask your customer here is: "In the end, what would tell you the time, money, and/or effort invested in this was worth it once this project/task is done?" This gets them thinking about the finish line and considering what they're left with after you provide your service instead of getting caught up in telling you how to do your job.

3. **Determining Expectations** — What are the nice-to-haves and need-to-haves for your customers? They may have a laundry list of how and what they want you to do for them. But you need to help them sort through that list and figure out their real priorities. You can help by asking questions such as, "What's the one thing you don't want to go without?" or "What's the main thing you don't want to see happen?"

   Even asking these questions can be a service. Often, people are looking for something but haven't quite figured out what it is yet. If you're able to help them get clarity, they'll trust you understand what they're trying to achieve.

4. **In-the-Meantime Communication** — This is one of the most powerful things you can do to create that best-in-class service experience — and the most overlooked. This came to life for me when I was working in call centers. I realized while you may be busy doing all you can to help customers, they often experience nothing but waiting. The longer the silence, the more they assume you are not doing anything for them. So

call centers train their staff to touch base with customers at frequent intervals.

What's funny to me is other functions don't employ this simple but effective approach. No matter what you do, whether you work in IT or janitorial services, whether you're an executive beholden to shareholders or an assistant managing an office, you can buy time — and patience — from your customer by simply touching base and providing periodic updates. Don't assume they don't want to hear from you until you deliver the final product.

5. **Connecting the Dots** — People absolutely love it when you are able to connect the dots of seemingly disconnected aspects of their problem. This can happen in a lot of ways, such as when you identify resources they hadn't thought of using or accessing, suggest leveraging previously created tools or processes to make things more efficient and cost-friendly, or simply point out how something they hadn't thought of could hinder or help them reach their goals.

6. **One-Stop Shop** — One of the more frustrating experiences for people reaching out for your help is hearing "That's not what I do" or "That's a different department." Of course there are times when they may be better off speaking to a different expert. But if you want to be a one-stop shop for them (and you do), then never, ever respond in the negative. That means you respond positively by setting them up with all the information they may need.

If you need to connect them with someone else, be sure to shepherd them over to that other person. You'll want to set the new person up for success by giving her or him all the details of your previous discussions with the customer. Remember, I'm using the word *customer* to represent anyone you may partner with on the job. This could be your manager, direct report, or a customer in the traditional sense. By transitioning things smoothly with the new person, you ensure customers don't have to repeat themselves or feel abandoned. Also, be sure to follow up to make sure they had their needs met.

7. **Making It Happen** — At the end of the day, the core of any service is getting stuff done, ideally right the first time. You can be as thoughtful as you want, but if nothing ever gets delivered, you're wasting everyone's time and money, including your own. This seems like an obvious point, but I've seen employees do almost everything but deliver because they take a detour or hit a roadblock.

    The obstacle can stem from our own mental blocks and show up as procrastination, fear of accountability, or resistance to making a decision. Often it's the fallout from the relationships we have damaged or not built in the first place. We hit roadblocks because we don't know how to get support from people we've had conflict with, so we let things get put on hold, thinking it's the other person's fault. No matter who's at fault, the customers don't get what they were promised. Or we may have overestimated our capabilities. Whatever the reason, once you realize you're not delivering as expected, it's critical to bite the bullet and alert customers.

8. **Elevating the Conversation** — Anytime you're speaking with someone you work with, you have an opportunity to elevate the conversation. It can be as simple as asking questions that drive more creative and optimistic thinking. Or you can shift the focus from what's wrong to what's possible. Helping people work through personal challenges or conflicts creates a more positive work environment and helps

build trust in your capabilities and intentions. A key aspect of service is how people feel about working with you. Do they feel judged or supported?

9. **Providing Options**—Too many times we focus on what we think is the "right" thing. We think we can push someone into making a decision if we have the right answer. The reality is people make decisions based on their comfort levels first. Sometimes they need more facts before deciding. But it's hard to know what you don't know. When someone can view two or three options, they get to react and figure out what matters and what they're willing to do without.

When you are helping people decide on the best approach to making a change, I recommend you provide an option A. This option is the ideal version. It covers all the needs and creates the best results. It also usually requires the largest amount of commitment and investment. But it does help them see the big picture first.

Then I present an option B. It's a scaled-back version of option A. I discuss what they lose with this option but highlight how it reduces risk, commitment, and/or investment.

Finally, I present an option C. This is the bare bones of what they can do and expect to see any results. We discuss what the best option is based on the level of resistance or buy-in they have to make a change happen. Often, discussing the options ends up creating an option Z, something that takes elements of all three approaches and comes together in a way customers feel comfortable committing to.

Through this process, you may have to do a little bit more work, but you will have demonstrated you are flexible and have helped customers come to a solution that works for them instead of forcing your viewpoint on them.

10. **Determining the Main Service** — Ideally, white glove service goes above and beyond what customers expect. If you can hit all the preceding points, it's fantastic. While that's not always possible, you always need to be clear on what the main service is customers expect from you.

     Imagine you take your car in for a routine oil change. When you arrive someone greets you and escorts you to the waiting area, while another attendant whisks your car away. In the waiting area, you're handed sparkling water, offered a chair massage, and given access to the snack bar of your dreams. Your car is done within the hour, sparkles like never before, and smells great. But on your drive home, the service light turns on, the engine starts to sputter, and you have to pull over.

     Yes, you received white glove service, but you only got the nice-to-haves. And as nice to have as that massage was, the need-to-haves were woefully deficient. Nothing can offset missing the mark on the need-to-haves. That's why it's so critical to get clear from the get-go what customers view as the primary service they are engaging you for.

No matter our title or level — everything we do, we do in service to someone else. Approaching your work from a service perspective sets you up to operate as a partner, be curious about the people you're working with, and focus on the bigger picture. Without a service perspective, we risk becoming robotic in what we do, working just to put a check mark on some proverbial list. Where's the fulfillment in that? Satisfaction comes from providing truly exceptional service, which helps connect what we love to do with those who can benefit most from our services.

CHAPTER 13:
Embrace the Creativity and Opportunity of Conflict

"Creativity comes from a conflict of ideas."

—Donatella Versace

What do you think of when you hear the word *conflict*? For most people, the word conjures feelings of discomfort, stress, frustration, or angst. But maybe you're not most people. Maybe you enjoy the competition that inevitably accompanies conflict. Or you recognize going through conflict often results in a certain amount of relief, creativity, and sometimes even deeper levels of trust.

The truth is our brains crave conflict. After all, conflict means we are encountering a different way of thinking. And nothing quite makes our brains light up like the Fourth of July than variety. Think about it. Some of your friends and family think differently than you do. You probably have debates about all kinds of things—politics, where to eat, the best movie, whose sports team is the best, etc. This is what makes life interesting. Variety truly is the spice of life.

Then why so much angst over conflict? What's driving us to recoil at the thought of conflict is not the difference of opinion but the struggle that accompanies it—the idea that the other person threatens us in any way is the real source of our stress and discomfort around conflict. While we are wired for variety, we are also wired for survival.

In the workplace, our survival senses are dialed up to high. And no wonder: our job not only represents our ability to provide food and shelter (think security), but our workplace is also the main venue where we connect to a "tribe." No matter how sturdy you are, the possibility of being kicked out of the tribe strikes a chord of pure fear in all of us. After all, if the tribe shuns us, we'll have to survive on our own. Probably not half as hard as it was back in caveman days, but still…

But we rarely get to choose who we work with. In fact, one of the key skills of succeeding in business is this ability to foster functioning, working relationships with just about anyone, regardless of how they may show up. What this means is not that we swallow our pride and simply tolerate others' poor behavior. The goal is to stay in strategic and helpful mode and not get triggered by our own fear. If that happens, our fear can pull us into a reactive and defensive place where our actions are driven by safety or looking good.

So how do we take the most strategic road when—let's be honest—so many of our bosses and colleagues seem to live to piss us off, behaving like they have no sense. I'll explain that in a moment, but here's why it's so important: when we are being defensive, we are less objective, and therefore are more likely to make bad decisions.

The most important step is to understand how we process conflict in the first place. Here's a model I use when coaching that I call the Conflict Navigation Map.

Conflict Navigation Map

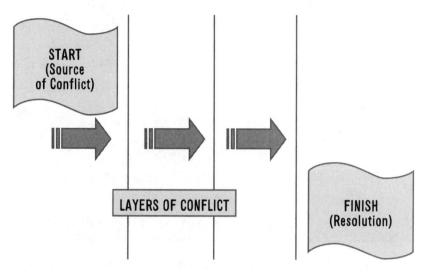

When someone brings a conflict for me to mediate, I look to see how people are navigating along this map and where they are currently operating from. I'll walk you through each component.

1. **Starting Line: Source of the Conflict** — This is typically how people describe the source of the conflict. They're not wrong. The conflict *is* about this. It usually boils down to two people operating from different values. This can show up in how someone approaches work, time, money, people management, etc. The list is endless. But the source of the conflict is not the real problem or they would have resolved it through some easy dialogue and negotiating.

   If someone is coming to a person like me for help, that means there's some level of "fight" in the conflict. There's a reason why the conflict isn't resolved through a simple conversation, and it usually boils down to a problem in the quality of the relationship between both people.

So it's critical for me to understand how they think about the source of the conflict. What I do is look at where their head is in regards to the layers of conflict.

Layers of Conflict

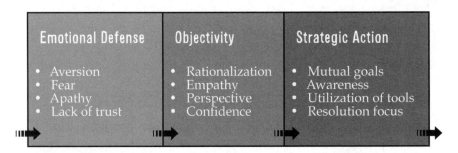

Emotional Defense	Objectivity	Strategic Action
• Aversion	• Rationalization	• Mutual goals
• Fear	• Empathy	• Awareness
• Apathy	• Perspective	• Utilization of tools
• Lack of trust	• Confidence	• Resolution focus

This reveals how they view the world and lets me see what matters to them.

2. **First Stop: Emotional Defense Layer** — The most important thing to uncover is the "why" of the conflict. Why is this a fight instead of a simple disagreement? And I'm not saying a fight always looks like a WWF match. Most of the conflicts that occur in the workplace are subtle and prosecuted using passive-aggressive behaviors. Even so, the people "fighting" and everyone around them can tell there's a level of unrest.

   The emotional defense layer is where the fight lives. Something occurs. We see a behavior of some sort — or don't see a behavior we expect from someone — and our brain sets about evaluating it to determine whether it's dangerous or safe. But here's the tricky part: Our brain is always telling stories. It's how it interprets the world around us. We use our memories to inform what kind of stories we tell about a situation.

   If we have developed a certain level of trust for the situation, we will craft positive stories. That trust can come from anywhere. It could emanate from our trust in the relationship with the other person developed over time or from our trust in our own ability to handle the situation or from the trust we have in the universe that things always work out for the best. In any case, we are practicing positive storytelling about the situation so our brains travel easily through the emotional defense layer and move on to the next step. Emotional defense tends to be a speed bump on the way to our resolution.

But if we harbor negative stories—or no stories—about a certain behavior or situation, our brains tend to veer toward the defense. This means we start weaving tales about how this person or people don't have our best interests in mind. Maybe we start collecting a list of things they have or have not done on our behalf. After all, our brain is built to prove the story we tell, whether it's positive or negative. The lower the trust level in the other person, situation, or even ourselves, the higher levels of fear we have.

Now here's the thing: our emotional defense layer is not necessarily a bad thing. It helps us. Imagine you're walking down a dark alley and someone starts walking behind you at a quick pace. Your brain will probably recall some scary stories before you've even seen whom this person is. In this case, we've been told negative stories by our family, teachers, and media, and our brain is simply retelling us those stories to keep us out of danger. We may clutch our belongings tighter, we may take off running, or we may turn around and confront the person. In this case, going into defense mode, whether we choose fight, flight, or freeze, is probably not the worst idea.

If we turn around and see someone that our stories and memories tell us should not be dangerous, we will immediately start to relax. Imagine you turn around and see a five-year-old girl. Most of us would relax. What if we see a cop? Our reaction will depend on what our experiences have been with police. If we see them as public servants who are here to protect us, we will feel safe and calm. But if we've experienced police as oppressors and violators of family, friends, or ourselves, our stories will tell us we have encountered someone dangerous. And we haven't exchanged one word with this person yet.

It's an interesting dilemma. We're told not to judge a book by its cover, but the reality is our brain is designed to judge and tell stories by how a person fits into our memory patterns. So how do we prevent ourselves from getting stuck in the emotional defense layer? Well, the first step is recognizing that, no matter what, the brain is going off past experiences and patterns at all times. The act of observing how your thoughts are creating stories and acknowledging they are simply stories helps stop us from being overly reactive.

Now when you're driving in traffic, walking alone down a dark alley, or surviving out in the wild, having a quick-to-react emotional defense layer probably works in our favor. However, in the workplace, we are rarely in physical danger, even though our emotions and ego often feel like they are one bad meeting away from being under attack.

The hard part is workplaces rely on staff being able to work together and build functioning and healthy relationships based on trust. Yet these same workplaces are steeped in fear-building cultures and practices. Not because leaders are bad people but because they are more adept at avoiding the things they are afraid of — such as failure, losing face, or going under — than knowing how to thrive through creativity, chaos, and diversity.

The best way to use our emotional defense layer is as a filter to assess our level of fear and the other person's level of defensiveness. When we feel safe and there are high levels of trust in the relationship, this is how we naturally operate.

However, when our ego is threatened within an interpersonal relationship, we are usually responding to feeling rejected or controlled. Think of these two fears as sitting in the back seat of your "brain car." Your behaviors, when not operating in the emotional defense layer, are being driven by hope and desire to reach certain goals.

But when in this layer, fears of being rejected and controlled hop to the front seat. They may even switch seats rapidly. One minute your behaviors are selected to help you avoid rejection, so you may withhold an opinion that might rock the boat, self-punish to avoid the ridicule of others, or obsessively hunt for ways to win someone over who seems uninterested or disapproving of you.

What	CONSCIOUS WHY	SUBCONSCIOUS WHY	CONTROL REACTION	REJECTION REACTION
Controlling Approaches				
Attack — overtly aggressive behaviors such as yelling, sarcasm, insulting, shoving, publicly ridiculing, finger-pointing, etc.	Put someone in their place for daring to go against you	Push away threat	Attack back, bigger and better	Avoid or cower
Sabotage — passive-aggressive behaviors such as agreeing to do one thing and then purposely doing something different, colluding with others to go against a person, spreading negative gossip, etc.	One-up someone who has offended you	Push away threat	Revenge	Sulk or complain to anyone but the offender

Fix—providing advice or doing things because you perceive the other to be broken or less than	Demonstrate superiority to the "less than" person and to others	Push away threat	Attack and put down	Self-punish or over-function to win favor
Rejecting Approaches				
Justify—evasive behaviors such as explaining and excusing vs. focusing on the other person's reaction or experience	Prove your "goodness" to the person expressing disappointment	Hide from threat	Become irritated and offended	Put own needs aside
Minimize—downplaying the importance of a complaint, trying to cheer someone up who is clearly upset with you before hearing them out	Avoid letting things get uncomfortable	Hide from threat	Try to bring person down to same level	Minimize own feelings as an overreaction
Self-punish—avoid receiving someone else's disappointment or ridicule by self-criticizing, self-deprecating, repetitive apologies, downplaying of own strengths, etc.	Prove your worthiness through martyrdom or sacrifice	Hide from threat	Withhold approval and add to criticisms	Put aside own needs so you will be liked

The next minute, you may get the sense that this person is causing you to live or work in a way you don't want to, and fear of being controlled jumps into the driver's seat and fear of being rejected moves into the passenger seat. Now you are finger-pointing, rebelling, or trash-talking the other person. This switch can happen in one conversation or over a period of time.

When we are coming from a fear of rejection, we tend to approach the conflict like a turtle. While the turtle may snap once or twice, its primary defense is hiding in its shell. For us, we may avoid tough conversations, keeping our thoughts and needs to ourselves, and just hoping the problem will solve itself. We figuratively shrink ourselves down to avoid being fully seen.

When we are coming from a fear of being controlled, we tend to react a bit more like a tiger. We lash out and view things in terms of territory. We may focus on how much people respect us. We become consumed by the fear that they don't respect our authority. We may finger-point, push others away, ridicule, or speak down to others. We puff ourselves up to appear bigger and mightier than what we are feeling inside.

Though we may seem stronger and more confident behaving like a tiger instead of a turtle, our behaviors are still emanating from a sense of fear and survival. So we are choosing reactive vs. proactive and strategic behaviors. Why does this matter? Because it almost always hurts our credibility with others.

Here are some clues to tell whether you are operating from a place of defensiveness:

- **Body Language**—We feel the "fight" in our bodies first, before our brains start to translate the story and explanation to us. You may feel it in your stomach. That icky, nauseous feeling when someone rejects you or says something that lands a bit too close to your own insecurities. You may feel it in your chest or shoulders. Someone does something that leaves you feeling attacked or insulted, and your fight mode gets triggered. Or maybe you feel it as a lump in your throat or flush to the face and head. You may freeze, not knowing what to say.

  Whatever your body clues, it's good to start observing and taking note. If you're tuned in to what your body is telling you, you can start to get a feel for when your brain is going into defense mode. This is a good place to be, because then you can question whether what your brain is telling you is helpful or if it's keeping you from building relationships that will help you.

- **Reaction Behaviors** — Once your body feels something, your brain goes straight into story mode. At lightning speed your body starts to exhibit behaviors. Common reactive behaviors include looking away and not being able to make eye contact. Our feet tell us a great deal too. If you find yourself walking away from people or taking the long way around the office just to avoid running into them, this is an obvious clue that your defensiveness has been triggered. Sometimes it's in our shoulders. We turn away and talk over our shoulder at people because we just can't bear to interact with them. All of the preceding is our animal instincts at work.

- **Apathy** — This is the toughest and most damaging aspect of staying in the emotional defense layer for too long. The longer we stay there and don't experience genuine resolution, our brains start to tell us there's no hope. So we start to disengage. We may even say things such as, "I don't even care anymore" or "Whatever; they don't even matter." But this isn't the sign of someone who doesn't care; it's the sign of someone who has stopped hoping for a better outcome.

A carefree person has lightness about them. They are not defensive or angry. They are calm instead of withdrawn. But people who are apathetic have chosen a certain level of numbness to ease the pain and frustration that comes from living in the story that they are being rejected or controlled by someone else.

For example, if my best friend and I are set to meet for dinner and a movie and she runs late, I will start crafting a story about it. My brain will ask for memories regarding similar situations. Maybe I'll recall how I was stood up for a date and had to dine alone. Maybe I will remember all the times she has been late and start to tell a story about how "people like her" don't care about others. By the time she shows up, I'll have had a few imagined fights with her. I may respond coldly to her no matter how friendly and apologetic she is. Of course, this will most likely trigger her defensiveness and fuel the cycle of distrust.

However, if my brain selects a story that describes good intent, the outcome will be different. Maybe my story about punctuality focuses on time as a continuum where things just happen when they need to. Maybe I recall a story about my self-worth that says how other people behave has little to do with how important and valuable I am. Or maybe I have a story about my friend that focuses on all her wonderful qualities and that punctuality just isn't one of them, that our friendship can withstand a few human flaws, and that if it matters to me I can talk to her about it and work it out.

This time when she shows up I'm just happy to see her. Her reaction will most likely be to enjoy me that much more and feel relaxed and safe to be herself.

We don't have control over how others perceive us or behave toward us. However, when we become aware of our own thinking and actively choose the stories that set us up for the results we want as opposed to the fears of what *might* be happening to us, we are more likely to attract the behaviors and results we want to see.

Exercise: Imagine someone from your current world or from the past with whom you've had a troubled relationship. Maybe you were afraid, irritated, or frustrated by her or him, or maybe something else made your relationship less than ideal. Write down three descriptions of what it was like to work with this person:

✓ _____

✓ _____

✓ _____

✓ _____

3. **Second Stop: Objectivity Layer** — How did you describe the person in the previous section? Did you write anything positive, or was it all negative? Was it kind of positive but not outright? The more negativity in the description, the thicker your emotional defense layer. The more neutral or positive it is, the more you are stepping into the objectivity layer. There's nothing wrong with being in the emotional defense layer. As mentioned earlier, this can help us identify and react to dangerous situations. However, *staying* in the emotional defense layer is a recipe for disaster.

Often the way out of the emotional defense layer happens when our minds cross over to the objectivity layer. Objectivity involves viewing things from a more balanced perspective. While operating from the emotional defense layer, we tend to tell stories with victims/heroes and villains. We usually cast ourselves as victims or heroes and other people as the villains. Then we tell stories like a prosecuting attorney. We do what we can to prove them guilty and us innocent.

In fact, we are so good at this our brain focuses solely on finding proof of their guilt, ignoring anything else, including the other people's experiences and perspectives.

Interestingly, it can feel almost painful to move from defensiveness to objectivity. In the emotional defense layer, we tell stories with the drama and emotion of a horror movie or emotional saga. However, in the objectivity layer, we start to tell the story like a well-wrought documentary. There are still interesting aspects, but both sides are represented, and there is a perspective that almost feels like an outside observer vs. the hero/villain dynamic. Being objective requires the following:

- **Rationalization** — We resist rationalizing people's behavior because we see this as synonymous with excusing their behavior. In reality, rationalizing is simply allowing our brains to explore their side of the issue. We don't just imagine they are focused on doing us wrong; we also start to examine how they might be seeing things. What might be triggering them? What about us is not easy to work with?

  The advantage of this type of examination is our brain is forced to tell a more well-rounded and unbiased story. This causes it to calm down. It moves from short-term, reactive thinking to long-term, proactive problem-solving. This is the kind of thinking that will support us focusing on what we want to achieve instead of getting obsessed with putting another person in our place.

- **Empathy** — Even though most people use them interchangeably, empathy and sympathy are not the same thing. The reality is sympathy tends to come to us easily and reactively, while empathy takes work, conscious effort, and thinking.

Sympathy comes from a shared experience (someone who has lost a parent can sympathize when a friend's mother dies) but empathy forces us to commiserate and "be there" regardless of having a shared experience or not (for example, someone who has never been fired empathizing with their friend who has just gotten the ax

Imagine I'm new to your team. I just started this week. I happen to sit near you, but we've spent little time getting to know one another so far. It's lunchtime and most everyone is gone. You're busy catching up on work, and all of a sudden you hear me slam my phone down and let out a loud sob and then shout, "No!" Next thing you know, I come over to you. I'm crying uncontrollably. I say I have to go home immediately.

What are you thinking about me right now? Do you think I'm a bit off? Are you uncomfortable with this much emotion in the workplace? Do you wish you had left the office for lunch? Or maybe you feel concern for me. Maybe you feel bad that I'm upset.

Now imagine that I blurt out, "I'm sorry, but I just found out my mother died." Now what are you thinking? Am I still a weirdo or basket case? Some of you may still be uncomfortable dealing with this level of emotion, but most people will no longer be judging me as crazy. Instead, you will show a level of concern and understanding. After all, my mother just died.

Now let's imagine I blurted something else entirely. Instead of saying my mother passed, I say, "I'm sorry. I have to go home. My boyfriend just broke up with me. We've been dating for a whole week. He was my soul mate." What are you thinking of me now? Are you uncomfortable? Do you think I'm an idiot? Do you think they hired the wrong person?

Here's one more. Instead of my mother passing or my week-old boyfriend dumping me, I say, "I'm sorry, I have to go home. I just found out my husband left me. We've been married fifteen years. I didn't see this coming. He's taken the kids." What are you thinking now? You may still be thinking this is too much drama for the workplace, but you're probably also calculating my fifteen-year investment in this guy and the fact that kids are involved, and will be more willing to cut me a little slack.

These examples show sympathy in action. My definition of sympathy is when we agree with the reactions and choices made based on the situation and context. We dole out sympathy after sitting as judge and jury to the person's right to be upset.

My interpretation of empathy is much harder. Empathy is identifying with people's emotional experience, regardless of whether we agree with their way of handling the particular situation. Think of the boyfriend scenario. Have you experienced a painful level of rejection and disappointment? Have you ever felt like the rug has been pulled out from underneath you? Have you ever felt betrayed? When using your empathy, you connect with the person based on this mutual understanding.

Why do we favor sympathy over empathy? Because, much like rationalization, we fear if we go there, we are somehow condoning the people's behaviors and choices.

- **Confidence** — This is where the third, and arguably the most critical, element of the objectivity layer comes in. Without confidence, we can't venture into rationalization and empathy. We will be swallowed alive by the needs and motives of the other person.

Confidence enables us to still respect our own needs, perspectives, and choices. This means I can identify with my coworker's anger and frustration. After all, I've felt anger and frustration. Maybe not in the same context or for the same reason, but I know the feelings and what they can do to you. And at the same time, I can still stand in my own truth of what I need from the scenario.

In these examples, I can empathize with the coworker who is sobbing and demanding to go home. I can rationalize she or he is operating from a severe reactionary place. But I may still hold to my truth that behaving this way is hurting his or her credibility as a brand-new coworker and makes me feel uncomfortable.

Objectivity helps us remain calm and allow other people in. We stop judging and move toward understanding. We recognize we don't have to agree simply because we are taking the time to connect with them and understand how they are feeling.

Let's put this to the test. Based on the same person that you imagined and described in the previous section, write three descriptions of what you think it felt like for that person to work with you:

✓ _____

✓ _____

✓ _____

✓ _____

Did you struggle more with this exercise than the other one? Was it tougher to imagine the other person's experience of you instead of the other way around? The easier it was for you, the more time your brain has spent operating in objectivity mode. The more difficulty you had with this, the more your brain has been focused on prosecuting vs. understanding the other person. Don't bother criticizing yourself over how you did. The point is simply to recognize whether or not you've taken the necessary steps to balance out your perspective.

4. **Third Stop: Strategic Action Layer** — The funny thing about this layer is it presents itself effortlessly when our emotional defense layer is thin. We easily see the other person's point of view while respecting our own. Our brains are open as opposed to defensive, naturally thinking of possibilities instead of defensive maneuvers. We are expanding vs. contracting.

This is an important point. While navigating conflict, we often make the mistake of jumping to the strategic action layer too early. When we pretend to be at the strategic action layer but we're still at the emotional defense layer, we tend to act in a passive-aggressive manner.

We don't acknowledge the fight between ourselves and the other person, yet the other person can always sense something is off. She or he feels the lack of trust and often assigns that feeling to mean you have bad intentions toward her or him. So any solution, no matter how creative and useful, is viewed as an attack. She or he senses you aren't prioritizing his or her needs and therefore don't trust anything you say.

This is when people describe others as inauthentic or fake. They usually deem the feeling they are getting from someone saying they are in the strategic action layer, but the behavior and tone is coming from the emotional defense layer. They'll end up thinking people have character flaws. However, it's just the product of people avoiding the tough work of moving themselves out of the defensive mode, through objectivity, and earning the right to engage in creative solution-building.

5. **Final Destination: Resolution** — This is the goal. If you enter into your conflicts with resolution as the goal, you will naturally pull yourself through each layer at the correct pace. The resolution feels right to both parties, and the outcome is deeper levels of trust, productivity, and collaboration.

   Too often we settle for the pat answer. We pretend everything is fine because all we want to do is move on. But that's like putting a Band-Aid on gangrene. Too gross for you? Well, think about how gross it is to work with someone you don't get along with and have to fake nice with every day.

Each time we skip self-reflection and elect to stay in prosecutor mode, telling our villain and victim stories, distrust and defensiveness grow like a festering wound. Contrary to the old saying, time does not heal all wounds. For relationships to work well, especially in the workplace, we have to roll up our sleeves and do the hard work.

If you're still with me — and not retching over my disgusting metaphors — then you'll be happy to hear there's a path toward healing...and it's paved with dialogue. More on that in the next chapter

CHAPTER 14:
Communicate with Actual Dialogue

*"A conversation is a true dialogue, not a monologue.
That's why there are so few good conversations: due
to scarcity, two intelligent talkers seldom meet."*

— Truman Capote

The toughest part of relationships is knowing how to have authentic, direct, and trust-building conversations. I think we have such a hard time with this because we've been taught people are not capable of receiving the truth. We assume if they were, they'd have no reaction other than agreement. So instead, we're taught to "sandwich" our communication, slipping the bad stuff between two slices of fluff. Hide the liver under the mashed potatoes. Of course we are the ones who are often not willing to deal with reality. Instead we want to *control* reality. We want it to look a certain way, and for that to happen we need people to behave a certain way.

So we don't engage in dialogue with people. Instead, we hold forums. Our own personal TED Talk with one person as our audience. All this in hopes that our words, if carefully chosen, will convince the other person how wrong she or he is and how much she or he needs to get on board with how we see the world. The problem is, the only thing those we're lecturing can hear is a droning stream of white noise.

They don't hear what we're saying, but they do receive a message. And that message is our lack of respect for their minds, needs, and capabilities. They feel the pressure we're applying as we try to control them. And they feel the imbalance of the conversation, with us being at the top and them being at the bottom. This is not a dialogue. This is, at best, a tennis match—a competitive conversation where there is a clear winner and a resentful loser.

Rewarding relationships are not built on this type of interaction. What this type of behavior does engender is the P-word—*politics*. And politics is at the center of most of the complaints I hear. People hate dealing with workplace politics. In truth, what they're saying is they hate having to navigate all the minefields we humans plant around the truth. We make it unsafe to say it like it is. We imply if we speak up to anyone with perceived power we will get smacked down, possibly kicked out.

On the one hand, this is a reality. As I mentioned, there are a lot of people swimming in the looking good lane, and hearing anything that's not complimentary feels like a direct hit to their safe little world. In general, though, most of us fail to recognize the importance of how we share the truth. We don't hold ourselves accountable for how we tell our story, our version of events. We are lazy. We want to just blurt out whatever comes to mind and call that being authentic. Because we're telling the truth here, what it should be called is thoughtless and reactive.

If this sounds tragic, it's not. All we need to truly communicate is to create a safe two-way exchange of stories. And the best way to start doing this is to recognize our point of view is merely one take on a situation. Of course, we have a right to honor our version, but we also have to respect other people's point of view. It's the respect for the other people's version of reality, and the ownership of our own, that creates the foundation for building something together. But this magic, and the trust, alignment, and progress that comes out of it, can't happen unless we shift our focus from controlling the other people to controlling our minds and behaviors.

So how do we do this? First we have to understand how our brain engages with dialogue.

1. **We observe the world.** The first thing we do is take in the world around us. We all use our own set of filters and frameworks to make sense of the world. Some of them were given to us. Some of them we pieced together on our own to make sense of things.

2. **We craft our story.** Based on what we see, we create a story of what happened, what it means to us, and what it says about the people around us. Many of us have a pattern of crafting horror stories instead of stories of success and happiness.

3. **We check for a pattern.** We look for a previous experience to compare with what's happening. If we've seen this before, we feel safer because we tell ourselves there is predictability in our circumstances. Even if that predictability is an undesirable outcome.

4. **We choose our behavior.** Behaviors tend to be chosen by our subconscious vs. our conscious brain. This means we pick whatever seems easiest and common instead of what might be the best strategy.

5. **We try to control the outcome to reinforce our story.** Our brain is obedient. If the story says the other person is out to get us, then our brain will do what it can to gather proof of that. If the story says the other person has good intentions, our brain will do what it can to gather proof of that.

The hard part is we draft our story so quickly and effortlessly that we tend to miss what part of the world is our story and what part happened. We experience our story as if it is fact. Then we make the mistake of telling our story as if it's everyone's story, accusing others of bad intentions if they don't confess to thinking the way we've decided they should.

Brain Storytelling Process

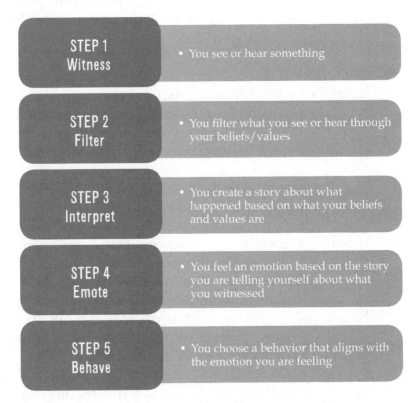

STEP 1 Witness	• You see or hear something
STEP 2 Filter	• You filter what you see or hear through your beliefs/values
STEP 3 Interpret	• You create a story about what happened based on what your beliefs and values are
STEP 4 Emote	• You feel an emotion based on the story you are telling yourself about what you witnessed
STEP 5 Behave	• You choose a behavior that aligns with the emotion you are feeling

The best way to approach this, then, is to own the fact that no matter what occurs in reality, our brain will automatically try to make sense of it. Let me make something clear: There's nothing wrong with that. It's how we connect to what's happening around us. We have a right to our story. We have a right to the emotional reactions our story evokes in us. However, we don't have the right to say our story is an absolute truth. We don't have the right to say our story should be everyone's story. Well, technically, we can say whatever we like. But it won't help us have a quality dialogue.

So accountability has to start with owning our human process of existing in and making sense of the world.

1. **Own your stories.** The beginning of accountability is practicing the ability to identify the difference between what we see and the story we create about it. To say someone came in at two p.m. is a description of the fact. To say someone strolled in as if she or he could care less that the meeting started at 1:30 and she or he had made everyone else late...that's our story. Neither is necessarily wrong or more important. But they are two different things. One is fact; the other is our own personal fiction. And we need to own our fiction. Maybe the other person did stroll in without caring about others, but we will never know. When you are venturing to describe someone's thoughts, feelings, or intentions, you are always drafting a fictional proposal of the truth. We need to own that.

2. **Respect other people's story.** Know as we are crafting our story, other people are busy doing the same. We must be accountable for honoring the existence of their story and their right to experience life through that story.

3. **Identify the facts.** Look for the neutral, indisputable meeting points. What occurred that was visible and tangible to both of you? Not what *should* be obvious but what is actual fact. "Twenty reports were issued on Friday." "The project was late by fifteen days." "The cost has increased by 40 percent." These are all tangible facts. This is green language, as discussed earlier. It's the tangible details that both sides can agree is reality. Using green language is a great way

to get yourself grounded in what occurred. It can also be a meeting place for both of you to see there are commonalities in each of your stories.

4. **Determine your judgment/interpretation of the facts**. This is where your story comes in. Your story focuses on yellow language. It's fictional but valuable. It supplies insight into what the facts mean to you. This can include your views on results, approaches, proposals, ways of doing work, and so on. This is where the "It's business, not personal" gets truly honored. You clarify that your interpretation is about your values and not about trying to judge or attack the other person. Yellow language also tends to create a more calm, cool, and collected emotional state for dialogue.

5. **Beware of judging/interpreting people and their motives or capabilities.** This, my friends, is dangerous territory. This is where we stop gauging facts and recognizing our opinions, and start handing down verdicts of innocent or guilty. This is red language. We start to voice conclusions about how smart people are, how willing they are to do something, how motivated they are. Whether, in fact, they hold any value. This is where we tend to label others. Our focus moves from the "what" and the "how" of the discussion to the "who" and their value as an individual. This is where our story can breed a lack of partnership and absolutely makes it personal as opposed to being about business.

Even if our conclusions are complimentary, they are still problematic because they set us up not to hear what the other person is saying. Instead, our brain picks out the little tidbits that prove the other person matches our judgment of her or him. We stop listening and start hunting for our version of the truth.

Sharing Your Storytelling Process

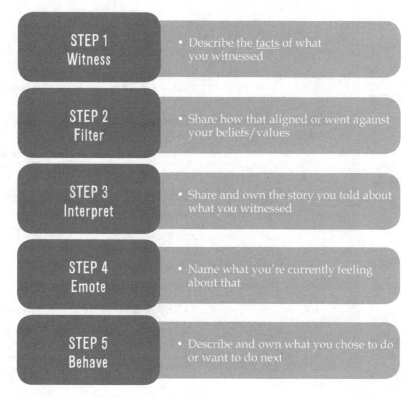

STEP 1 Witness	• Describe the facts of what you witnessed
STEP 2 Filter	• Share how that aligned or went against your beliefs/values
STEP 3 Interpret	• Share and own the story you told about what you witnessed
STEP 4 Emote	• Name what you're currently feeling about that
STEP 5 Behave	• Describe and own what you chose to do or want to do next

Communicate to Build Partnerships

So how do we dialogue so that we stay accountable to owning our story and behavioral choices? I'm not gonna lie to you—it's no easy task keeping our mind from running willy-nilly with whatever stories pop up, especially when they trigger strong emotions. Reining in our mind is a skill you'll be refining for the rest of your life, but with a little discipline, you can reap the rewards.

INVITE
- Goal: Create Clarity
- What is the purpose for having the dialogue?
- Provide context, behavior, and impact; include one brief example.

CONNECT
- Goal: Build Connection
- Why would they care?
- Describe how having the conversation would align with what's important to them as an individual.

LISTEN
- Goal: Foster Understanding
- How do they see things?
- Ask at least three open-ended questions to gain a better understanding of their side of things.

CREATE
- Goal: Collaborate for Solutions
- How would they ideally want to approach solving this?
- Ask for their ideas before adding your own.

COMMIT
- Goal: Plan for Action and Accountability
- What next steps need to be taken by each person in the near future?
- Ensure each person has something to do that can help move the new approach forward.

Try these tips to have genuine two-way dialogue:

1. **Invite people to the party you plan on throwing**. This is about clarity. When you ask someone to speak with you, be sure you are clear as to your intentions for the dialogue. Most of us don't even take the time to think about what we're looking to accomplish when engaging in a conversation with someone.

   Caution: When we're struggling to initiate a conversation and have already crafted several negative stories about the topic, we tend to invite people to a conversation under the guise that we are going to discuss something simple such as a project, deadline, or report. The reality is we are planning to lecture them about how they should do something or think more like us.

So when people agree to attend our "party," they are understandably disappointed. They may also be shocked and feel underdressed for the party they are attending. This sets up resentment and defensiveness. So the chances they are listening to you and your carefully crafted lecture are slim. Instead, they are most likely crafting their own comeback or exit strategy.

When you invite someone to a conversation, come clean about the real topic at hand. If it's something simple, you'll probably feel pretty comfortable plainly stating what you want to discuss. But if you've been angrily plotting the conversation, you'll most likely feel a bit uncomfortable articulating what you want to talk about.

But authenticity and clarity are the two ingredients that need to be present for you to have a snowball's chance at experiencing real dialogue with another person, especially if the relationship is strained in any way.

To make sure the "invite" doesn't get muddied, you want the invitation to be brief and to the point.

Example: "I wanted to discuss how we work together. I've felt tension between us for some time now."

Notice the topic was clearly and simply introduced and the story involved is being owned. "I've felt tension" vs. "There has been tension." The first is someone sharing his or her story and taking accountability for it. The latter is stating a fictional story as fact, and you can be sure the other person will receive it as an accusation.

When inviting someone to a dialogue, keep it brief, one to two sentences max. Anything else sets us up to start lecturing or attempting to control the other person's reaction. This is about an invitation, not forced conversation.

But let's take a moment and recognize why we don't tend to issue genuine invitations. In a word: rejection. What if the other person says no? What if we show our hand by letting her or him know we are struggling with the relationship and she or he pulls a poker face and refuses to play? Well, no one ever said it was easy. If it were, I wouldn't have to write a chapter about it. Being authentic and accountable, swimming in the strategic and helpful lane, is definitely a vulnerable place, and the possibility of experiencing rejection is the price we pay for the chance at real dialogue.

2. **Earn your right to invite someone to the party**. If you're going to invite people to a party, you damn well better have considered why the hell they'd want to even show up. What benefit is there for them in attending your little get-together? You may not have thought that far. You may have been so focused on your story that you didn't even consider what other people would have to hear in order to want to come to the party.

The more engrossed we are in our need to speak with them, the more likely we will create a list of why they *should* want to fix whatever we perceive as broken. They *should* care about the work. They *should* want to do a better job. They *should* want to do things my way. *Should should should should*. Be careful. Don't throw a party and then *should* all over everybody.

Instead, take the time to look at the other people. What do they care about? What motivates them? What scares them? Not what someone in their position *should* care about. But what, as unique individuals and human beings, do they genuinely care about?

This is how you connect with what they care about and signal they have equal weight in the dialogue. This isn't an employee speaking with a manager, an executive sparring with another executive, a plumber talking to a disgruntled customer. This is people speaking with one another and making a genuine connection.

Any good host or hostess would know and understand something about their guests. They would take those needs into consideration when throwing the party. This means connecting the reason for the dialogue to what we've learned matters to the other people. Most of us think, "Well, they're my manager, they *should* want to discuss my career with me." Instead, focus on them as people. Try something like: "I wanted to discuss how we work together. I've felt a great deal of tension between us for some time. I know you've mentioned how critical making deadlines are to you, and I want to make sure how we work together supports this goal rather than making it difficult."

Notice that connecting to what they care about is referencing something they have said or exhibited through their decisions. If you are going to say "you know" what the other people care about, be sure you are basing that on their words or actions, not on what you assume they *should* care about.

Sometimes we have no idea what matters to the other people. Either the relationship is too new or we have to admit to ourselves we haven't bothered to consider the other people. So we have to state that. Take accountability for not knowing.

"I wanted to discuss how we work together. I've felt a great deal of tension between us for some time. I'm hoping you and I being able to deliver on deadlines together is as important to you as it is to me. But I must admit I've been so absorbed in the issue of the deadlines I haven't seen things from your perspective."

This isn't about blaming them, and it sure isn't about blaming yourself. But taking accountability for what you know and don't know is critical to set the stage for a genuine dialogue.

3. **Listen so that the other person feels understood.** You will fail at this at first. Trust me. We all do. Our impulse is to dive headfirst into *our* experience of things. I get it. We want things off our chest. We want to feel better. We want to be understood, validated, heard. We also think way too highly of our capacity to speak and be understood. We think if we say things in just the right way, other people will magically convert to our way of thinking.

Well, guess what? So do the other people. When we prioritize listening, we not only help build trust, we also allow ourselves to hear both sides of the story before diving in.

There's a reason they say listening is an art— because it's damn hard to do well. We tend to listen selfishly—either because we are interested in collecting information we think we'll need, because we are entertained by what's being said, or because we are playing the agree/disagree game. Guess what these reasons all have in common? They're all about us.

To listen for the other people as opposed to for us is to focus on making sure *they* are heard. To do that, we need to see the situation from their point of view. What does it feel like on their side of things? What might they be looking for from us? All of the preceding is about listening with empathy. Remember, empathy is about identifying with how other people feel about the current state of things, not about agreeing with all their decisions and behaviors.

But it's not enough for you to listen so that you genuinely hear other people. The other people have to be able to *experience* that feeling of being heard and understood. This isn't about just nodding your head and paraphrasing what they say. A parrot can do that. It's about curiosity. It's about compassion. It's about attention.

So set aside your agenda. This simple but powerful act will help you see their humanity and be in the moment with them. Now, just because you are taking this moment to genuinely connect with and understand them does not mean you are giving up your right or opportunity to discuss your version of things. But for now, it's about them and your understanding of them.

Below is a visual for the three types of listening.

Type #1 Information

- Focus: Listening to obtain information in order to learn how to perform a task
- Use When: Trust is established and purpose of working together has been clarified

Type #2 Legitimacy

- Focus: Listening to determine what you agree or disagree with
- Use When: Trust is established and all parties are ready to collaborate on coming up with the best solution

Type #3 Understanding

- Focus: Listening to ensure the other person feels heard and understood
- Use When: Trust either needs to be built or repaired

4. **Remember the rule of thumb, "three strikes until you're out."** This means you need to go at least three levels deeper in your understanding of them before you dive into your side of things.

    The best way to convey understanding is through genuinely curious questioning. Genuinely curious questions aren't about leading other people to a preconceived conclusion you want them to have. Those are leading questions, and they tend to be close-ended and focused on our version of events. They look like these: "So why don't you care about our customers?" "Why do you struggle with getting your work done?" "Why do you make things so difficult?"

    This is also not yet the time to start problem-solving. Jumping to a solution before building trust based on mutual understanding is no better than putting a Band-Aid on a wound full of gangrene.

    So instead, ask questions that invite other people to share their story. You can inquire about how they've experienced things in the past or how they are currently experiencing things. What are their biggest pain points? What is working for them? How are they experiencing you? Remember, you don't have to agree with any of it. But you do have to get as close to reality as possible. Your job is not to try to shape their story but to hear it as they are telling it to themselves in their own minds.

    Prepare yourself to receive what they have to say. If they criticize you, don't go on the defensive. Instead, get curious. Where are those perceptions coming from? If they attack your character, don't get hurt or offended. Instead, get curious. Why are they experiencing you that way?

    The questions you ask should be open-ended: "What has this been like for you?" "How are things on your end?" "What's your view on how we work together?"

The idea is to make it safe for them to be honest and forthright about how things feel on their end. Make sure that is your genuine goal. If it isn't, trust me, no matter what kind of poker player you fancy yourself, your nonverbal ticks and verbal slips will advertise whether you genuinely care about them or if you're just collecting tidbits to use against them later.

Whatever they share, use your questions to connect to what they're saying and demonstrate a genuine desire to learn more. If your questions help them self-reflect and increase their own understanding of themselves, all the better.

Once they've shared, then you need to muster the confidence to be as candid and vulnerable as you just asked them to be. Don't go on the attack or use any of what they just shared with you against them. Trust is the only thing that will keep the dialogue balanced.

There are three types of questions I recommend using to help build trust and understanding quickly. Ask about their experience of things. There is no right or wrong answer to this. Their experience is their experience. Learn about the pain points they are experiencing. Demonstrating comprehension and empathy to their responses shows a genuine interest and care for their side of things. And finally, help them clarify their viewpoint by having them paint the picture of what their ideal version of things is. This leaves things focused on the possibilities and moving forward.

Experience	• How has your experience been? • What's your take on the situation? • How did you see things?
Pain Points	• What challenges are you currently dealing with? • What has been the biggest roadblock to your success? • What has been most difficult when working with _____?
Viewpoint	• What would tell you that the work we do was worth the time and investment ninety days from now? • What would feel the most helpful to you while we work on this together? • What would have been the ideal way this could have happened?

5. **Create a new future.** The best outcome of any dialogue is a meeting of the minds to collaborate and create a new, mutually satisfying outcome. Once you've arrived at a genuine understanding of one another, the next step is to look forward...together. To work, this step has to be a joint effort.

Ideally, what the other person has shared, coupled with your curiosity, has expanded your perspective, if even just a little bit. If you sense that's the case for the other person too, then it's time to use that expansion together.

This is the good part, where you start looking for solutions. Here again, questioning and listening are your tools for making this successful. But this time around, the questions should focus on driving creative thought about the future. With your better understanding of one another, the problem-solving isn't about "fixing" the other person and how she or he thinks but about the two of you thinking about new possibilities.

Questions should be focused on what you both want vs. what you both want to avoid. Ask things such as, "What would be an ideal solution?" "What would tell us that things were better this time next year?" "What would we do if we didn't have limits such as budget or time?"

Then the two of you could throw out options. Remember, this isn't about immediately coming to a conclusion. First, just see where your brains go after hearing ideas.

6. **Take action.** Once you both have had the opportunity to try out this new reality, it's time to move the ball forward. That can only be done through action. Your next move doesn't have to be dramatic or revolutionary, but each of you does need to take something on. Both of you need to demonstrate mutual accountability toward building a better future. This can be as simple as scheduling a follow-up meeting, while the other person does some research on a topic.

Ideally, both of you are doing something to support your new, expanded reality within forty-eight hours of the dialogue. Too often, after an exhausting dialogue, we're so glad the emotional roller coaster has come to a stop that we call it a day. The reality is without this follow-up activity, we risk going right back to our previous patterns that produced such crappy results. We'll feel betrayed that the other person hasn't changed, even though we most likely haven't changed either.

Dialogue that creates genuine communication is the glue that keeps your business together. How people feel working with you makes or breaks how much influence and continued viability you have in your chosen field. This isn't about playing office politics; this is about knowing how to connect with the humans you wish to do business with. And if you think that's soft or fluff, then you don't get what makes a businessperson successful. It's not power. It's not money. It's not control. Those are just tools. It's the ability to influence your own environment without having any of those as guarantees.

CHAPTER 15:
Inspire Commitment from Others

"Individual commitment to a group effort — that is what makes a team work, a company work, a society work, a civilization work."

— Vince Lombardi

You've heard me say it before: influence is key. Too often we wait for a title or position to supposedly endow us with some great power over others. But it never fails: the further up people go in an organization, the more they realize they now just have more people to get on board with rather than tell exactly what to do.

But our ego — oh, our ego — wants to believe we are in control. We strive to convert people to our way of seeing things. Maybe it's natural to think if only we had enough letters in front of our title, then we could *make* them see it our way. The problem is life doesn't work that way. I've never met a person who said things got easier with each move up the ladder.

Instead, what I hear is, "Wow, there's so much politics the further up you go." The truth is it's not about politics. It's about humans. And no matter where you sit, you have the opportunity to influence outcomes around you. What's most important to understand is influencing is a skill, a muscle you can build. But that muscle doesn't magically appear just because you managed to get into a certain role at a company. There are countless VPs complaining about SVPs who don't listen to them, countless CEOs lying awake at night because their board or Wall Street seems to be turning against them. The title is not enough. The ability to influence is what matters. And you can start developing your influencing skills right now. In fact, the earlier you start conditioning that muscle the better.

The good news is you're already doing it. You started influencing your environment the day you were born. You used your cries to get attention, food, and playtime. You moved on to "reading" your parents and playing on their sympathies, ego, and mood swings. Then you learned how to play by the obvious rules in school and the unspoken rules of the playground, and so on.

So what happens once we get to the workplace? Why aren't we better at influencing on the job? It comes down to a simple misconception concerning power. We think the person with all the resources has all the influence, so if we don't have any resources — that is, any overt power or control — then there's nothing we can do. It's a cop-out. We *choose* that as our reality because we've committed to playing in the looking good lane and minimizing our risk. If we can blame others for our misery, then we never look bad. Victims are rarely the villains.

It's risky to be influential. If you are influential, it's inevitable that someone will feel uncomfortable about what you're making happen. You have to put your views out there. People get to see how you view the world. People can critique what you do or don't do. But if you fly below the radar, you can just sit back in the passenger seat, bitching about how others are flying the plane. It's a weak play, but if that's all the bravery you can muster, then so be it. But don't pretend it's because you don't have any influence over your reality.

You Have to Give a Shit About Something

To be influential, you have to start with being clear about your cause. What are you trying to make happen? What do you believe the outcome is? Why does it matter?

Don't try to influence others just to move up a rung on the ladder. Eventually, people will figure it out and you'll leave them feeling gross about being involved with you. They won't be able to put a finger on it, but they'll sense they're being manipulated and they'll do whatever they can to get away from you.

You have to give a shit about something. You have to genuinely care about something enough to fight for it. That something needs to be bigger than yourself and your meager survival on the planet. If you're trying to make something happen because you think you know the answer, that's not enough either. Doing the smart thing is never enough to inspire anyone. That's why people who face death while surviving a heart attack don't magically change their lives. Unless they have something greater than themselves to change for, they'll continue on as they always have.

If you are going to influence others, make sure it's for something worthwhile. That's the only way you'll have the passion and resilience to fight the good fight. Your cause has to be about more than being right or doing a good job. If you're a plumber, it can be that you believe everyone deserves clean running water. If you're a photographer, it can be you believe everyone deserves the opportunity for peace and understanding that seeing the world through the eyes of others can afford. If you're a teacher, your cause can be you believe each child is a miracle waiting to unfold. If you're a screenwriter, it can be you believe film is how people can better connect to their emotions and the world. Whatever you've chosen to do for a living, attempt to influence others in a way that helps you deliver on your POP.

If you don't, no matter how much money and "success" you collect along the way, you will be living a life disconnected from an inspiring purpose. And you will have difficulty inspiring commitment from others.

To be influential, you have to understand what true influence is. Most of us think we've been influential if we get the room to agree with us. But genuine influence is about spurring others into action in alignment with what we want to see happen. It's about inspiring commitment from others.

What is commitment? Commitment is all in. What does that look like on the job? Well, when people are committed, they are on board not for you but for the cause. They are thinking about the cause and not just your conversations. They are putting energy and action toward making things happen beyond what they've been asked to do.

What's hard about this process is for it to work, you must relinquish control. When you influence others to this level of commitment, you have to leave room for others to influence the outcome of the cause, and even to influence you.

Commitment Levers to Pull

Here are some of the pathways toward gaining commitment from others:

- **Agreement** — There's something attractive about getting others to agree with us. It strokes our ego. It makes us feel right and smart. The trouble is agreement is just that and nothing more. I can agree nobody should go hungry, but that doesn't mean I'll take action to help solve the problem. Ever wonder why it seems easy to get agreement during a conversation but you never see anything change or happen afterward? That's because agreement just means they're not *against* what you're suggesting.

  What's important is agreement is still useful. Give someone who agrees the easiest job possible — give them the task of sharing their agreement with others. You can do this by simply bringing them along to meetings or discussions to help show there are others who think like you. Or they can serve as ambassadors of your message as you roll out the proposal.

- **Compliance** — This is what we think we get when we have power: the right to make people comply. But compliance is just a small version of what commitment can get you. I comply with the speed limit, as long as the threat of a ticket is imminent. But if I'm not *committed* to road safety, for myself or others, then the minute the road is clear of speed traps, it's lead foot all the way.

  But compliance can be a great way to throw folks into the pool. If what you have will genuinely help other people, then sometimes it's useful to just force them into the experience. A lot of the people who show up at my workshops were basically "thrown into the pool" by their managers. The key is to make sure that once they're in the pool they have a meaningful experience that connects with them on a deep level. If you do this, you can sometimes convert a "resistor" into a fully committed participant.

- **Disagreement** — This is my favorite area to work in when building commitment. Not because I like to tussle with people but because people who disagree with you tend to be expending energy around the cause. That energy is simply working against you rather than for you, but it's out there. Energy from someone is your best friend. If you can avoid getting overwhelmed by the idea that people might be rejecting your idea and, in part, rejecting you, then you can find a future that redirects their energy toward the cause. Most likely they disagree with the "how" and "what" of your cause vs. the "why" of your cause, if you're genuinely coming from a strategic and helpful mind-set.

- **Sabotage** — This is the most damaging to your cause. This is people who have energy to expend toward the cause but don't feel their disagreement or input will be heard. So instead they deliver that energy via passive-aggressive attacks. These can be everything from not sharing helpful information to talking trash about you behind your back to creating minefields that will impede your progress. Minefields can include not prepping you for problems they know are coming up, planting seeds of doubt in other people's minds, or simply not doing their job well and causing extra problems where there were none before.

This isn't about some evil guy twiddling his mustache as he plots your demise; this is about someone who doesn't trust you and your intentions. Maybe he has his own issues, but maybe you've inadvertently shut him down or perhaps come across as playing for yourself instead of the greater good. The best thing you can do when you discover sabotage is to focus on getting the person to openly disagree. That's right. Don't try to get him to agree. Make space for him to share his story and to be genuinely heard.

Package Your Pitch

The next part of the equation is knowing how to package what you're pitching. Make no mistake about it—you are pitching your idea or recommendation. It's a mistake to think you don't have to get the other person to buy in to what you're saying. And it's pure arrogance to think you are right and everyone should just see that. Nobody is inspired to commit to someone who is bullying them with facts and data or scaring the crap out of them with how the world is going to fall apart simply because they didn't heed your words.

So instead, figure out the pitch that best highlights the benefits of what you are proposing, making sure it clearly shows how it connects to what others care about. This doesn't mean sugarcoating anything or withholding difficult-to-hear information. This means clarifying why your proposal is important by telling a story of optimism vs. fear. You want people moving to a strategic and helpful position alongside you, not to a safety or looking good position.

Boil down the key points into the three core areas that will need to be agreed upon. The world is chock-full of details, chaos, and complexity. Boiling things down to their essence, while a lot of work, helps people pull back and look at the bigger picture, to focus on what matters, and to get their minds wrapped around what you're trying to do.

Remember, you are pitching they run a marathon with you. You can't be frustrated they are hesitant to start the race at the start when you're standing at the finish line. You have to go back and meet them where they are. You have to have the patience to watch their mind make the connections on the journey you've already taken.

When setting out to influence people, take a phased approach. This works whether you are influencing an individual or a group or shifting an entire culture. The first phase is simply getting your message out there. See this as planting the seed. Pick the best seed you can and plant as many as you can — with more than one person and on more than one occasion.

One of the biggest roadblocks I see people throw up for themselves is holding the misconception that if they pitch their idea perfectly it will instantly gain commitment. Instead, recognize the brain will need time to convert your idea into one of its own.

The next phase is helping people make the idea their own. This is part of why I love disagreement. We take the seed and start to pick it apart, rebuilding it with little pieces of everyone's ideas, creating something that wasn't possible without the various viewpoints of other people. But now they've been able to mark it up and shape it. This is what makes the idea start to feel like their own.

This is also where many of us struggle. What was once our precious little idea whose DNA was 100 percent our own starts to mutate as it takes on the input of other people's minds. How to handle that? Simply determine the top two or three aspects of your idea that you will champion and select a few nice-to-haves that you can give up, if needed, throughout the creative process.

The final stage is moving things into action. What's great about this is action doesn't have to be dramatic. Sometimes your best bet is to pick a small but enjoyable aspect of the change and get people to give it a shot, trusting the more they engage and experience things the more they will want to participate in the shift.

In my workshops, if I sense I've got someone who hasn't bought in to what we're teaching, I do an exercise that's low-risk and almost guarantees they will be able to participate successfully. It's about building trust and getting them to engage in a way that shows the change isn't all bad. This could be something as simple as debating ideas.

If you feel like there's been way too much talk and not enough action, then see if you can arrange some level of mandatory compliance. If people *have* to engage in the process, then that's half the battle. But remember if you're throwing them in the pool, you better make it enjoyable and safe to swim there. Be sure to provide the right amount of communication and/or training around the change. Depending on the change you're proposing, you might even consider a competition or some type of reward for participating.

In the end, there is no magic trick for getting people to commit to your vision or proposal. Your best bet is to avoid or remove the roadblocks that set people up to resist. Thinking that your way is the right way and that's that will do nothing but garner you a reputation for being a nag. Assuming that your title is enough to mandate your proposal into existence might get you a certain level of compliance but will eventually lead to behind-the-scenes sabotage.

If there's nothing else you get from this chapter, I hope you fully commit to the belief that influencing requires you to respect the people you are trying to influence. Your goal should be to bring them along for the ride rather than seeing them as obstacles or less than because they don't think like you.

From Sabotage to Commitment Model

COMMITMENT

Taking action and putting discretionary effort towards furthering goals and success regardless of reward, recognition or penalty.

AGREEMENT

Aligned in thinking but no real action or investment being made. Potential to convert to a vocal champion.

SABOTAGE

Actively tearing down or creating disruption, usually behind the scenes; difficult to work with since hard to identify or even know it is occurring.

DISAGREEMENT

Overtly sharing opposing views. Opportunity to convert energy and passion toward the work.

COMPLIANCE

Taking action only as required to adhere to policies or avoid penalties. Can be an opportunity to engage if able to create a positive or useful experience during compliance.

PART 5:
For the Veterans

CHAPTER 16:
My Veteran
Transition Story

"Unthinking respect for authority is the greatest enemy of truth."

— Albert Einstein

ecause of my experience as a veteran, I wanted to make sure I included a section that focuses on the unique aspects we face as we transition out of service from the military. Though everything in this book is applicable to veterans, the following chapters address veterans in particular to help with what I've experienced, through my own transition and coaching other vets, to be a different experience than the strictly civilian workplace experience.

What follows is my own personal story and experience of serving in the military and eventually transferring out. I want to emphasize my experience is just that, mine. All people have their own experiences. Some have had nothing but a genuinely wonderful time serving their country. Others, not so much. To be honest, I've had a little of both.

Not having experience on the battlefield, I don't know what it's like to lose close friends, take a life, or fear for my own. I served during peacetime, before 9/11, and held a desk job for the majority of my service. I share my story, as honestly as possible, only to provide insight into how I thought about things and how that thinking helped or hindered me in job-hunting and career choices.

If you prefer to jump ahead to the more practical advice that follows, feel free to skip this chapter.

Why I Joined

I grew up with a father who was retired from the US Army in a mostly low-income town surrounded by military bases. In my hometown, the military was viewed as the primary way for young people to escape their situation or pay for school. My brother had joined the Air Force right after high school, was stationed in Vegas, and from all appearances was living an easy, college-dorm kind of lifestyle. I was steeped in the military my whole life. Add the fact that my last name is MacArthur, and it seemed an almost inevitable step in my life to sign up with the armed forces.

The only thing is I didn't want to join the military. I saw the military from a slightly different angle than my peers did. I remembered my father, who suffered from Parkinson's, spending a large part of my childhood in military hospitals. He devoted more than twenty years of his life to the military, serving in the Korean War and driving tanks, which possibly contributed to his Parkinson's. But when he showed up at the VA hospital, he was a retired vet, which meant he had to get in line behind active-duty service members. At least that's how the hospital in our area ran its affairs.

This meant my dad would sit shaking violently in the waiting room while an active-duty service member with the sniffles went ahead of him. As a child, this outraged me. I was angry at the military for treating my father as if he didn't matter as much as another human being simply because he was retired. Today, I get that someone was probably trying to stick to a process at the expense of adapting to real-life situations, but this was my first taste of how the military got stuff done, and I was not impressed.

I also grew up in the Reagan era. To some, the 1980s were the essence of the high life. Everywhere you looked, Americans were living the dream with their MTV, neon clothes, workout videos, and teen angst movies. But that wasn't my life. My family was struggling, not strutting, through the 1980s. There are a lot of reasons for that, so I'm not blaming anyone. All I know is what I saw on TV wasn't what I saw in my world. And when the Iran-Contra hearings hit the airwaves, I became that much more suspicious of the powers held by our government.

I also did my growing up in the post–Vietnam War era. This meant service members weren't hailed as heroes the way they were before Vietnam and, to some extent, after 9/11. The country had gotten comfortable with viewing soldiers as if they were drinking troublemakers and not much more.

You'd often hear people say things such as, "We should make criminals serve in the military." Even as a disillusioned and skeptical teenager, I understood there was something wrong with that sentiment. The idea that serving your country had gone from being an honor and source of pride to something that should be served up as punishment for lawbreakers was, as far as I was concerned, a serious problem.

Just watch the beginning scenes of *Rambo*. Sylvester Stallone strolls into a small town, his military-style jacket announcing he's a vet but doing nothing wrong. He's immediately picked up by the sheriff and told they don't want "drifters" like him, looking like he does, in their town. Then a whole movie unfolds where this unassuming veteran with PTSD is hunted by law enforcement for no other reason than being an out-of-work vet. I think the country has forgotten just how much the military had fallen from grace in the public's eyes for the majority of the post-Vietnam era.

So I was conflicted. On one hand, I resented how broken the system seemed to be and how that affected my father. On the other hand, I got that when you're a country that's basically the richest house on the street, you need a good security system. I understood that having a strong military was vital.

And despite my disappointment in how things were being run in our country, I still believed in doing my patriotic duty. Hearing my mother's stories of living in post–World War II East Germany imbued me with a major appreciation for the liberties and freedoms that came from living in a democratic country. I believed you didn't get to enjoy those freedoms without contributing to them in some major way.

I didn't sign up right away. The day after graduating high school, I moved out and began working three jobs while I completed two years of junior college. As cliché as it sounds, the trigger that threw me into making this decision was a major relationship breakup. "Major" because I was nineteen, and all breakups are major at that age. I found myself needing to do something that would propel me forward and out of that town and all that hadn't worked for me up to that point.

But I didn't just wake up one morning and go to a recruiter's office. I spoke with women and men who were already serving to try to get a sense of whether this was the right move for me. Some stories were worthy of a recruiter's pamphlet, but others spoke to being miserable and disappointed with how the military was run. In the end, it came down to what usually drives my major life decisions—my gut. Something was compelling me to join, even though I had spent most of my life harboring conflicting views of the military.

Something that would be critical to me later was the fact that, prior to enlisting, I already had more than six years of work experience. This meant I knew what it took to get a job. I knew how to secure my own employment. This is a skill many young men and women don't acquire before joining the military, and I think this lack of job-getting skills can prove to be a major handicap for them when trying to make it on their own after their military contract is over.

I also had raised myself for the majority of my life, so I always had a clear connection to my own voice and sense of purpose. I'd already made several decisions for myself and had taken risks where I had no backup plan or resource to bail me out. This all played into why I didn't always mesh with the military culture, but also why I was able to secure work for myself after my contract was up.

I knew I wanted to be badass, so I signed up for the Marines. I remember walking into the office with an intense sense of taking on the world. I was a woman on a mission. I asked if they would guarantee me a job assignment, so I could ensure my time in the military would leverage my brain and I wouldn't get stuck in some repetitive job that wouldn't be useful in the civilian world. They laughed at me and said, "When you join, you work for the Marines. You'll find out your job while in boot camp. No guarantees. You go where we need you to go."

Tough talk worked well with me. I was nineteen and out to prove I was just as tough as any guy. So I said fine. I then asked if I needed to shave my head. I figured if the dudes had to, I did too. They laughed at me. No, I could keep my lovely locks. I asked about going in as an officer. But that would mean a two-year delay while I finished up a bachelor's degree, and I was desperate to do something right then and there. After all, I was already nineteen. So much time had already passed me by, right? So I agreed to sign up for the enlisted path.

My actual enlistment was delayed, because it was February 1994 and I was going to be graduating with my AA degree in December. During that time, I had to come in for monthly visits to make sure I hadn't gotten fat. Yup, talk about an ego check.

The recruiters I was working with tended to show up late for my weigh-ins. One morning in October, I was waiting outside the locked office. It was windy and cold. An Air Force recruiter showed up. He asked whom I was waiting for. I explained I was in delayed enlistment with the Marines. I had no interest in the Air Force, because they were considered the least hardcore. (This tendency to initially write things off and then later pursue them shows up a lot in my life. #stubborn.)

The Air Force recruiter said I could wait in his office because it was cold and he had coffee and donuts. I love donuts. So I went inside. I may not have drunk the Kool-Aid, but I ate the donuts.

He asked what my military test score was. It was in the high nineties. He lit up and asked what job I'd be doing in the Marines. I said I didn't know yet. Then he explained he could get me into the Air Force as a top-secret linguist if I passed their language test. Guaranteed. He talked about me being able to be an undercover agent and work for the NSA. Since I hadn't completed bootcamp with the Marines, I could easily switch over to the Air Force if I wanted.

Now don't get me wrong: I was fully aware that recruiters tended to up-sell to get you signed up. But I liked the idea that I'd be "guaranteed" to do something worthwhile and meaningful, that my brain as well as my body would be actively engaged in protecting our country. And who wouldn't want to be an undercover agent?

I went home to think about it. I remember talking to my brother. He asked me why I wanted to go into the Marines. I said I wanted to be disciplined and hardcore. He said, "Well, then run up a hill because you want to, not because someone is yelling at you. Sign with the Air Force. Take the guaranteed job." Even with this advice, I still struggled with my decision. I'm sure anyone in the Marines would have said, "Go with the Marines." I'm not here to make a case for which is the better branch. I think each serves its purpose, and therefore each has its own culture. In the end, I went with the guaranteed job.

I took the language test down in San Diego and scored very high. Turns out I remember patterns pretty well, and I've always been a good test taker. (I credit growing up in a highly dysfunctional home, where it pays to stay alert and see the answers early and often. Plus it made me good at making lemonade out of lemons.) So come January 1995, I was on a bus to the airport and off to Air Force boot camp at Lackland Air Force Base.

Why I Ultimately Didn't Fit

My initial game plan was to stay in for twenty years. When I do something, I tend to do it all the way. I figured that would set me up with retirement benefits that could come in handy, and I was ready to make a difference for my country. I remember sharing this with a sergeant my first month in and getting that look that says, "Let's see how you feel a year from now." He was right.

I breezed through boot camp. I had been training at home for the demands of *marine* boot camp. And let's face it: Air Force boot camp was about as physically challenging as freshman PE. But what I did find challenging was being stuck in a room with a bunch of fresh-from-home girls who were crying about missing their mommies and daddies. From what I hear, the men are no different. Makes sense. The military tends to target kids just as they're leaving high school and their parents' homes, the idea being they're moldable and open to obeying commands. They are hoping to find people who aren't used to thinking for themselves. After all, you don't want someone questioning orders on the battlefield.

But I'd lived on my own for more than two years by the time I joined. Not to mention I'd been working since I was thirteen. So I had no problem thinking for myself and came fully loaded with viewpoints and opinions. Which is why my friends were shocked to hear I'd even considered joining the military in the first place. But I did.

While boot camp was pretty uneventful, I did find it interesting how removed from the world you feel. It's as if time stops. You go from living in the world to living in the barracks, as if nothing else exists. And at the end of the six weeks, which was one of the shorter boot camps at the time, I did notice I had lost a bit of my identity. I couldn't seem to remember how to apply makeup. Picking out clothes felt odd. After all, I'd been in uniform this whole time. I'd stopped identifying as Heather and now only answered to Airman or MacArthur.

After boot camp, they send you straight to tech school. For me, that was the Presidio of Monterey in Northern California to the Defense Language Institute. I had ten months of learning Russian ahead of me. I had hoped to get Chinese or Arabic, because I scored high enough on my language exam to get either. To me, those seemed like the most practical for a job after the military. I was always thinking about how things would affect my ability to get a job even back then.

But alas, I didn't get to choose. They had let too many Russian linguists exit early after the Berlin wall crumbled — and supposedly the Soviet threat along with it — in 1992. It turned out they needed a few after all, and my timing couldn't have been better for them and worse for me. So I was assigned the one language I felt would be the least helpful for getting a job after I got out. But I had twenty years. I figured I'd be doing all kinds of different things during that time and things would work themselves out.

I remember flying into Monterey and seeing all the trees. My eyes almost hurt taking in that much greenery. I'd grown up in the desert and hadn't traveled much. I was excited. I'd struck out on my own adventure and I was poised to see the world. I remember the shoreline of Monterey like it was yesterday. All the stuff of my childhood — the desperation of that small town I grew up in and the lack of opportunity — was behind me. I was finally free to follow my calling, to be something great.

Within the first few months, 80 percent of those who started language school "rocked out." Rocking out meant they couldn't hack it and got reassigned to a different job. From my original class of thirty, only two of us graduated. The other guy already knew Russian. And then there was me, with my freaky ability to remember patterns, which happens to be useful in learning a language. Not that I was some hot-shot at it, but I was good enough.

One of the first experiences that chipped away at my respect for those in charge happened the second month of language school. I was summoned into the office, where the sergeant in charge had about a dozen airmen, all rocking out, lined up. I walked in and saw all these faces of airmen who were already defeated because they couldn't figure out why they weren't succeeding, and here he was humiliating them. He asked, "Airman MacArthur, why don't you help these losers and explain why they are failing and you are passing your exams?"

I guess he assumed I'd get off on him treating me as if I were special or something. But I hated him instantly. I loathed anyone who relished making others feel small. Not only that, but shaming people doesn't help them learn faster. I just thought he was a pompous asshole.

So I answered honestly. I said, "Well, sir, with all due respect, the reason I'm passing and they're failing is because I do the opposite of what you're telling them to do. Instead of spending eight hours in class and then spending my evenings ironing uniforms and shining boots, then studying till midnight, I go to the beach. I pay to have my uniform pressed and boots shined. Then right before class, when my brain is fresh, I study for one hour." This didn't please him one bit, so I was promptly excused from that little meeting.

Needless to say, the phrase "with all due respect," became a common caveat preceding things I tended to say to those in higher-ranking positions. And the reality is you don't get fired in the military. Sure, you could lose favor and maybe get in trouble if you didn't know how to word things, but my mother was the queen of rapid-fire attack fighting, so I was pretty quick on my toes.

That attitude never got broken out of me, no matter who or what I came across during my four years in the military, which included encounters with generals and, at one point, President Clinton (not that I ever had to "with all due respect" POTUS). I'd see everyone else scrambling in fear when someone "important" was coming, and I kept thinking,

"Why are they more important than any of us? If they're not nervous to meet me, why would I be nervous to meet them?"

Why I Decided to Get Out

So how did I go from wanting to spend twenty years in service to my country to counting the days till my four-year enlistment was over? Well, it wasn't one thing. It was several things. Some big, some small.

One of the events that had a big influence over my experience happened during my sixth months at tech school. I was raped by an officer. I regretfully assure you my experience is not unique. But it was my experience.

What was five times worse was the climate I was in during that time. Sexual harassment and date rape were just starting to be discussed across the military and political system. We were caught in the tailwinds of the Anita Hill vs. Clarence Thomas hearings. The military was still reeling from the Tailhook scandal and was about to head into the Aberdeen scandal. Unfortunately, the undercurrent made it abundantly clear that if you reported any kind of sexual abuse, rape or otherwise, you'd get tagged as trouble and sent to another base with a mark on your record.

I had a decision to make. Some may think I took the coward's route. I sometimes do. But in the end, I took what I consider the survival route. If I reported it, I had no proof. It would be my word against his, and I doubted any of his buddies were going to take my side. Also, if I reported it, I'd most likely lose my security clearance and my job as a linguist. I'd just started a new life, and it was about to be taken away from me.

I went on and graduated from my training and was eventually assigned to work in the NSA as a Russian linguist. I had a top-secret security clearance and I felt like I was making something of myself. I tucked away what had happened and moved on. Little did I know how this would affect me for years to come, including being diagnosed with PTSD once I finally got into therapy.

But from that point on, my experience in the military was pretty uneventful. But it was an interesting time to be in the armed forces. Most civilians weren't happy about the military, and when I went somewhere in uniform, I was usually greeted with odd looks or an aloofness. If I were in civilian clothes, people treated me much more warmly. When I told people I was in the military, their response was almost always, "You don't look like a lesbian." Women in the military were still a relative rarity. So the public's perception of us was pretty skewed as well.

Once I arrived at my station in Maryland, working for the NSA, I had a great sergeant who saw something in me and made sure I was able to balance my work and complete my college degree. He recognized that as fast a learner as I was, I was also a talker. I'd bring in *Cosmopolitan* magazines and have the men and women on my shift take personality quizzes and discuss their motivations. Clearly, I was destined for what I do now. But I was distracting people from their actual jobs. So he'd send me on projects that had me working with people all over the place. He also put me up for competitions that involved being interviewed on current events by high-ranking officers.

I loved those and tended to win. Not because I was any better than those I was competing against—I usually wasn't. Because I didn't care about getting an award, I came to it much more relaxed and confident. I had nothing to lose. As far as I was concerned, the military had already let me down in a big way. The leadership was just as flawed as other humans. So I went in and used these opportunities to share my opinion. I think that made me stand out as confident and sure, which isn't what they were used to. Most of the competition came off as nervous soldiers hoping to make a good impression and win points. I couldn't have cared less. I just wanted to have my brain engaged.

My master sergeant saw that, and he engaged it. Sadly, he ended up retiring a year before my enlistment was up. The new guy in charge was not at all interested in whether I was going to complete my college degree, and he stopped allowing me to work my schedule around school or work on projects that took me far and wide. I ended up getting an assignment that made it difficult to attend school. Luckily, I was a month out from graduating and was able to pull off a few miracles with help from my professors.

The truth is while my job was top secret, it was boring and pointless. I was wasting government dollars, and I knew it. I was living near DC and could read all these amazing job opportunities that were previously unknown to me in the paper, but I couldn't just quit the military and get a new job. They own you for the duration of your enlistment. Most civilians don't get that.

During my last year they offered me a reenlistment bonus of $12,000 and a guaranteed tour in Germany. Now, to someone who makes less than $20,000 a year (which I did at the time), $12,000 is a nice chunk of change…and I'd always dreamt of going to Europe. The thing is I hated my job as a linguist. And in the military, it's not like I could just get a new one. I was not in control of my job or how they leveraged me.

A close friend of mine had joined a few months after I did. She was from my hometown and now, coincidentally, was stationed with me at NSA. She took me aside and asked why I was considering reenlisting. The story I was telling had to do with the money and location. She said if I wanted to go to Germany, I could get out and take myself there. I didn't need the military for that. I had to admit she had a point.

What I didn't want to admit was I was telling just half the story. The other half was I had no idea what I'd do when I got out. I'd heard all these stories about people becoming homeless or not being able to make it as a civilian and then having to reenlist. I didn't have family I could go back to. I didn't have parents who had gone to school, ran a business, or even been employed full-time. Oh…and I was broke.

I had spent most of my money to pay for college since I was saving my GI Bill for a master's degree. Let's face it: the enlisted ranks don't get paid that much. And Maryland is an expensive place to live. So I got two additional jobs. I used my security clearance and took one job providing security to construction crews. I'd sit there in a top-secret government building reading *Cosmo* while making sure the workers didn't steal any secrets or try to access parts of the building that were off-limits. My other job was installing office cubicles in buildings that required a security clearance. Both were primarily male-dominated fields, and I had to spend every shift convincing the newly assigned crew that I wasn't a liability and would work just as hard as any guy. It was exhausting but paid more than any other part-time gigs I could find.

What was more exhausting was how little time I had for sleep. I worked a night shift at the NSA for nine hours. Then four hours at security. Then another four in office installation. That left me four to five hours for sleep, if that much. I remember coming home at one point and trying to take my pants off but being so exhausted I just broke down crying and passed out on my bed with them barely unbuttoned. But I had six months before my enlistment was up, and I needed a nest egg because I had no idea what I was going to do.

The sergeant in charge of my squad was trying to convince me I should reenlist. First he reminded me of the bonus and travel that was on the table. Which I admit was tempting, considering my situation, but I knew my friend was right: I had to believe I could get those things on my own terms if I wanted them.

When that didn't work, he asked me about my patriotic duty. Was I ready to just abandon my country? That's when I knew I needed to get out. Because they had me for four years, and not once did they use me in a way that was truly serving my country. So I said, "I want to make sure I can serve my country. And the only way I can guarantee that is if I'm in charge of how I'm leveraged and where I work."

How I Transitioned

With no idea what I was going to do, I turned down reenlistment and kept at my three-job hustle to scrounge up some savings. Once I officially declined reenlistment, I was immediately signed up with the office of transitions. Their job was to square away my paperwork, help me write a résumé, and assist in finding a civilian job for me.

It was the winter of 1998. As popular as the Internet had become by then, it was still relatively new, and job-search sites were pretty useless. So I was going to have to rely on the office of transitions. Only they weren't as helpful as I thought they'd be. I quickly realized the office was staffed mainly by people who hadn't transitioned all that well themselves. There wasn't a soul who had any job-hunting mojo or who had successfully navigated the private sector in any meaningful way. Sure, they were all friendly, but they were processing hundreds of us.

They sat me in front of an antiquated computer and ran through some basics on how to write a résumé. But the samples they shared were primarily geared toward government positions. Which meant they still had a lot of military jargon in them. They were full of acronyms I knew weren't going to mean a damn thing to a corporate recruiter.

So I bought a book and started to put a résumé together. I also looked at what government jobs might be out there that would leverage my experience as a linguist, so I didn't have to start at the bottom.

In the meantime, I applied for everything under the sun, including a job I wanted—FBI agent. I know: still with the undercover agent stuff. Clearly, I had watched *Silence of the Lambs* one too many times and was determined to be Clarice Starling. I'd gotten my psych degree with a minor in criminal justice and read every book there was on serial killers. I was destined to be a criminal profiler, and with my security clearance, linguist experience, and stint at the NSA, I figured I'd be a shoo-in.

I took and passed the initial tests. I thought for sure things were golden. What with the Russian Mafia running large in New York and spreading to California, they'd pick me up in a heartbeat. But the truth was, they weren't looking for linguists. Which is hard to imagine in this post-9/11 world, but back then, it was true.

You have to remember that during the Clinton era we were coming off a few decades of peace. Sure, we had Desert Storm a few years before he stepped into office, but most of America didn't even notice that was going on. So white-collar crime, not terrorism, was the FBI's biggest concern. They'd keep my application on file for one year. I was to call in every month to find out if they needed a linguist. After a year, my application would be thrown out. Then I'd have just one more opportunity to apply again.

In the meantime, I had two choices: apply for the civilian version of my job at the NSA, which I hated but for which I'd get paid four times as much as I did as a member of the military, or move back to California and take a chance at getting a job doing something I might like. But who knew what that was? I decided to head back west.

My friend who had served with me at the NSA had already moved back near our hometown in California with her boyfriend. She let me rent a room from her while I looked for work. I was certain I was going to land a job in no time. I had a college degree in psychology and a security clearance, and I worked for the NSA as a Russian linguist, for crying out loud. Did I mention my top-secret security clearance? Oh, okay.

It turned out nobody cared. At least not in California. Maybe all that would have landed me a government job in DC, but in Cali, I was more of a novelty than anything else. I had gotten out the week after New Year's in 1999. I had enough savings to pay for two months of rent at my friend's place, and that was it. So I needed to land something quickly.

That first week back, another childhood friend of mine, who was living nearby with her parents while she went to

USC, invited me over for dinner to catch up. They had all been good to me when I was a kid and struggling with my home situation. Her dad was a retired Army officer himself. We got to talking, and he shared he was an executive at a Sears collections call center nearby.

I remember thinking, "Seriously? You used to lead missions and now you run a collections call center?" That wasn't going to be me, that's for sure. So when he offered to submit my résumé for a lower-level manager job at the call center, I didn't exactly jump for joy. But out of politeness, I agreed. While I loved this family for all they'd done for me, I was meant for greatness. I'd had a badass job for the NSA. I couldn't end up in some call center, could I?

In the subsequent weeks, I would drive down to San Diego and work my way up the coast, applying for jobs and going on a few interviews, discovering I didn't know how to connect what I did in the military to what I *could do* on the outside. All the jobs in California that required a security clearance were in the technology field. I'd get the interview because of my clearance, and then they'd apologetically tell me I wasn't qualified.

Suddenly, that call center job was looking pretty attractive. What was initially me "being polite" turned into, "So any word on the call center job? Huh? Huh?" At the same time, I started to apply for anything I could find—a gas station attendant, fast food shift lead, the highway patrol. I needed a job.

My friend's father got my résumé to the right people at Sears, but I still had to go on three different rounds of interviews, and with each passing week, my bank account was dwindling. They were more thorough than the people who did my military background check, and even slower.

During this process I received a call from the civilian sector of the NSA back in Maryland. They were calling to offer me the civilian version of my old job. The pay: $85,000 a year.

Now, to someone who had no job and only about $20 left in her bank account, and who had never made more than

$18,000 a year, that was one hell of an offer. So what was the downside? I had been miserable as a linguist. I hated living in Maryland. I suffered from seasonal depression and couldn't stand the cold. But the money looked good. Real good. Not to mention I was still at my friend's place, and I could tell she wanted to get on with her life with her man sans roommate Heather.

I remember being alone in my friend's guest room and staring at the phone. I could pick this up and say yes and I'd be set, my problems solved. Or I could gamble on myself. Somewhere inside me a voice said, "You can make the money you want doing something you love. You just have to find it. Don't give up." So I called them back and told them I was declining the job offer. Trust me, I pissed myself a little over that decision, then cried myself to sleep out of sheer panic.

Then I put all my focus on landing that call center job. I needed a paycheck. This wouldn't be a job I'd get locked into for life, but it could get me out of my friend's house and pay the bills. Luckily, I had some interview skills from my days in retail and fast food that I could dust off. I also had management experience from before and during the military. It's that management experience that landed me the job. I had never worked in a call center, and my only experience with collections was on the wrong end of things. But I knew how to lead and build teams.

Even though I was desperate for work, I knew I needed to make a certain amount of money to get a place of my own and do more than just get by. So I negotiated. I threw out a number I'd picked up from the job postings for managers in similar companies. I went from potentially making $18,000 a year to $36,000. It wasn't the $85,000 I had turned down, but I had doubled my previous salary.

Their first response to my counteroffer was no other new manager was making that high of a salary, to which I replied: "You're not getting a new manager. I'm coming in with more than eight years of management experience." Yes, that management experience started when I was fourteen working fast food, but I saw no reason why it wouldn't count. And as it turned out, neither did they. Maybe it was the fact that I had just turned down a job that was willing to pay me $85,000 that gave me some negotiating confidence. Who knows? But it worked. I started in the call center the second week in February 1999.

Even with my new negotiating moxie, my ego had been properly checked. I saw now that the family friend who had gotten me in the door was doing something just as important as he did while in the military. He was leading teams and helping people. That hadn't changed. He was providing a nice home and life for his family. And he'd saved my ass... once again. I will be eternally grateful for his generosity and belief in me.

I realized this job would be a solid paycheck until I was able to get accepted into the FBI. But just six months later, in August, my one year in the application-hold period was up. I had my last call with my FBI contact. They let me know, unfortunately, the FBI just didn't need linguists at the time. If I wanted to go to law school or get an accounting degree, that's who they were hiring. I was devastated.

I had taken a chance and joined the military. Fought tooth and nail, worked tirelessly to complete my bachelor's degree, and didn't report or attempt to prosecute my rapist all just to secure a better job and future for myself. But here I was, living no more than an hour outside the hometown I had been so desperately trying to get away from...and I worked in a collections call center. I could have done that without a degree or the military experience.

After several nights of crying away my misery and bruised ego, I decided I'd get a law degree. So I bought a bunch of books on being a lawyer and signed up to take the LSAT. I did okay considering I hadn't studied for it. I started to look into how I could put myself through law school. But I just wasn't fired up about it. I remember complaining to a friend about not knowing what I wanted to do now that the

FBI was off the table and not being that motivated to go to law school.

She said she didn't think careers happened that way. That most people just kind of fall into their careers without realizing it while they're busy working and trying out jobs. Once again I thought, "Not me. I was meant for greatness."

That same month the call center posted a job for a training manager. The job had a legit Monday–Friday schedule. Up to that point, I'd never had a position with weekends off. So I went for it. I'd done a strong job as a manager and was able to secure the new role based on my reputation for being able to turn poor performers around.

I was in the role for about a month when I met with a woman who had come in to teach us presentation skills. When she shared that she worked for herself as an independent consultant, made her own hours, and made more than six figures, I was sold. *I wanted that.* I wanted that kind of freedom with my time and money. Little did I know it would open up the path to what I believe is my true calling. Much like my friend had said, my career kind of found me while I was busy finding work.

Shortly after that, I realized if I wanted to do that kind of work, I needed to take the risks that came with it. I wasn't in the military anymore, so there was nothing to stop me from applying for work elsewhere. Within a month, I began applying to other jobs in the Los Angeles area. I was moving to the city and I was going to get the experience I needed to eventually go out on my own. And thus began the adventure that would eventually evolve into the career I have today.

That is my story as briefly and honestly as I can tell it. Hopefully, you get that I didn't have a clear path laid out for me, but I still managed. I didn't have all the tools that are available now, but I still managed. I also didn't have a lot of help in some ways but had lots of help in other ways. Believe it or not, you have a lot of help available to you too, even if it comes from nontraditional places. If there's one thing life has taught me, it's that you're never truly alone in this world unless you choose to insist upon it.

I want to be one of those people who help you. I hope the previous chapters have already done that. But I understand being a veteran has some unique aspects to it that don't always get called out. The following chapters contain practical tips for veterans based on my own experience as one, my years of career-coaching experience, and countless hours counseling vets on how to successfully transition into the private sector. I hope my words play some part in helping you reach your own unique greatness in this new leg of your career and chapter of your life.

CHAPTER 17:
Support the
Troops, Right?

"I shall return."

—General Douglas MacArthur

We are in an interesting climate. For the first time in decades, our country is back in love with its troops. Where before it was customary to cast an uncomfortable eye toward those in uniform, we are now awash in bumper stickers, airport hugs, and "Thank you for your service" spilling out of every passerby. Even companies have made it their mission to hire veterans. But are we helping?

Working as a consultant, I partner with leaders and HR professionals. I'm often brought in to work with transitioning veterans. The common message I get is, "We hired them because of their leadership experience, but they just don't seem to know how to mesh with the culture."

I had a feeling this would occur when, starting in about 2008, I saw company after company promoting their campaigns to "support our troops" and "hire veterans." Few if any were doing much to prepare themselves and their culture for hiring veterans, especially those straight out of the military.

Some organizations at least held training classes for recruiters and hiring managers on how to interpret résumés and assess experience. But I heard little mention of the mental and emotional transition a veteran goes through while shifting out of the service. I also didn't hear anyone talking about how different the military and private sectors are in terms of organization. I saw no training for leaders on how to build inclusive environments for the diversity military veterans brought into the workplace.

When a company hires me to coach veterans on how to better acclimate to an organization, the expectation is the veterans are the ones doing all the changing. There's little interest or awareness from the organization that if they are to integrate this new brand of "work ethic" and discipline, they need to change a bit themselves.

While this chapter provides veterans with strategies on how to transition successfully, here are some tips for those of you who are hiring, managing, and/or working with veterans recently transitioned from active duty.

1. **Understand just how strange transitioning can be.** Depending on what veterans did for the military, they may have quite a road ahead of them to transition from their previous reality to the private sector. Even for veterans who have had jobs that closely resemble civilian ones, you have to remember the military is a culture all its own.

    Yes, every workplace has its own culture. But the military has a lifestyle culture that goes beyond the workplace. There's a level of order, command and control, enmeshed living arrangements, and common identity that holds troops, divisions, etc. together. There are pluses veterans will bring to your workplace from that, and there are minuses.

    No matter what the experiences of the former service members, they'll more than likely be going through a bit of "self-discovery." Most people join the military straight out of high school. Many have never lived on their own. They may have gone from the rules of their parents' homes to the rigidity of the military. This is as true for people getting out in their mid-twenties as it is for long-term vets retiring in their early forties. All of which can lead to a search for identity that can show up in a variety of ways—strange clothing choices, radical appearance changes, mood swings, etc.

2. **Know they can be struggling with a sense of lack of belonging.** No matter how friendly their new teams are, after work everyone goes home to their separate lives. For some veterans, this can be difficult. They are used to a community that centers on the workplace but fully extends into their personal lives. In the military, it's common to play on sports teams, go to barbecues, drink, and even raise families together. Having a team luncheon once a quarter just ain't the same.

   If they don't have an already-established community outside their workplace, they may try too hard to build that connection on the job. Your other employees may find that somewhat intrusive or even unprofessional. Military vets may think it's perfectly fine to invite coworkers and employees out for happy hour, where drinking outflanks professionalism. To veterans, it's them showing support for their "troops." To those in the private sector, it can scream "legal risk."

   It may not always be that extreme. Sometimes it can just be people who don't get what's appropriate to invite others into. Their social media presence may be unrestricted, and though it may not reflect anything illegal, it may reveal more of a personal side than most are used to seeing from their coworkers and leaders.

   On the other hand, it may be worth exploring how veterans can help bring teams together beyond the day-to-day work. They've witnessed firsthand how well people gel when some of the traditional boundaries are softened.

3. **Leadership may hold a different meaning to them.** Yes, the military focuses heavily on training and developing its leaders. But their charge is different than that of a private-sector employee. In the military, there is a heavy emphasis on following orders. That goes all the way up the chain of command. So you could have hired a previously high-ranking officer in the military and be shocked at how uncomfortable they are with setting direction for teams. Most leaders in the military are implementing orders as opposed to coming up with them.

   Vets are used to a high level of organization and structure, whereas most private-sector companies aspire to agile change and are comfortable with a certain level of chaos. Hierarchy is more nuanced, which in turn affects decision-making. Many former military leaders are looking for the black-and-white rules of engagement, and they can be surprised to find those clear-cut rules just don't exist for them in the private sector.

4. **Authority used to be absolute for them.** Some may be coming from a position where their authority was absolute. If they said jump, guess what their direct reports used to do? They may create a great deal of conflict and disturbance with their team if they have those same expectations in their new roles. Prepping them for this is essential. It's essential to demonstrate just how important relationship-building and -influencing are to the way work gets done in the private sector.

   Related to this is how they view their own bosses. They may think their direct leaders wield complete authority. For instance, you may recommend they interview a candidate and they may interpret that as you *directing* them to *hire* that candidate. Understand, at least for a while, they may interpret most of what you say as "direct orders" instead of suggestions or ideas.

They may also struggle with giving feedback to "superiors." Collaborating with those in higher positions can feel foreign and borderline disrespectful. Additionally, they may see their own employees' hearty discussions or debates as undermining their own leadership.

5. **Their level of formality can be off-putting.** At first it may seem charming that you have someone so polished on your staff. But if all the *sirs* and *ma'ams* and impeccable posture aren't part of your culture, veterans will start to seem out of place and risk being ostracized. Trust me, most veterans are proud of these behaviors. So while they may recognize they act differently than others on the team, they may view that as a good thing. Be prepared to discuss what level of formality aligns with the culture you've hired them into.

6. **They may speak a completely foreign language.** Not literally, but close. Veterans may have a way of speaking that employs lots of unfamiliar acronyms, curse words, and/or code words. It all depends on the role they held before. Understand this may be the first work environment they've had to adapt to. Without your feedback, they could go on to damage relationships simply by trying to connect with a "language" that doesn't translate.

7. **They may miss feeling significant.** No matter what they did in the military, they were part of something.

They may have faced death on a daily basis or simply filed paperwork. But their uniform bespoke a certain level of gravitas in most circles.

Even holding a high-level executive role can come up short in this area. Their identity was drawn very large for them, and now they may feel like they're swimming in a sea of average. They may not feel what they do is connected to a bigger purpose.

Others may be hunting for an adrenaline rush, even though they chose more stable and safe work than what they did while serving in the military. I've seen this play out with veterans creating a certain level of chaos where none existed before. They may overstress about menial things or go on and on about the "days on the front line." Again, at first this intensity may seem refreshing, but my experience has been that it wears thin and starts to alienate vs. endear them to others.

8. **They are more mission- than profit-driven.** On the surface, this is an admirable quality. But having basically worked for a nonprofit their whole lives, some vets may lack the experience of managing the financial side of things. The idea of cost controls and profit-driven decision-making may be completely foreign to them.

   This is an easy one to overlook, both for employers and veterans. I've seen many situations where the issue takes a while for both parties to recognize. Too many times veterans are then seen as lacking "common sense" or intelligence. The hiring manager starts thinking they made a bad hire. So discussing it up front and providing some internal training on the finance side of the business can give veterans just what they need to focus and make informed decisions.

9. **They are used to guaranteed employment.** The military, so far, has not done "layoffs." They either repurpose people into other roles or offer early separation with bonus. Military veterans don't spend their time during their service thinking about job security.

    This can play out in several different ways. On one hand, you may have someone with a higher level of commitment and staying power than you're used to with today's workforce. On the other hand, you may find veterans in leadership roles have no experience terminating others for lack of performance. Or they have an unrealistic sense of job security and do not notice when their performance, or lack thereof, is putting their own employment at risk.

10. **They are used to career paths and continuous development.** This is one of the main benefits of hiring veterans. They've been heavily invested in by the military. Depending on what they did in the service, they've received more on-the-job training than any Ivy League college graduate.

    However, they struggle with entering a workforce where training is not part of the day-to-day and where there is no clear path to success and promotion. Time in service counts for very little. And as interesting as some of their war stories may be, people will tire quickly of hearing "how things used to be."

So what does this all mean? Are veterans bad hires? Absolutely not. At least not because they are ex-military. At the same time, it doesn't guarantee successful hires either.

How Do We Support Our Troops?

You want to help our returning troops? Good. They deserve it. They signed up for the chance to risk their lives for our freedom, and many did. They've given their time and made a multitude of other sacrifices for, in most cases, little pay.

But assuming their military experience is enough to prepare them for their new lives is naive. Let's definitely keep hiring them. Let's keep looking for opportunities to leverage their unique experiences on the job. But let's do so in a way that sets us, and especially them, up for success.

Here's what you can do:

1. **Train your managers on how to create inclusive environments.** This has benefits that go way beyond this topic and is a major contributor to successful workplaces in this age of collaboration, diverse customer bases, and fluid project teams.

2. **Understand the difference between skills and cultural norms.** Many of the veterans being hired have their skills underestimated because they need some time to adjust to cultural norms. To increase the pace of that learning curve, the best thing to do is engage in frequent dialogue. Sharing feedback and hearing out their perceptions and concerns will help them build a deeper understanding of the culture and how best to navigate it.

   A healthy respect and acknowledgment for the differences of the military culture vs. that of your company is a good place to start. How do people socialize? What is the level of formality? What nuances exist around hierarchy? These types of questions should be a dialogue. Remember, veterans need to acclimate to your company's culture, but that culture should include their style and what they bring to the table as well.

3. **Invite veterans to share what worked for them before.** Our workplaces are struggling with teams that don't have each other's backs. Veterans come

from a different team culture. The majority walked out with a strong sense of unity and partnership, even if they didn't particularly care for the other people.

4. **Provide support.** This can come in several different packages. If you are hiring a large number of veterans or putting them in high-level positions, it's worth the investment to get them a coach. The cost of turnover or the damage done by poor on-boarding can hit pockets deeper in the long run. Consider a training consortium where veterans can get together to learn from each other's on-boarding experiences and leaders can coach one another.

5. **Practice open-mindedness and a growth mind-set.** One of the key differences I see between what I experienced in the military and what I tend to experience in the private sector is the presence of a growth vs. a fixed mind-set. The military assumes they will have to train and develop their personnel. The private sector prefers to "buy" talent instead of build it.

    This means many civilian leaders have not been trained on how to develop others. They are quick to throw the baby out with the bathwater, meaning at the first sign that employees are not performing up to expectations, the leader sees these as bad hires and writes them off.

    Learning something new takes time, trial and error, and the space to take risks and learn from mistakes. Those first stressful ninety days on the job for any new hire are critical. However, for someone coming from such a drastically different work culture, they can be that much more confusing. Leaders who not only understand but also know how to coach new hires through this precarious time can help your organization get the biggest return on its investment.

These are just some basic, common-sense recommendations. And that's all it should take — it's not rocket science. It *should* be common sense. It shouldn't be difficult for veterans to move into the next chapter of their careers. It's sometimes just our lack of awareness, sensitivity, and patience that makes or breaks their ability to do so.

Not that veterans are some helpless population that can't handle challenging situations. Of course they can. But I'm constantly struck by what I've experienced and witnessed: often the very thing we thank them for while passing them in the airport, we condemn them for when applied on the job.

CHAPTER 18:
Veteran Transition Tips

"In the middle of chaos lies opportunity."

— Bruce Lee

Don't Believe the Hype

One of the hardest things about transitioning is all the fear. Fear of the unknown and fear of all the "hardships" everyone talks about nonstop. It creates anxiety and doesn't help with solving anything. Just like in life, yes, there are real challenges; yes, there are unexpected speed bumps and road-blocks and heart-wrenching disappointments possible. But just as possible are completely unplanned and unexpected opportunities, helping hands from people you've yet to meet, and heart-fulfilling surprises.

This is life. I love that for the first time in decades, the country is back to embracing our veterans, wanting to thank them for their sacrifices and lend a hand by creating job opportunities. But there is an underlying message that seems to be weaving itself into all the commercials, job fairs, and even documentaries: veterans have a difficult time finding work after the military.

But here's the truth: If you've read the previous chapters, you know getting work is the new skill all people need to acquire. Technically, veterans are no different than anyone else going through a career change. Looking at it from that perspective—as a job change vs. a veteran's transition—will help you eliminate some of this extra "challenge" that isn't there.

Now that's not to say there aren't some unique challenges and opportunities connected with changing your job out of the military. There are, and I'll do my best to highlight them and provide tips to make them work to your advantage as much as possible.

Also, I want to be clear. I'm not being flippant about today's employment challenges. They are real, and depending on what you do, you may find a shrinking job pool or even discover your particular field has dried up altogether thanks to advances in technology. Or you may have done something useful but also particular to the military and find that work just doesn't exist in the private or government sector. But that doesn't make you any different than a million others who are challenged by their own jobs becoming less relevant. It's not a handicap; the mistake is assuming you are not first and foremost a business owner.

Even while serving in the military, you were still a business owner. You got paid for being in the military. Yes, it was probably not equal to the value you provided for our country. Just like teachers, police officers, and other civil servants, service members rarely get paid for the real value of their work.

We can complain a reality TV star famous for nothing more than stunts and a reckless life makes a hundred times more than the men and women who protect our country, but that's capitalism. If you create the demand and sell the value, then you get the money. Supply and demand. It may be oversimplifying, but it's essentially the truth.

Now, you can resent that or you can embrace the freedom that comes with it. Personally, I love the fact that no matter your class, race, gender, beliefs, or station in life, if you can come up with a product or service people want to buy, you can make money. The demand is what dictates the monetary value even if others don't see it as a cultural or moral value. But that also creates the opportunity for anyone to create anything and take a stab at building his or her own destiny.

Does that mean everyone has the same opportunities? Absolutely not. No matter who you are, there are things that are working to your advantage and things that are not. Some of us have more roadblocks to success than others, but at the end of the day, we all have the freedom to create success for ourselves. That is something too many of us take for granted.

Don't believe the hype about all the difficulties you'll supposedly face as a transitioning veteran. Just like with any major life change, you will eventually have to face your own demons in terms of fears, challenges, handicaps, and limitations. But you will also discover your resiliency, creativity, passion, determination, and transferrable skills and talents. This I guarantee you.

To set yourself up for success, keep a few things in mind:

1. **Don't be afraid.** Now, I know some of you reading this have stared fear in the eyes and shot it in the head. You have seen unspeakable horrors and possibly participated in the taking of lives of other humans. You have witnessed friends being maimed or killed. You may not be leaving the military completely intact, physically and/or emotionally. But that doesn't mean you don't have some fear over what will happen to you after everything you've known for the past few years is gone.

   You are not alone. What you're feeling is a normal human reaction to wondering what's next. Like I was, some of you may be eager to get out and carve your own paths. Others of you may be reluctant to leave behind your friends and fellow soldiers.

   However, while fear is useful when faced with life-and-death situations—keeping you alert, heightening your senses, and sharpening your focus—it doesn't help much in the civilian world, where you need to feel safe. As I mentioned in the beginning of the book, the mind-set that leads to the most success in the civilian workplace is strategic and helpful. This is the mind-set that causes your brain to create ideas you hadn't had before, connect the dots in ways no one has thought of before, and embrace others in a way that makes them feel welcome and connected with you. For that to happen, you have to be relaxed, open, optimistic, confident and, above all else, hopeful.

2. **Don't assume someone else will take care of it.** Let's be honest: the military overwhelmingly recruits a certain demographic of young and moldable people. For the majority of you, the experience has been a seamless move from having your life dictated by teachers and parents to having it dictated by the leaders in charge of you, right down to where you lived, what you ate, and what you wore. Yes, the longer you were in the more you may have earned back some of those freedoms, like choosing your off-duty attire or the furniture in your home.

But your career path was handpicked for you. You may have had a say in how quickly you were promoted or whether certain training opportunities were offered to you, but by and large, things have been determined for you. As a business owner, you handed over the majority of operational responsibility to the military.

What you need to recognize is now you are about to move into a phase of business ownership where you will be in control of everything. For some of you, this will be the first time you are experiencing this level of ownership. This is exciting. Enjoy it, but also accept the responsibility.

This is where we veterans tend to create challenges for ourselves that don't need to exist. We just don't realize someone isn't coming in to tell us what to do. It's like our brains don't flip that switch until something harsh happens and we have to jump into action.

It may seem like I'm pointing out the obvious, but I want you to set this book down, close your eyes, and just let the following statement roll around in your head: "I'm a business owner, the CEO of my lifelong career, and I have to start creating what that looks like."

I want you to let these words sink in early and often. If you're still in the military, one of the most important things you can do is start to take that control back. Even if you have to do it behind the scenes by researching opportunities or laying out a plan for what you'd like to do once out of the military. You want your brain to rewire around anticipating and creating your future instead of waiting for direction from someone else.

I don't say this condescendingly. Even though I was used to making my own decisions from a young age, I was surprised to discover how conditioned I'd become to waiting for someone to give me a command before taking action. Everyone will have an amount of this reaction. You need to tune in to yours.

Depending on your branch and base, you may receive an extremely detailed, personalized transition package or a loose, scattered, and largely administrative one. After you finalize your decision to end your contract, you may feel a sudden drop in support or you may get that as soon as you confirm your plans not to reenlist. For me, it was the latter, but I'm hearing more stories of support before and after the transition date.

No matter your situation, never forget that you are the sole business owner of your career. You've simply been allowing the military to take on some of the overhead so you could focus on the delivery of service.

Another thing to keep in mind is your age. The older you are when you separate from the military, the more likely people will assume you know what you're all about. The irony is the longer you've been in, the more this self-awareness muscle may have atrophied. This doesn't mean it can't be developed. Just know people tend to view self-knowledge as a sign of wisdom, and they are looking for it in people in their thirties and beyond.

The truth is finding yourself is a lifelong journey. So be gentle with yourself and start where you are. As long as you are taking full responsibility for your life and where it's headed, you will already be leaps and bounds ahead of the majority of the population, civilian or otherwise. As I mentioned before, even those in the private sector have grown accustomed to a certain level of abdicating power and allowing others to drive their careers. So it's not completely unique to the military.

3. **Don't be afraid to ask for or receive help.** Just because you are back to being a fully responsible business owner, that doesn't mean you should go it alone. The help may not be as structured, and where it might come from may not be as obvious, but help is available almost everywhere.

You are exiting the military at a time when companies are investing heavily in demonstrating their support of the troops, and it's not hard to find organizations that exist solely for the purpose of helping veterans acclimate and integrate into the civilian workforce.

Not only that, but people love helping others. I know it doesn't seem that way, especially if we've experienced a particularly dark side of humanity. But

I can tell you from experience: for every one person who doesn't want to risk putting his or her hand out for you, there are many more who would like nothing more than to be a part of your journey, whether you were in the military or not.

The thing people like to help with is a cause. And if it happens to have a high return on investment, all the better. So you want to make yourself a high-return-on-investment kind of person. That means not taking for granted the help being offered, even if you're not quite sure it can assist you in that moment. Be someone who is up to more than just getting work for yourself and getting paid.

You just got done serving your country, and whether you put your life on the line or you were a pencil pusher like me, you committed your life during that time. That's reason enough for someone to want to invest in you. But you don't want to stop there. The minute your time is up, your military life is a past-tense story. Sure, people will care about it, but what they want to know about is what's next. They can't help you get someplace if they don't know where that place is. For you to maximize the help available to you, you need to have a clear story about what's next for you, whether that's a new career, being there for your family, or realizing some other dream.

Another thing I highly recommend is leveraging your military benefits to get therapy. Some of you will be suffering from PTSD, but even if you weren't traumatized in any particular way, going through therapy can help stimulate and foster increased self-awareness. This is invaluable when carving out your life path. Therapy can also help you build tools to increase your resilience, which you're going to need for your job search.

4. **Don't be afraid to work.** I know many of you did ridiculously hard and sometimes laborious work while in the military. There's an element of purpose to even the most mundane task in the military. I could have cleaned bathrooms, but if I did it for the military, I was still part of something big, something vital, something heroic. But doing that type of work in the civilian world doesn't have the same level of heroism attached to it. Though it should.

Any job that serves others and makes people's lives better is worthy and respectable work. But our country has lost sight of the dignity inherent in doing this type of work. We've gotten too attached to titles, pay, and fancy cars. (Don't get me wrong: There's nothing wrong with going after wealth either. To me it's all about purpose.)

Remember the gentleman I met in the Caribbean who worked on a resort doing maintenance and chauffeuring the owners around? He had dignity in spades. He was doing this work for his family, and the pride he took in executing it well was his own.

I say all this so that you don't get hung up on what kind of work you take on. Be ambitious. Be a dreamer. Be unstoppable. But be grateful and humble in the process. That means you may need to start with work that seems like a step back from what you've accomplished so far. Trust that everything will lead you to where you need to be if you keep moving forward.

Remember, you're making a career change, so you may need to take on work you didn't ever expect to do again. But if the job isn't at someplace you want to stay, know you can take that time and experience and make it work for you in driving your career. And unlike in the military, you can quit when it's time to move on to the next opportunity.

5. **Don't be too attached to being a hero.** There's an ego check that happens to us when we leave the military. I didn't serve during a time when people came up to you in the airport and thanked you for your service. I didn't save anyone's life or go anywhere near a battlefield. But even I had a sense that I was a big deal in some way, and it was a bit tough working in the civilian world, where your work is rarely referred to as heroic.

I mean how many times have you heard someone say, "Wow, that call center manager saved my life. Thank you for telling me I haven't paid for that washer I charged on my Sears credit card"? Never. Or, "Wow, if it wasn't for that Walmart greeter, I just don't know where our country would be"? Yeah, no. Doesn't happen.

Now, some of you will be hired right into leadership roles. I've worked with people where this has happened, and even with a fancy title, they can still struggle on the job. One minute they were in the field making life-and-death decisions, and the next they're in a boardroom dealing with a bunch of suits and their passive-aggressive communications.

What's dangerous is these people often create drama without realizing it, because they are so used to dealing with high-stakes situations. Their peers, not looking to have their stress levels unduly escalated, can find this need for action annoying. In fact, the majority of vets I have coached who work in office settings struggle with just this problem.

For those of you who take jobs in police or fire departments, or with agencies such as the FBI or CIA, you may experience less dip in hero status. But for the rest of us, it can be a real issue.

The beauty is, in the civilian world, you can craft what kind of hero you want to be and how you want to ultimately contribute to the world. Your impact can be small or even global. When I think of someone who has led a heroic life, both inside and outside the military, I think of my friend's father, who helped me get my job at the Sears call center.

He was a hero to the troops he commanded while he served in the Army, and he is a hero in the way he manages his team and helps others in his civilian roles, whether in a call center, raising a family of his own, or by opening up his home to me when, as a teenager, my home life was too much to bear. He has lived a heroic life regardless of what capacity he happened to work in.

Start Where You Are, but Start Now

If you're just starting the sign-up process for the military, now is the perfect time to begin proactively planning for what you'll do afterward. If you're halfway through your contract and you're not sure if you will reenlist or not, now is the perfect time to plan and practice for your post-military career. If it's your last week in and someone just handed this book to you, now is the perfect time. If you're already out and you wish someone had told you about all this months ago, now is the perfect time. Start where you are. But start now.

A couple things you can do proactively, no matter where you are in your transition timeline, are build good habits and foster connections. All business owners should do these throughout their lifetimes. But because many military members experience a more dramatic shift in their careers than others, it's more important for us. What follow are some tips that can be leveraged early or much later in your career journey. As mentioned, start where you are, but start now:

1. **Build your self-awareness.** As I said earlier, this is a lifelong journey. But I'm finding that fewer and fewer people in the workforce have a strong sense of who

they are as individuals, and therefore have difficulty tuning in to their own voice. What this means is they find it difficult to form and voice their own opinions. Even executives struggle with cultivating their own vision for their department or company. The more you've been rewarded for being obedient and following orders — as an adolescent and as an adult — the more you will struggle with this.

And don't think self-awareness is a by-product of age. It's a habit, a practice that needs to be cultivated. Some things that help with this are meditation, solo adventures or trips, therapy, personality assessments, etc. It comes down to cultivating an intimacy with one's own thoughts. If you struggle with spending time alone, you may want to brave into that.

Self-awareness is one of the primary leadership traits people look for, especially in the private sector. Leaders are expected to be able to identify and manage their emotional reactions to life. They are also looked to for a viewpoint on how things should be done, now and in the future.

I find self-assessments that ask questions about how you view the world not only give you insight into how you think, but they also provide a terminology and language for how to describe your thought process. You can often find these types of assessments as part of books that help you explore why you view the world the way you do.

Some common assessments I've used in my coaching practice and seen used in the civilian workforce include the MBTI/Myers-Briggs, DISC, Birkman, PQ assessment, ESCI/Emotional Intelligence, and the Thomas-Kilmann Conflict Mode Instrument. There are many more, and you can easily look these up online and get familiar with the terminology and how you score in terms of communication and preferences.

In the military, it isn't as common for someone to ask, "What do you think about all this?" or "What do you think we should do?" especially of the middle to lower ranks. But in the private sector, it's becoming more and more prevalent, no matter your title or position.

2. **Stock up on supplies and skills**. There are certain things you should have and be familiar with using by the time you transition out of the military. Some of these may be issued to you by the military, but that depends on your job, so you'll want to make sure you have them as your own by the time you separate.

   • Laptop and Cell Phone — You need to have your own by the time you separate. The private sector will expect to be able to reach you no matter what. They will also expect you to be connected to the Internet and possess basic computer skills, irrespective of your role.

   • Computer Skills — For many of you, the military will have trained you above and beyond what most civilians need to know about technology. The problem is you may lack familiarity with what are considered the basics in the civilian world, such as the Microsoft Office Suite. For others, your job may have had little to do with technology, and you may only use a computer for emails or chatting with friends and family when away from home. For most private-sector and government jobs, the minimum is a fundamental fluency in the Microsoft Office Suite. Also, in the corporate world, quite a bit of communicating gets done with spreadsheets and PowerPoint presentations. If this is part of your military job already, great. If not, leverage online resources to get familiar with the tools.

- <u>Public Speaking / Meeting Presence</u> — If you're looking to work in an office, expect that most work will get done and decisions made in meetings. Professionals are expected to be able to present their views in concise and engaging ways. The better you are at this, the easier it will be to influence how things get done.

  If your military role doesn't require you to do any of this, you can take courses on public speaking or even just look for opportunities to speak up in group settings. If you are out in the field the majority of the time, then during leaves or when you have access to the Internet, watch and learn from TED Talks that are available for free. Don't assume you have to be a master out of the gate. Just be aware that there will be a great deal of this in any corporate setting.

  Also, it's important to note that passion and emotion are often viewed as un-soldier-like in the military. Stoic expressions, sternness, and a certain intensity tend to command higher levels of respect in the military. In the private sector, they are looking for a more relaxed and casual demeanor than what may have been customary during your service.

- <u>Managerial Skills</u> — Managerial skills are the number one transferrable skill you can cultivate. No matter what specialty you worked in, managerial skills can get you into a company much faster and at higher levels than any technical expertise all by itself. This is a definite plus we get for serving in the military. Most civilians are assuming you are coming out with leadership skills. Regardless of your role or rank, you will want to practice and cultivate your ability to get work done through, and with, others. Even as a frontline, lower-ranking enlisted member, you can volunteer to take on projects or missions that enable you to practice managerial skills.

But you will also want to practice the civilian best practices and language around leadership. The easiest way to do this is to take a course, whether online or at a university. A course gets you in a conversation with a diverse population, ideally one that has plenty of private-sector workers. Another option is to simply read leadership books. These are usually written for the private sector and discuss common challenges faced in the workplace, using terminology you're sure to encounter once you enter the workforce. As you read them, pay attention to ways you can translate what you do in the military to what you can do in the civilian workplace.

- Business Savvy — Too many military members lose touch with the day-to-day cultural norms of the population they are defending. The military world is like its own planet. It comes complete with its own industry trends, language and acronyms, and priority topics. As humans, we tend to pay closest attention to the things we believe directly affect us. But thanks to the Internet, we have the luxury of easy access to just about any topic we may be curious about, no matter where it's taking place. You'll want to cultivate not only your business savvy but also your understanding of what's going on around the world.

A great way to keep in touch with business is to use social media. You could set up a Twitter account, if you don't already have one, and follow companies such as *Forbes*, Business Insider, *Fortune* magazine, Inc., *Harvard Business Review*, Fast Company, TED Talks, and others. You can also keep up with key people who regularly discuss business trends and insights, such as Daniel Pink, Simon Sinek, Brené Brown, Jeremy Gutsche, Arianna Huffington, and many others. This is a fast, convenient way to get the latest articles and keep in touch with the private sector.

- <u>Interview Skills</u> — If possible, take on part-time work. The money will not only help you add to your nest egg for when you separate, but you'll get a chance to practice job-hunting and interview skills in a low-risk environment. And if you're just looking for a gig that you work over the holidays or on certain days, you won't feel as rejected if you don't land the first few. Also, you'll get to practice being yourself in an interview.

  One of the main things veterans need to learn to do in an interview is talk about their transferrable skills in civilian speak. For this reason alone, I highly recommend working in nongovernment roles. Many government workplaces speak a lingo similar to the military. Ideally, you're able to do something off the base.

  Depending on your situation and security limitations, you may not be able to take an additional job away from base. If that's the situation, try doing some freelance work online, where you write articles for little to no money. The benefit is you still have to do a phone interview, etc. Plus, you get practice expressing yourself.

- <u>Build a Network through Giving and Receiving Help</u> — I admit, the thing I absolutely hated hearing the most while transitioning was, "You have to go out there and network." I loathed the idea of prostituting myself out to people, begging them to talk to me, and hoping they'd offer me a job. For one, I didn't even know how or where to begin to network. And job fairs, which seemed like a legit place to start, felt so strange and desperate.

Later in my career, people would often comment on how well I networked. What I realized was I enjoyed connecting with people in non-pressure situations over common interests, and in these situations felt—and came off as—completely genuine.

An easy way to find such situations is to join private-sector clubs or sports teams, or participate in hobbies outside the military. Mingling with the nonmilitary in these situations lets you be authentic without needing something from anyone. People can get to know you for you.

A key part of networking is keeping in touch with those you already know. For veterans, this means staying connected to those you served with in the military. Thanks again to the Internet, this is much easier now than it was when I exited. Besides Facebook, Instagram, Snapchat, and their ilk, you'll be able to find several online communities for ex-military. These are ideal for giving and receiving help. You'll find people who have already transitioned and can make introductions for you.

This should absolutely be a two-way street. Look for opportunities to help others as well. Don't make the mistake of waiting until you need something. People love helping others, but they absolutely hate being used.

- <u>Financial Literacy</u> — This has a lot to do with whether or not you grew up with parents or caretakers who were financially literate. Chances are your parents were somewhere between financially responsible and financially illiterate. That's not a knock; it's just a commentary on the nature of our country.

  But you becoming financially literate will help you in a multitude of ways. It's not just about saving your pennies for a rainy day. It's about learning how to generate money and knowing how to make it work for you.

  Many of you will be limited in how you can earn extra money either because policies prevent you from getting outside work or you're stationed in an area that doesn't provide such opportunities. So learning how to manage and invest what money you do have is invaluable.

  I recommend taking online courses and reading articles and books that focus on personal financial planning and creating wealth. This isn't about being greedy; it's about creating financial freedom for you. What can financial freedom buy? It'll get you such luxuries as a stress-free job search and the ability to take risks to get you closer to doing what you love once you separate from the military.

  This, of course, is an important life skill for everyone, but what I want to emphasize is the importance of learning financial literacy as early as possible in life. I knew — and know — few people who think about making money work for them. The majority of people in the middle to lower classes tend to see things from a "work for money" standpoint, viewing saving as the number one strategy for survival.

  Some great books to read on this topic include *Rich Dad, Poor Dad* and several others by author

Robert Kiyosaki. Tony Robbins has also written some good ones, and let's not forget the most trusted financial voice, Warren Buffett.

Another thing to consider is practicing your entrepreneurial skills while still serving. This might involve creating an online business or presence. I've known many people who have turned their hobbies into a revenue stream via sites such as Etsy, eBay, and Craigslist. You can even self-publish your own novel and sell it on Amazon. The important thing is not to assume there is only one way to generate money on your road to financial freedom.

3. **Tend to your emotional health.** Emotional well-being has become an everyday topic of discussion, and no wonder. It's essential for succeeding in life and in your career. However, I will say it seems to be more of an expectation for those in the private sector than those in the military. Depending on your upbringing, you may also have varying degrees of comfort with focusing on this side of your health.

One of the biggest hurdles I encounter when coaching people in the workplace is overcoming the habit of negative self-talk. Either they are limiting themselves based on a negative self-image or a desperate need to be validated, or they just have a garden-variety negative outlook on life. Either way, this attitude sends a message that they would be difficult to work with, and that's kryptonite in the civilian workplace.

Coming out of the military, you may be struggling with disappointment or working through a sense of loss. This is all the more reason to address this issue and practice positivity while you're still in. Because it's not like you can just walk into the private sector with a smile and all of a sudden have a positive way of viewing things. It takes practice. And like I said, there's no better place to start than where you are.

Don't Underestimate the Job-Hunt Hustle

If you didn't have to get a job before you joined the military, then it can feel uncomfortable having to secure your own employment. Make no mistake about it: finding, securing, and creating demand for your work is a hustle and will require energy and focus. To prep yourself, consider the following:

1. **Time will feel different to you than to others.** When you're looking for work, one of the biggest challenges we face is time. It can feel like we don't have enough of it, especially if we are financially challenged. But what you have to understand is those who are interviewing you don't feel the same way about time. Their days are most likely filled to capacity with meetings, projects, and deadlines. One week to you is an eternity. To them, it's a blink of an eye.

   You will need to cultivate patience while still knowing when to reach out and follow up. Be sure to be careful what you're telling yourself while waiting for a call or email. Tell yourself things such as, "The perfect opportunity is making its way to me." Don't tell yourself, "They're not going to want to hire me. They're probably avoiding me, and I'm bound not to get a job." Negative self-talk will only chip away at your confidence, thereby limiting your effectiveness at marketing yourself during actual interviews. So pace yourself and don't put all your eggs in one basket.

2. **Transferrable skills can be your greatest advantage.** As I mentioned earlier in the book, your transferrable skills and unique talents matter more than your work

experience. But you'll need to know what these are and how to convey them to others.

Management, business, finance, and technology experience is almost always transferrable to most jobs. However, so are such skills as the ability to quickly learn processes and procedures, make sense out of chaos, multitask, build relationships, and navigate conflict. All of the preceding are industry- and job-agnostic, so spend some time thinking about how you can highlight them.

3. **Secure living arrangements for ninety days or more.** This may seem like common sense to some of you, but for many, especially those who went straight from their parents' home to the military, this can be a huge issue. Some of you have family who are waiting for you to come home, and others of you have friends you know will take you in. But some of you may not have either. If you are in the latter category, you can reach out to organizations such as US Vets Transitional Housing, which operates in some parts of the country. Knowing where you will live for the first few months, and having an address where employers can contact you, will make things a lot easier.

4. **Translate rejection to directions.** When you haven't had to sell yourself or market your skills, going out on an interview and then not getting the job can feel devastating, especially if you are doubting whether or not you can make it in the civilian world. But here's the thing—not getting a particular job can be the best thing for you. It's a bit like dating. Some people end up living happily ever after with the first person they go out on a date with. Others go on multiple dates before they click with someone. Well, job-hunting can be a lot like that.

Instead of dissecting what happened in a way that focuses on how you failed or didn't do something right, look at the situation through a learning lens. What worked for you? What didn't? What about the job sounded like a great fit, and what would have been a stretch for you?

Believe it or not, your career is sending you information with every job offer and every decline. It's about where you fit best, not about your worth as a human. In a society where we so identify our sense of self so closely with our work, it's difficult to separate the two. But you need to in order to experience the adventure and fun of job-hunting. Believe it or not, it can be a blast if done right.

5. **Apply for jobs early and often.** When you're separating from the military, my advice is to apply for a multitude of jobs. You can always say no to a job offer you decide isn't the right fit for you. It never hurts your confidence to receive a job offer even if it's not what you want to do. And as my own story illustrates, you may be surprised what experiences end up being right for you and leading to your ideal career or field. Plus, you'll get the opportunity to practice your interviewing skills.

Understand Perception vs. Reality

Recently, I was meeting with the head of the human resources department of a large corporation. She was struggling with supporting an operations department transitioning from one VP to a newly hired one. They had hired several veterans for leadership positions, assuming they would get the place in order. "But they don't seem to do well without structure and clear direction," she said. "And you know in this world, nobody is going to tell you what to do. You've got to figure that out for yourself, or you're not going to make it." She went on to tell me about how her organization changes way too rapidly for there ever to be a stable structure. Vets, she said, need to be agile. "It looks like they just aren't going to work out."

Yes, people are much more willing to hire ex-military, but they are no more prepared for what that experience will be like for their company or for the veterans. And unlike the military, they are usually not steeped in a culture that focuses on skill-building, training, and development. They prefer to hire ready-to-go talent instead of building it. Therefore, they don't always comprehend the difference between someone who is acclimating and someone who is not a good fit. Here are some ideas to help you guide your own acclimation effectively:

1. **Expect a bit of an identity crisis.** I don't want to assume you will go through this, but it happens to quite a few of us. You've had much to identify with and create a personal identity around by being part of the military, and a lot of that is about to go away. Think about it. You were trained to be a fully immersed member of the military. You were steeped in the culture of the branch you joined. You dressed and wore your hair in a way that identified you as part of a tightly knit community.

   Now you are going out into the civilian world, which by and large expects individuality. I've worked with hundreds of vets, and many tell of trying to connect with their civilian coworkers in the same way they did with their military brothers and sisters. And it tends to go poorly.

2. **Don't expect the same level of structure.** Most organizations in the private sector have gone through massive shifts over the last ten years and have settled on a "nimble" way of doing things, which can

seem chaotic. You may struggle with navigating the workplace because things won't be as orderly as they were in the military. I say use that to your advantage. In the midst of chaos there is room for creativity. In this environment, you can often make things happen without having to get fifteen people to sign off on it.

3. **Don't wait to be told.** Taking initiative is critical to the private sector. That's not to say that you don't have to share what you're doing or get buy-in. But those are different than getting permission. Reread chapter 16 on how to inspire commitment from others.

4. **Separate your personal from your professional life.** In the military these two things are one and the same. We usually sleep, eat, party, and do everything else with those we work with day in and day out. In the civilian world, your personal and professional lives can be separate, with a gray area determined by the local culture and the culture of the company. Some workplaces are more casual and tend to do things such as happy hour after work, while others frown on any mingling outside the workplace.

5. **No one actually cares about your war stories.** This sounds harsh. And it's not entirely true. People like to hear these stories as an interesting aside but not as a constant refrain when discussing work. "When I was in the military, we would…" Nobody cares. You're not in the military anymore. You are working in their world now, and they want to know you have both feet grounded in their culture. Could you imagine saying to your marine buddies, "Well, when I was in the Air Force, they would…" Yeah, not so much.

Now, this doesn't mean they don't respect your experience or want to leverage it. But if you constantly live in the past, you will start to teach them you are not one of them. On that note, they also don't care what your rank was or how many high-ranking people you used to run with. Titles do mean something in the civilian world, but not nearly what they do in the military world.

6. **Authority is not absolute.** In the civilian sector they expect you to take direction and guidance from people higher on the food chain than you, but not in the same way you did in the military. They expect a certain level of discussion and discourse, especially if you see things from a different perspective, rather than treating everything they say as direct orders.

    Now this doesn't mean you can completely ignore their requests or be disrespectful, but there is room to collaborate. In fact, you'll often need to push back for them to get a sense you know what you're doing.

7. **You can get fired or laid off.** In the military, you can get in trouble, you can get demoted, and you can even be sent to a military prison or dishonorably discharged. But those consequences are rare, and the rules are clearly laid out and defined. In the private sector, you can get fired and not understand how it happened. Ideally, leaders are good at giving feedback and plenty of opportunity to course-correct, but there's no guarantee that will be the case. Also, you could be a great performer but still get laid off because the need for your function or service has dried up.

    No matter where you end up, you should never stop seeing yourself as a business owner. This means consistently creating demand for what you do, building financial literacy to create a safety net (so you are not solely reliant on your job), and keeping your eye on trends and how they may affect your job security.

8. **You can quit.** That's right. Remember every day you show up on a job in the civilian world it is purely by choice. Sure, it may feel like you don't have another choice because you have convinced yourself you don't have other options, but you always do. You gave up your personal freedom to serve your country. You signed your life away. Literally. But now you get to enjoy that very freedom you helped protect for everyone else. Exercise that freedom.

    Don't sit in a job you hate and then blame how miserable you are on your boss or the organization. They don't own you. You don't have a contract anymore. You can quit anytime you like. And if you choose not to, that's your choice too.

9. **Become a cultural linguist.** Every place you work has its own language and way of discussing things. You are going to be extremely fluent in military speak. But if you can't translate into their language, you'll once again appear as an outsider. Start by losing the acronyms that only fit in the military.

10. **Pick up on cultural norms that don't match those of the military.** A big one I see a lot is the level of slang and curse words that can be a common part of day-to-day dialogue in the military but are seen as highly unprofessional in the private sector. You may not agree with me here. Some may say a little cussing is fine. I say err on the side of not doing it until you understand the culture. This is definitely a case-by-case situation. If you're someone who doesn't use foul language, then this is not an issue for you. But for many, cursing was the motherfucking norm, and the degree to which it was acceptable in the military will probably never be the same in the private sector.

Also, gauge the level of formality. You may charm a few people by calling them sir or ma'am, but in most private-sector jobs, that level of formality is just not normal and, in fact, can make people uncomfortable. If you're thinking, "Well, I don't care. That's how I was raised," that's fine. But I guarantee you, in most work environments, using that kind of language will set you up to appear separate from them as opposed to one of them.

Hopefully, these chapters have given you some insight into how to prepare for and tackle your transition successfully. Of course, it's natural to still have questions and concerns. Your journey will be similar to that of many vets yet unique to your own personal purpose. I hope you understand it's up to you whether you see this time as an exciting adventure or a treacherous turn of events. Here's my two cents: thinking positively will set you up for more opportunities for success, so you might as well approach it the way.

Once again, thank you for all you've done and what you will do for our country. I wish you the best of luck.